ENCYCLOPAEDIA OF PSYCHO-
ANALYSIS
1

Drawing the Soul
Schemas and Models in Psychoanalysis

edited by

Bernard Burgoyne

REBUS PRESS

© Bernard Burgoyne to the edited collection, and the individual authors to their contributions 2000

First edition 2000

Printed in Great Britain

All rights reserved

No part of this book may be reprinted or reproduced or utilised in any form or by any electronic, mechanical or other means, now known or hereafter invented, including photocopying and recording, or in any information storage or retrieval system, without permission in writing from the publishers.

Rebus Press
134 Dukes Avenue
LONDON
N10 2QB

ISBN 1 1900877 25 2

CONTENTS

Foreword   5

Notes on Contributors   7

    Introduction
    Bernard Burgoyne   9

1 Donald W. Winnicott's Diagram of the Transitional Object and Other Figures
    Margret Tonnesmann   22

2 The Significance of Bion's Concepts of P-S↔D and Transformations in 'O': A Reconsideration of the Relationship between the Paranoid-Schizoid and Depressive Positions—and Beyond
    James S. Grotstein   34

3 Three in One: Fairbairn's Volatile Trinity
    Eleanore Armstrong-Perlman   57

4 The Flow of Narcissistic Energies: Kohut's Diagram in *The Analysis of the Self*
    Phil Mollon   77

5 How to Square the Medicine Wheel: Jung's Use of the Mandala as a Schema of the Psyche
    Michael Whan   92

6 Turning a Telescope on the Soul: Freud's Interpretation of the Structure of the Psyche
    Sharon Morris   117

7 Freud's Infernal Trinity: on the Vicissitudes of the 'Tripartite Model'
    Dany Nobus   150

8 The Schema L
    Darian Leader   172

9 Autism and Topology
    Bernard Burgoyne   190

10 A Calculus of Convergence
    Nathalie Charraud   218

Bibliography   227

Index   242

FOREWORD

The time is shortly before Christmas 1994 and three dreamers are ensconced in the comfortable leather armchairs of the staff bar at University College, London. The dreamers are Kirsty Hall, Oliver Rathbone and Sharon Morris. We like the idea of starting a publishing company. Single authored books, we calculate, will take three months to produce. Edited collections are a little more complicated, we note, and so might take up to six months... Our abject ignorance is a kind midwife to our project... Yet now our original idea has finally flowered. *The Encyclopaedia of Psychoanalysis* has been born. And, despite all the delays and setbacks, our vision is still intact.

Rebus Press is a non-partisan publishing company. We aim to bring a range of psychoanalytic ideas to a wide readership, namely: the experienced psychoanalyst or psychotherapist; the student, in the guise of either clinician or academic; and, last but certainly not least, the interested person in the street. We pose the question: are the original ideas which psychoanalysis brought to the world now dead, or are they alive and kicking in the work of subsequent writers, waiting to be brought forward afresh and anew for each generation of readers? In turn, we hope that through *The Encyclopaedia of Psychoanalysis*, Rebus Press will stimulate the next generation to take up the baton and produce further creative thinking.

The *Encyclopaedia* series does not set out to tell people what to think. It encourages readers to be fascinated, lured into reading 'just one more chapter', to puzzle over conflicting points of view and, on occasion, to grapple with difficult and complex ideas. Why? Well, if psychotherapists and psychoanalysts encounter the Byzantine complexity of human suffering in their daily work, then our view is that the practitioner will find assistance in this supremely difficult task by being gently helped to think for him or herself. Being told what to think and what to do does not produce good psychoanalysis or good psychotherapy, and it seems there is far too much 'instruction' of this kind already in circulation.

I wish to thank all our contributors to the *Encyclopaedia* series—past, present and future. As they have discovered—or, indeed, will discover in due course—Rebus Press is unique. We do not settle for statements such as: 'following Melanie Klein it is clear that...' or 'as Jacques Lacan has demonstrated...' We insist on *explanation*, wherever possible. As a result many of the people who have written for this series have had long, passionate, interesting, and—very occasionally—acrimonious discussions about their papers with the individual editors of our books, with the chief editor of Rebus Press, Duncan Barford, and with me. Consequently, where ideas do seem unclear, this is often because it is the intention of the author to leave the reader in doubt. Doubt *can* be a productive position from which to carry out an analysis of one's own thought, or an assessment of one's opinion about a book and—indeed—is regarded by some as the only viable position from which to conduct good psychoanalysis or psychotherapy...

The *Encyclopaedia* series has a consistent format. In most of the books you will find papers which are informed by Freudian, Jungian, Kleinian, Lacanian and Object Relations perspectives. You may also find papers where the perspective of the author is hard to pin down... Good! Keep the 'doubt' working! In each volume we attempt to offer a wide range of opinion, and the majority of papers have been specially commissioned and written for the series. In a few cases, we have published work which has already appeared elsewhere but perhaps in a format which has not been easily accessible. In some instances a paper has appeared in another language, and has been specially translated for this series.

The aim of the *Encyclopaedia* is to present a coherent body of ideas, yet within a structure sufficiently loose to allow the reader to interpret the papers for him or herself. We are hoping and aiming for a wide-ranging reaction to the contents of these volumes. Feedback, constructive criticism, ideas for future projects in the series, possible papers for future inclusion—all of these and more are most welcome.

Kirsty Hall MA
Commissioning Editor
e-mail k.hall@rebuspress.co.uk

NOTES ON CONTRIBUTORS

ELEANORE ARMSTRONG PERLMAN is a psychoanalyst in private practice. She is a member of The Guild of Psychotherapists and the Site for Contemporary Psychoanalysis. She has contributed many papers on Fairbairn in both books and journals.

BERNARD BURGOYNE is a psychoanalyst, a founder member of the Centre for Freudian Analysis and Research, and a member of the Ecole Européenne de Psychanalyse, and of the Association Mondiale de Psychanalyse. He was educated at the University of Cambridge, the London School of Economics and the University of Paris. He is Professor of Psychoanalysis, and Head of the Centre for Psychoanalysis in the Institute for Social Science Research at Middlesex University. His current and pending publications include 'Interpretation' in *The Klein-Lacan Dialogues*, (1997) eds. Burgoyne and Sullivan, London: Rebus, and 'From the Letter to the Matheme' in *The Cambridge Companion to Jacques Lacan*, (2001) ed. Rabaté, Cambridge: Cambridge University Press.

NATALIE CHARRAUD is a psychoanalyst and a member of the Ecole de la Cause Freudienne and of the Association Mondiale de Psychanalyse. She is currently a lecturer in psychopathology at the University of Rennes II, having previously taught mathematics for many years at the University of Paris XIII. She has published widely on the relations between mathematics and psychoanalysis: amongst her publications are *Infini et Inconscient: Essai sur Georg Cantor* (1994), Paris: Anthropos and *Lacan et les Mathématiques*, (1997), Paris: Anthropos.

JAMES S. GROTSTEIN MD is a professor of psychiatry at UCLA School of Medicine and a training and supervising analyst at the Los Angeles Psychoanalytic Institute and the Psychoanalytic Centre of California.

DARIAN LEADER is a psychoanalyst and founder member of the Centre for Freudian Analysis and Research in London. He was formerly Senior Lecturer in Psychoanalytic Studies at Leeds Metropolitan University, and is currently Honorary Visiting Academic at the Centre for Psychoanalysis, Middlesex University. He is the author of *Lacan for Beginners, Why do Women write more letters than they post* and *Promises lovers make when it gets late*. His most recent book is *Freud's Footnotes*(Faber, 2000).

PHIL MOLLON is a psychoanalyst of the British Psycho-Analytical Society and a psychotherapist who trained at the Tavistock Clinic. He has been interested in the work of Heinz Kohut for many years and has written two books on this topic: *The Fragile Self: The Structure of Narcissistic Disturbance* (Whurr

1993) and *Releasing the Self: The Healing Legacy of Heinz Kohut* (Whurr 2001). He works primarily in the NHS.

SHARON MORRIS trained as a visual artist at the Slade School of Fine Art where she now teaches. She has recently completed a PhD in the relation between words and images in the act of self-reference using the theories of C.S. Peirce and Freud and has published an an essay on the collages of Höch and Cahun and has a forthcoming paper on the writer H.D. Sharon Morris is a Research Associate of the Centre for Freudian Analysis and Research.

DANY NOBUS is a Lecturer in Psychology and Psychoanalytic Studies at Brunel University. He is the editor of *Key Concepts of Lacanian Psychoanalysis* (Rebus Press, 1998), and author of *Jacques Lacan and the Freudian Practice of Psychoanalysis* (Routledge, 2000), alongside numerous papers on the theory and practice of psychoanalysis.

MARGRET TONNESMANN is a member of the British Psycho-Analytical Society and a retired consultant psychotherapist.

MICHAEL WHAN is an analytical psychologist with the Independent Group of Analytical Psychologists. He is in private practice. He has published in several journals such as *Harvest, Spring* and the *European Journal of Psychotherapy, Counselling and Health*.

INTRODUCTION

Bernard Burgoyne

Some phrases shock; some disquieten; and some beg for explanation. In any such event, there always turns out to be something within the context of the phrase that indicates a lack. In each of these cases, the separation of curiosity from disquiet can be a very fine affair.

Wilfred Bion's work is guided by a particular quality: a determination that insists on questioning even the most extreme experiences of human love and pain. His questions are serious, and he has the courage to follow up the directions indicated in his answers—even if this takes him along pathways that are far removed from those of common sense. And if authors such as Bion, in extending their themes, repeatedly put forward mathematical terms as they deepen their journey into the human soul, it seems that these terms have been imposed by the clinical problems to which they are responding. Commentators often choose to be tacit about such details, reacting to such problems with a studied mutism. But if any analyst persists in giving such a formalising direction to their work, what can one conclude about their seriousness, and its consequences? 'Projective geometry'; 'algebraic calculus'; 'deductive system'; 'transitional space': what exigencies force Winnicott and Bion to bring such phrases into their work?

Not all psychoanalysts formalise their work, even in an implicit way. Do human passions gain by having such instruments trawled through them? Or are these structures spurious and unnecessary extravagances which add only distortions to the settings appropriate for the analysis of the human soul? In the history of the analytical movement there has been a split response to this question. On the one side there have been those who wanted to give a central focus and primary importance to formal structures determining the human condition—Freud, Bion, Lacan, Hermann, Matte Blanco, and others; and on the other side there have been those who give priority to common sense over the action of structure—Anna Freud, Hanna Segal, and almost all of the schools which base their technique on the functioning of counter-transference.

The aim of this book is to give some clarity to the issues involved in this dispute. There are some psychoanalysts who define their position as that of being faced with problems of working with structures that in some sense bring with them a demand for formalisation. Other analysts give to formalisation a more restricted position, lest it take over the experience of the analytical encounter. In this book, there are ten essays, each of which gives a sharply drawn characterisation of the place and functioning of formalisation in analytical work. The analysts whose work is addressed here cover a wide field: Winnicott, Fairbairn, Bion, Kohut, Jung, Lacan and Freud. The questions being formulated in these essays are very central: so central that in each case it has seemed necessary to assess their bearing on clinical work, that is, on the question of the nature, and of the direction, of analytical treatment. By these means, some ways forward may be found that can give co-ordinates—formal or informal—to the basic analytical problem of the relation between the analyst and the analysand.

In the history of the analytical movement, each school, each sub-school, each individual psychoanalyst has taken up a position—more or less clearly present in their published work—on the functioning of formal structure in the analytical situation. Reconstruction from this perspective of the various threads to be found in the psychoanalytical literature will often produce an emphasis different from that usually stressed in the existing histories of the field. For instance, the centre of the conflicts that came to be known as 'Controversial Discussions' within the British Society during the war-years of the 1940s can be seen to have been organised almost entirely by a dispute about the fundamental level of analysis[1]—that composed of unconscious phantasy and its effects in the school of Klein, as opposed to that resting on the authority of common sense in the work of Anna Freud. Whenever such a prism is applied to analytical work, it will split the field into a range of positions: each of these positions establishes a style of psychoanalysis—but one which can maintain its place in the analytical world only by keeping its claims closely linked to its prescriptions for clinical work.

A middle route has been proposed, stressing the clinical origin of the problem of formalisation, and avoiding what has been perceived as its extremes. In his commentary on the history of the Independent Group in the British Psycho-Analytical Society, Eric Rayner draws attention to the existence of a tradition dating from the early work of Ernest Jones, a tradition which claims that affects are accompanied by—are attached to—a local island of structure (Rayner 1990: chapters 3, 4). In this view of affects, they come equipped with a structure of symbols. The development and functioning of symbolism then plays centre stage in the analysis of affect. This is particularly evident in the work of Marion Milner and Charles Rycroft; indeed their work can be seen as addressing a number of themes widespread across the British Independent Group throughout the years of its early history. Structure in this tradition is given a place, and a serious investigation;[2] but it is kept subordinate to a range of assumptions about human nature, and particularly to notions of empathy, understanding, and common sense.

Some analysts try to amalgamate these two poles. In the lectures that he gave when he was the Freud Memorial Professor in London in 1979, André Green produced a metapsychology equipped with beautiful butterfly-like geometries. His work is full of structures, substructures, logics ... and people who enter into relations based on them. The people he describes—analysts and analysands—possess a considerable amount of power: dependent on, but separate from, the spaces that they are engaged with. In this respect, he works with the tradition of the British Independents, although his investigations of structure are considerably more extensive than theirs. His starting point is Winnicott's formulations on space:

> In order to study the play and then the cultural life of the individual one must study the fate of the potential space between any one baby and the human (and therefore fallible) mother-figure... (Winnicott 1971a: 100)

Both Winnicott and Green see spatial structures as active in the construction of reality (both in and out of analysis),[3] always involved in the effects of symbolisation, and always partially involved in the attempt to communicate. Winnicott ends the passage I have cited with a characterisation of the mother-infant bond in terms of love. So is love and its effects really supposed to inhabit these spaces? And are these the kinds of space that the geometer analyses? The structural pole that we are presenting says: *yes*.[4]

Green's work gives rise to the following question: in his account of the relationship between the analyst and the analysand does he intend spatiality to be taken as a formalisation of the analytical situation? The answer is fairly clearly: yes. He develops a notion that he takes from Bouvet of the functioning of distance in the analytical relation, and extends it so as to be able to introduce an algebra of 'reasonably small differences' within the analytical space (Green 1997, chapters 11 and 12). He asks why the structure of representation needs to be given a central place in the analysis of the clinical situation: 'Why not follow Anglo-Saxon analysts who have abandoned the differences Freud drew between word-presentation, thing-presentation, and affect?' (Green 1997: 307). His answer lists the defects of abandoning an analysis of the structure of language:

> ...censorship interferes to a minor extent when words are replaced by images, to a greater extent when words are replaced by affects, and to an even greater extent when acting out or bodily states come to the forefront (Green 1997: 307).

But he insists at the same time on having an opposite theme: since there exist 'limits to language', analysts must use their 'ego control, ...power of inhibition, and... ability to link and integrate... psychical layers' (Green 1997: 307). The power of the individual is here blended in with the spatiality of the relationship.

In the space whose elements are relations between people, let us go back to the early formulations of the problem of intersubjectivity, made by Bion and Rickman in their work at Northfields during the War. In the Northfields paper (Bion & Rickman 1961),[5] Bion had been concerned with the problem of how to restore to a group its activity: he claimed that the display of the causes of the group's distress will provide the group with an activity around which it is able to unite. In ordinary social conditions the individuals in the group will not have available sufficient insight to be able to appreciate the nature of their distress. If the nature of this distress can be demonstrated to the group, says Bion, then the functioning of the group will change. Now, whether or not this is true, why does Bion think that it is 'demonstration' that is needed? Why does he introduce such a term? Some commentators will imagine that he is invoking not proof, but a metaphor: if this is so, then the way that he develops his argument is surprising. Imagine, he says, that the various pathways that the individual can take form a 'framework'. This framework is 'included in a space', and 'enclosed within transparent walls'. Within this space, he says, 'conflicting impulses' produce a series of directions that the individual can move in. This preliminary formalisation of the space of human relations will then allow Bion to formulate, and then attempt to resolve, the problem of how to move away from the state of depression in the group. Bion expresses his determination 'not to attempt the solution of any problem until its borders have been clearly defined', and this attitude he describes as that of 'scientific seriousness' (Bion & Rickman 1961: 19). In the early 1940s, Bion was looking for a 'scientific' theory of the functioning of the group, and also of the motivation of the individual.

After the War, Bion returned to this theme: like the philosophers before and at the time of Socrates, he saw the individual as stunned and disorientated by the conflicts in the human soul.[6] He maintained that the fundamental problem of human relations was unconscious conflict—conflict demanding an intervention from specialists who are able to find a pathway through what previously had been simply an impasse and blockage in human desire. 'Full human development', according to Bion, involves scope for the development of human relations over a wide range of interaction with others: a person should be able to act in a group, says Bion, 'without being condemned to the frustration and atrophy of their ... desires' (Bion 1994: 344). The dereliction of the fabric of human relations—what he calls 'psychiatric disinheritance'—he seeks to remedy by formulating a science of the unconscious: in this paper he calls for a scientific study of this unconscious tension operative both in the individual and in the group.

Lacan agreed with Bion about the crisis in human relations, and the deserted condition of most psychiatric research. Lacan had visited England in September 1945 for a period of five weeks. A visit so soon after the end of the War put him in touch with the variety of initiatives that had been put forward by British psychiatrists during the war years: he had a series of meetings with British psychiatrists and psychoanalysts, in which he was impressed particularly by the work of Bion, Rickman, and Sutherland. He had a 'long meeting' with Bion and Rickman where they conveyed to him their concern to give a central focus to research on the structure of the unconscious. One (Rickman) said to Lacan that the Oedipus Complex was the 'equivalent of the three body problem in physics' (Lacan 1947: 293-312). The report that Lacan gave of these meetings was presented in Paris in the autumn of 1946, just a few months before Bion's appeal for a new psychoanalytical ethics in psychiatric research in Britain.

Like Bion, Lacan described the conditions of depression and loss of creative interaction in the modern social world; he talked of what he called 'the truly panic dissolution of the moral state of groups'.[7] The group, he said, used 'the same modes of defence that the individual uses in neurotic defence against anxiety'. Lacan agreed with Bion on a wide variety of points, and especially on two central themes—that group structure is in 'crisis', and that the cause of this crisis is neurosis in the individual. The remedy was to be sought in the development of a science of psychoanalytic intervention, based on the structures present in Freud's 'young science' of the structure of groups.

According to Lacan, the same structures which are present in individual neurosis introduce patterns of group dissolution that 'create destinies that will persist for generations'. He referred to the Lancet paper by Rickman and Bion as marking a historical step in the development of a science of individual and group identifications. When he outlined the structures Bion wished to become manifest in a space within 'transparent walls', he described them as giving a 'perfect readability' to the group's difficulties in coming to terms with the problems of its own existence. Although he was already developing his own studies in formalisation, he appealed to the work of Kurt Lewin. Lewin was able to formulate the properties of the social bond in terms of 'vector analysis' and of space. In the discussion on Lacan's paper[8] Lewin's 'topographical' investigations were again praised, this time by Pierre Turquet. When Lacan was asked to summarise his response to the work of Bion and Rickman, and to the movement to introduce the analysis of structure in general, he concluded by alluding to the words of Galileo: '*E pur si muove*'—'the structure is there: that's how it works'.

Lacan worked with specialists on formal structure for over thirty years.[9] Lewin—in pioneering work in the 1920s and 1930s—had investigated what he called the 'principles of topological and vectorial psychology' (Lewin 1936). Lewin had proposed investigating spaces the structure of which constitutes the psychological determination of the individual. His work analysed separation properties, inaccessible regions, frontiers and boundaries. In setting up this orientation in the analytical field, Lewin drew on work by Felix Hausdorff, Karl Menger, Georg Friedrich Bernhard Riemann, and Waclaw Sierpinski. What characterises these writers? They are all first rank mathematicians—all of them shifting the frontiers of work in mathematics in their time. Both Lacan and Bion would try to include mathematical work within the structure of an analytical school, eventually making immense advances beyond the development and extension of the methods and conceptual apparatus that Lewin and his school had been using in Berlin since 1926.

Lewin's School produced important results, many of them bearing on questions of clinical technique. One of his researchers, Bluma Zeigarnik, a Russian psychologist working with him in Berlin, produced a series of results involving uncompleted tasks. Any such task, she found, is remembered significantly better than work which is allowed to be complete. Since remembering is one of the aims of the analytical work, breaking the session in a variety of ways would seem to generate productive variations of technique.[10] Although these themes have been taken up by Hartmann, Bernfeld, Lagache, Lacan, and others, there has been little or no development of any of these issues in the UK.[11] In one of her contributions to the discussion of the theory of technique, Anna Freud was able to say:

> Logical as these regulations appear in the light of the definition of analytical technique given above, not one of them has remained unchallenged. I name as examples ... the break with regular hourly work advocated by Lacan (1953—1955); the distrust of the unlimited development of transference by members of the Chicago Institute (Alexander and French, 1946); the sole use of transference interpretations by part of the English school of analysts... (A. Freud 1998: 247)[12]

Naturally, analytical theory cannot be considered in isolation from questions of analytical technique; neither in turn can be considered in isolation from questions of structure. By the time of the Second World War, a fairly widespread recognition was emerging that analysis of structure needed to be explicit, and that any method for the investigation of structure would raise questions about the philosophy of science.

An outline of how work in this field developed in the 1940s can be seen in the work of Siegfried Bernfeld, Marjorie Brierley, and John Rickman. In a paper first published in 1941 (Bernfeld 1985), Bernfeld presented his work as an argument about observation: it is actually an argument about the far from simple relationship between observation and structure. In this respect Bernfeld is recapitulating themes that from the beginning Freud had located in the field of psychoanalysis.[13]

Bernfeld started off by seeking to establish the method of psychoanalytic investigation. He arrived at two results: the first was that any science started with 'the observation of facts', and the second was that the methods of observation are themselves made up of structures: there is some conflict between these two themes. Let me describe the latter. Bernfeld argued that Freud built psychoanalysis as an instrument through which a refinement of ordinary conversation is used as a method for the investigation of the unconscious. Conversation, particularly as it is practised in the analytical setting, has a structure: it moves from a usual state of discourse to the approach of a hidden secret; talk that goes round the place of what is hidden gives rise to a confession; after the disclosure of the secret, a new form of usual conversation begins. Bernfeld formalised this as follows: u-s-c-u (or more fully, u-s-i-c-u, where i represents the intervention of the analyst). This structure u-s-c-u now becomes a fact of psychoanalysis, and demands investigation, demands research.

The appeal for research that Bernfeld had initiated now started to lose its momentum: as he developed his argument he found himself caught between two poles. The first idea he put forward—that science is based on facts—is an old fashioned idea termed 'induction'. This was widely believed during the first half of the twentieth century (and certainly at the time Bernfeld was writing), but is now equally widely discredited. The second idea was much more subtle -that fundamentally central facts in a field of science are themselves structures. Thus his call for research—and for attention to the philosophy of science—can be interpreted in two ways. The first is to focus on the domain of fact; the second is to give priority to the domain of structure—as did, in fact, Bernfeld himself. The first of these two pathways was taken by Marjorie Brierley, the second by John Rickman and, later, Wilfred Bion.

Brierley set up a framework for the investigation of research problems in psychoanalysis which directed such work in Britain in a particular direction: the direction of facts.[14] She supposed that scientific theory was based on facts that could provide it with 'adequate evidence' (Brierley 1951: 92). Actually, little is evident or patent in any science, let alone psychoanalysis. She insisted that research in psychoanalysis be based on the inductivist tradition, and appeared to be unaware that the more general (theories) can never logically be deduced from the less general (facts). The aim of psychoanalysis, she claimed, was to establish what the theories were which followed from the facts: psychoanalysis should look for 'general laws which can be deduced from the specific clinical data. Correct observation of data is the first step' (Brierley 1951: 96).

In reality, the nature of logic is such that the level of fact can be deduced from theories, but never the other way around. Her message was repeated time after time. In the previous year she had proposed that psychoanalysis give itself the duty of becoming 'strictly scientific' (Brierley 1951: 89); by this she meant the introduction of 'strict definition' to allow the further establishment of 'adequate and valid... evidence'. She showed no awareness of the fact that 'the particulars of the consulting room' are already infused with theories, that facts are theory-laden, and not in any sense independent of the structures with which these theories are built. Later, rather than correcting these views by gaining closer access to the work of philosophers of science, she wrapped them in a protective film of humanism: 'metapsychology ... is derived by inference from the detailed study of living persons'; this produced, she hoped, a 'generalisation of science' relatively free from 'mathematical terminology' where a philosophy of life is directive of psychoanalytic research in general, and of metapsychology in particular (Brierley 1951: 156).[15]

This was the first signpost used as a direction finder by the British Society. It was a sustained body of work, all of it pointing in the wrong direction. A second—a different direction—was proposed by Rickman at the end of the decade. By research, Rickman meant something quite different. Towards the end of the 1940s , he started to construct what would become a series of articles on the problem of structure in analysis.[16] In these papers he devised a theory of the different structures present in 1-body relations, 2-body relations, and 3-body relations: 1- and 2- body relations represented the conditions of a range of research moving from 'reflexology' up to the 'sound-proof and social-proof' investigations of the consulting room. To these preliminary formulations of the structure that Bion wanted to become 'transparent', Rickman added the 3-body relations of 'all the derivatives' of the Oedipus complex. He also commented on the difficulties of formulating many-body psychologies at a level higher than three: the projection of these structures into the analytical relation Rickman hoped would provide the framework for the analytical work.[17]

Thus Rickman aimed to formulate the analytical relation as a 2-body laboratory where the 3-body relations of the Oedipus complex are transferred into the 'scientific reality' of the analytical encounter. His stress on the 'present' of the analytical interaction would have generated a range of difficult problems for his programme, but many of these would have produced creative developments of psychoanalytic research. And in terms of his seriousness in taking up themes of formal structure there can be little doubt about his intentions:

There are two kinds of mathematics I am led to understand; there is metrical mathematics and non-metrical ... The former ... has produced nothing of much importance to psychiatrists; the latter ...—I refer of course to topology—has not yet been developed well enough to be able to catch the fineness of the structure of the human soul. (Rickman 1957: 209)[18]

Rickman wanted to build such a web—to work with structures that could grasp the intricacies of human passion, and Bion—his colleague and analysand—followed him in this quest over the next thirty years.

Bion took up a root and branch investigation of scientific method. In his personal notes[19] he initiated a series of detailed investigations of the work of philosophers of science, starting with Braithewaite's work in the 1950s, and moving on to wider discussions of Popper, Quine, and Russell. He attempted to formulate and 'improve' classical scientific method, attempting to use the structure of scientific deductive systems in order to grasp the functioning of the analytical encounter. 'Psycho-analysis is a joint activity, of analysand and analyst to determine the truth': it is in this respect, said Bion, that psycho-analysis acquires the characteristics of a science. His phrase continued: ' ... this being so, the two are engaged—no matter how imperfectly—on what is in intention a scientific activity' (Bion 1994: 114).[20] He searched in classical presentations of the methods of science—Euclid, Galileo, Whewell—attempting to avoid the errors of his predecessors, by studying logic and in particular the logic of the sciences.

Marjorie Brierley was not happy with what Bion proposed. Even in the early 1950s—in her comments on his remedies to civilisation's malaise and discontent—she opposed any formulation of psychoanalysis that diverged from her own recipe for 'balance' in science. In commenting on Bion, she put it in the following way: 'psychoanalysis must preserve its own balance if it is to render any aid to the wider world crisis' (Brierley 1951: 117). One of the functions of the proper handling of metapsychology was, in her view, to give such a tempering perspective by blending scientific method into a liberal view of human nature. This movement towards a realistic 'fellowship' of social engagement will be inferred, she said, in the same way that she takes natural science to have already inferred properties of the external world, that is, by induction. Her basic orientation in psychoanalysis was then given by the acceptance of 'common-sense empiricism ... of whatever seems to be inescapably real for man'. The kind of formalisation that Bion was seeking upset what she wanted to establish as the ethics for psychoanalytic work.

Her conversation with Bion continued in 1967. In her comments on his paper 'On Memory and Desire' (in Bion 1994: 385), she accused him of 'departing' from psychoanalytical technique, and this on the grounds of the functioning of judgement and observation in analytical practice. There could have been a wide field of questions open up at this point, but in a sense this debate is only now just beginning.

In January 1959, Bion had talked of the light that clinical work in psychoanalysis can throw on common sense: common sense is revised by the formalisation of clinical problems—and so is observation, judgement, and 'that particular instance of scientific hypothesis and deduction known to us as a psycho-analytic interpretation' (Bion 1994: 15).[21] Bion thought that a psychoanalytical interpretation might have to intersect with points within a geometry in order to determine a direction for analysis (Bion 1994: 210): this concern with deduction and consequentiality, formal and informal structuring in the unconscious, led his work away from the direction appealed to by Brierley. In following-through Rickman's direction in psychoanalysis, Bion struggled with questions of common sense and formalisation, in order to set in place an ethics of psychoanalysis not imposed on it from elsewhere.

Rickman and Bernfeld, like Lacan, stressed the importance of the work of Kurt Lewin. 'The work of Lewin and his pupils' said Bernfeld, had provided exactly the right direction of research to be able to take up the delicate 'difficult—and fascinating' problems of the structure of the human soul (Bernfeld 1985: 351). Rickman had drawn on Lewin's formulations of the ways in which the analysis of structure can formulate and give approaches to what is real (Rickman 1957: 220). Lewin and Imre Hermann can be seen as the precursors in this field of investigation of the texture of neurotic pain. They placed human suffering within a matrix which determines real effects by a structural method: real passion, in many respects, can find its definition only by being located within the neighbourhoods of subjective spaces.

Neurotic suffering stems from a kind of error: an error in apprehending the past. A structure of error constitutes the mechanism of defence in neurosis, and the painful investigation of this structure constitutes the main direction of analytical work. When Bion searched for a method built from the apparatus of the sciences, it is such a method of investigation that he was trying to introduce into the human soul. As he said in the notes that he added to his compilations on 6th February 1960:

> The search for... method constitutes for the psycho-analyst the search for a scientific method. For him the scientific method is

that procedure, or series of procedures, by which error is made to declare itself. (Bion 1994: 123)

Notes

[1] An alternative view—one shared by many of the participants at the time—is proposed by Pearl King in her introduction to *The Freud-Klein Controversies 1941-1945* (King & Steiner 1991). She sees the central issue as that of how to incorporate 'new' analytical knowledge into the field of psychoanalysis: Marjorie Brierley held a similar perspective. The notion that the dispute was 'centrally' about the structuring agency of the psychic apparatus was less widely adopted, despite the fact that this is precisely the perspective which locates the issues in the work of Freud. These groups tend to assume the question to be largely one of 'adding' results to Freud's work.

[2] Rayner and Matte-Blanco, like Imre Hermann and large sections of the modern Franco-Hispanic schools, draw on mathematics in order to analyse relations of structure. In this respect, see, for instance, Rayner's appeal to the notion of 'isomorphism' (Rayner 1990: chapters 3 and 4).

[3] Green adopts Winnicott's notion of potential space and adapts it into a concept describing the analytical relation. He formulates the Freudian concept of the preconscious as a form of 'transitional space' between the unconscious and the conscious, and he relates this space-at-play in the analytical relationship to the Winnicottian space: the one is a projection of the other (Green 1997: 304).

[4] That love is operative within such spaces has in fact been known for a long time in the analytical movement: see Imre Hermann 1978, 1979, 1980. These texts originally appeared in German or Hungarian between 1924 and 1966.

[5] W. Bion and J. Rickman: 'Intra-Group Tensions in Therapy', in *The Lancet*, 27th November 1943 (subsequently reprinted in W. Bion, *Experiences in Groups*, London, 1961).

[6] W. Bion, 'Psychiatry at a Time of Crisis', a talk given as Chair of the Medical Section of the British Psychological Society in January 1947, and published in *The British Journal of Medical Psychology*, vol. 21, 1948, pp.81-89; it is reprinted in Bion 1994: 337-352.

[7] 'Le groupe... en proie à une dissolution vraiment panique de son statut moral' (Lacan 1947: 293).

[8] Lacan 1947: 313-318. The discussion involved Pierre Turquet, Eugène Minkowski, Adrien Borel, Henri Ey, and others.

[9] Lacan sought collaboration with a working mathematician. For many years he worked with Georges-Théodule Guilbaud, a mathematician who had worked with the epistemological study-groups developing the work of Piaget. Guilbaud took part, for instance, in a symposium held in June 1959, a round table discussion between psychologists, logicians, and mathematicians, on the relation between informal 'natural' forms of thinking and proof methodology; the discussion involved questions of structure and formalisation, ranging over questions in the metamathematics of Tarski, and order relations in structures weaker than lattices (Gréco, Grize, Papert & Piaget 1960). From 1951 onwards Guilbaud worked regularly with Lacan, Benveniste, and Lévi-Strauss.

[10] Any break in the session—holidays, a variable length of session, loosening the attachment the analysand has to their day-dreams—is evocative of broken love relations; the primary body of such broken relations are those of the repressed Oedipal loves. It follows that such breaks will bring the transference into being.

[11] Even today, in the United Kingdom and in the United States, many people are unfamiliar with the details of Lacanian clinical work. Things are very different in Latin countries, where in addition to closed presentations of clinical work in psychoanalytical and public sector institutions, clinical work is presented extensively in public conferences. Many hundreds of cases are presented annually in such contexts. For an introduction to the existing Anglo-Saxon literature, see Benvenuto 1989, Burgoyne 1990, 1996, Leader 1997, Burgoyne & Sullivan 1997. Good general discussions of Lacanian technique are available in Fink 1997 and Dor 1997. There are also now a number of Lacanian journals published both in Britain and in the United States which give the Anglo-Saxon reader access to details of Lacanian clinical work.

[12] Investigations of variations of classical analytical technique were widespread in the 1950s: Sacha Nacht in Paris and Kurt Eissler in the United States were prominent among those putting forward such proposals. Anna Freud approved of some of these innovations; she seems to have been unaware that Lacan's formulation of the variable session was based in part on the study by Lacan and Lagache of the Zeigarnik effect. For details of the situation at this time see the panel on variations in technique at the IPA Congress in Paris in 1957, in particular the contributions by Loewenstein, Eissler and Nacht, published in 1958.

[13] See for instance the themes of the relation between observational thinking and the structure of desire in Freud's 'Project' (Freud 1950a—or, better, Freud 1950b).

[14] Marjorie Brierley published a series of articles in the 1940s on the themes of metapsychology and scientific method. They were later developed in her book of papers published in 1951. See 'Internal Objects and Theory', 'Theory, Practice, and Public Relations', 'Notes on Metapsychology as Process Theory', and 'Further Notes on the Implications of Psycho-Analysis: Metapsychology and Personology', in Brierley 1951.

[15] This subordination of psychoanalysis to a world view other than that of the sciences is of course directly in opposition to what Freud insisted on. See 'The Question of a *Weltanschauung*', in Freud 1933.

[16] See 'The Factor of Number in Individual- and Group-Dynamics', 'The Role and Future of Psychotherapy within Psychiatry', 'Number in the Human Sciences', and 'Methodology and Research in Psychopathology'. All of these appeared in the collection of his papers *Selected Contributions to Psychoanalysis* (1957).

[17] Rather than project these structures into the analytical present, Lacan of course wanted to use them as pathways into the (Oedipal) past. See Lacan's comments on the 'ego-to-ego' in the analytical relation, as distinct from what he calls 'the reconstruction of the (psycho-sexual) history' of the analysand (Lacan 1988: chs. I-IV).

[18] Several contemporary developments in this area are published in the present collection of papers.

[19] Published as Bion1994.

[20] This is an undated fragment, but was probably written in early 1960.

[21] Interpretation is one of the issues that is now beginning to be debated in a series of discussions between schools of psychoanalysts: see for instance the articles by Catalina Bronstein and Bernard Burgoyne 'Technique and Interpretation in Klein' , and 'Interpretation' in Burgoyne & Sullivan 1997: 37- 64.

DONALD W. WINNICOTT'S DIAGRAM OF THE TRANSITIONAL OBJECT, AND OTHER FIGURES

Margret Tonnesmann

A diagram is an illustrative figure giving an outline or general schema of an object and its various parts... A diagram is a graphic representation of the cause or results of any action or process or its varieties. (Shorter Oxford Dictionary)

A diagram can be understood as aiming for a direct visual impression, without having to communicate data with the precision of a tabula. Donald Winnicott's diagrams are indeed direct visual impressions, presented in his personal style of 'squiggle drawings'. He was gifted—there are hundreds of his drawings in the archives of the Institute of Psycho-Analysis in London which bear witness to his talent. We have been informed that he made these drawings spontaneously, illustrating moods or thoughts. Some of them look like sophisticated, humorous cartoons. However, as James Hood (1996) has pointed out, Winnicott would have hated them to be taken too seriously.

Winnicott used diagrams in two papers written in 1951 and 1952. The first of these, 'Transitional Objects and Transitional Phenomena', was read to the British Psycho-Analytical Society. In it he presented, for the first time, his concept of 'transitional space', where the infant makes use of the first object of which he takes possession. In 1952 he presented a paper, 'Psychoses and Child Care', to the Psychiatric Section of the Royal Society of Medicine. Here, Winnicott presented his views on early emotional development. He stated, 'At first the infant is not the unit. As perceived from outside the unit is an environment-individual set-up' (Winnicott 1952: 221).

In the setting in which the individual starts, he/she 'can gradually come to create a personal environment' which 'becomes something that is near enough to the environment that can be generally perceived' (Winnicott 1952: 222). Winnicott prefaced his paper by stating that what he intended to say was controversial but – from his point of view—fully substantiated by his own analytic and other clinical work. Since his intention was to study 'the whole procedure of the early development of psyche-soma including the delays and distortions', Winnicott claimed that he would 'need to be dogmatic, and I hope to make my meaning clear by using diagrams' (Winnicott 1952: 222). Perhaps one could read this introduction as indicating that diagrams are used here as a 'short-cut', in order to cover the vast amount of material Winnicott had set out to present in a single lecture.

Nearly all the diagrams he used in this paper—and some others—can also be found in the posthumously published, unfinished manuscript which served as a basis for his lecture courses at London University and the London School of Economics. This was written in summer 1954, and was intended for eventual publication. Indeed, it was later included in the collection *Human Nature* (1988).

In the introduction to this book, Claire Winnicott described her husband's style of lecturing:

> His lectures could be free and seemed unstructured only because they were based on a central core of integrated knowledge and a carefully formulated pattern of the stages of human development which the students could comprehend. His rapidly constructed diagrams on the blackboard will be remembered by all who attended his lectures as an essential feature of his way of communicating. (Winnicott 1988: ix)

M. Jacobs has quoted a psychiatric social work student who found Winnicott's lectures difficult to understand. However, the student also commented that '…his drawings of the relation between the baby and the breast were impressed upon her memory' (Jacobs 1995: 20).

There is a passage in *Human Nature* that may throw some light on Winnicott's intentions when drawing the diagrams. At the beginning of the chapter which deals with emotional development characteristic in infancy he sets out to describe 'the stage of development at which the infant becomes a unit, becomes able to feel the self (and therefore others) to be whole, a thing with a limiting membrane, and with an inside and outside' (Winnicott 1988: 67). He then points out that:

> The concepts of the previous section (which dealt with health and instinct theory) were intellectual concepts in the mind of the observer… Now, instead, it is more profitable to use a diagram which could be a child's drawing. Let us say that a child is covering paper with lines and to-fro movements, and has been wandering round with pencil going from place to place, occasionally slipping incontinently over the edges and then something new

turns up, a line that joins up with the beginning, a rough circle is made and the child points and says: 'duck' or even 'Tony' or 'Anne'. The diagram we need, in fact, is the child's conception of the self, a sphere, which is a circle in a two-dimensional drawing. (Winnicott 1988: 67-68)

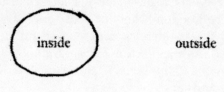

Fig. 1

Characteristically at this stage there is progress of the following kind: The idea of a limiting membrane appears, and from this follows the idea of an inside and an outside. Then there develops the theme of a ME and a not-ME. (Winnicott 1988: 68)

In a later chapter Winnicott suggests that it is possible

to examine a still earlier stage of individual development by once again employing a new method of presentation. We can make use of a diagram. The environment is now at its most important and cannot be left out either in theory or in practice. (Winnicott 1988: 126)

Winnicott reproduces, at this point, the same diagrams that he had already used in, as he put it, a more 'dogmatic' form, for his paper 'Psychosis and Child Care'.

André Green has pointed out that Winnicott's work 'reflects richly alive experiencing rather than erudite schematising' (Green 1997: 286). The point of reference for Winnicott's propositions remained the analytic setting, hence, Green says 'theory stays in direct touch with clinical practice' (Green 1997: 286). Jean-Bertrand Pontalis has contrasted the French preference for forging 'neo-concepts' with Winnicott's way of 'finding something – difficult cases that have forced him to find it and, as best he can… he puts words to his discovery' (Pontalis 1987: 142). [1981] Perhaps one can therefore understand the diagrams Winnicott used in his papers of 1951 and 1952 as additional visual means of communicating what he had found.

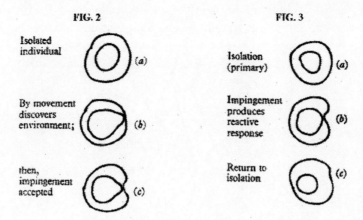

Figs. 2 & 3

Winnicott states that Fig. 2, above, 'shows how, by active adaptation to the child's needs, the environment enables him to be in undisturbed isolation. The infant does not know. In this state he makes a spontaneous movement and the environment is discovered without loss of sense of self' (Winnicott 1952: 222).

This is contrasted with Fig. 3, where the adaptation to the environment is faulty. The environment impinges on the individual 'so that the individual must become a reactor to this impingement. The sense of self is lost... and is only regained by a return to isolation' (Winnicott 1952: 222).

On other occasions, however, Winnicott stressed that the infant has an innate capacity to recover from those impingements which belong to the ordinary individual-environment set-up. In the paper 'Transitional Objects and Transitional Phenomena' he refers to the positive value of these impingements. It is only a faulty environmental adaptation which compels the infant to become a reactor. Consequently, it 'produces a psychotic distortion of the environment-individual set-up. Relationships produce loss of the sense of self, and the latter is only regained by return to isolation' (Winnicott 1951: 222). In the course of further development, it leads to 'more and more defensive organisation in repudiation of environmental impingement' (Winnicott 1952: 222).

Winnicott's Diagrams

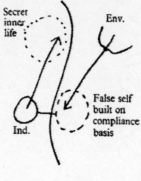

FIG. 4
BASIC SPLIT IN PERSONALITY

Fig. 4

Fig. 4, above, depicts:

how a tendency for a basic split in the environment-individual set-up can start through failure of active adaptation on the part of the environment at the beginning. In the extreme case of splitting the secret inner life has very little in it derived from external reality. It is truly incommunicable. (Winnicott 1951: 224/225)

A 'false self', therefore, develops on the basis of a compliance with the environment. Interestingly, this diagram was not included either in Winnicott's later paper, 'Ego Distortion in Terms of a True and False Self' (1960), or at the relevant places in the unpublished 1954 manuscript. However, in the latter, Winnicott refers to this diagram, and comments that:

By using the diagram that belongs to the extreme case one can easily illustrate the implications of this way of looking at early emotional development and apply what we see to the task of the ordinary normal person and the difficulties inherent in life. (Winnicott 1988: 108)

He suggests that, in lesser degrees of splitting,

there are objects in the secret inner relatedness of the true self and these objects have been derived from some success at the stage of the theoretical first feed. In other words, in lesser degrees of this illness it is not so much the primary splitting which is to be found as a secondary organisation of splitting which implies regression from difficulties encountered at a later stage of emotional development. (Winnicott 1988: 107)

FIG. 5
THEORETICAL FIRST FEED

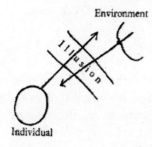

FIG. 6
POSITIVE VALUE OF ILLUSION.
THE FIRST POSSESSION =
TRANSITIONAL OBJECT

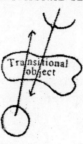

Figs. 5 & 6

Fig. 5, above, from 'Psychoses and Child Care' (1952) depicts this 'theoretical first feed', and – along with Fig. 6, 'the transitional object', the first possession—is conceived as a development which demonstrates the positive value of illusion. It is, however, in the paper 'Transitional Objects and Transitional Phenomena' that the development of the individual-environment set-up is discussed in detail.

Continuing our examination of 'Psychoses and Child Care' we encounter two diagrams which, notably, do not have the stamp of a squiggle drawing.

Figs. 7 and 8 (overleaf) are akin to ordinary verbal descriptions of the intermediate area of primary madness and its elaboration. Both depict the intermediate transitional space (and also process) between inner subjective reality and the external, shared reality, which, as Winnicott suggests, remains an important source of experiencing throughout life. The infant's subjective experience is *verbalised* here, rather than communicated by a squiggle drawing. It could be seen as another example of what Winnicott termed 'intellectual concepts in the mind of the observer' (Winnicott 1988: 67). Evidently he did not depict such concepts through a squiggle drawing diagram.

28 *Winnicott's Diagrams*

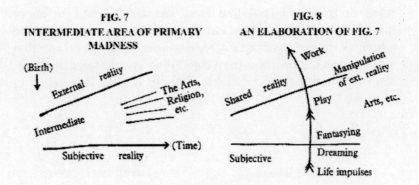

Figs. 7 & 8

In the paper 'Transitional Objects and Transitional Phenomena', Winnicott discussed the value of illusion and reasoned that from birth human beings are concerned with the problem of the relationship between what is objectively perceived and what is subjectively conceived of.

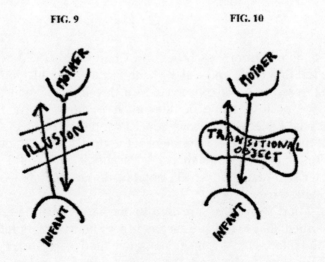

Figs. 9 & 10

Figs. 9 and 10 are slightly modified versions of Figs. 5 and 6 from 'Psychosis and Child Care'. Winnicott described the idea illustrated by Figs. 9 and 10 as follows:

At some theoretical point early in the development of every human individual an infant in a certain setting provided by the mother is capable of conceiving of the idea of something that would meet the growing need that arises out of instinctual tension. The infant cannot be said to know at first what is to be created. At this point in time the mother presents herself. In the ordinary way she gives her breast and her potential feeding-urge. The mother's adaptation to the infant's needs, when good enough, gives the infant the *illusion* that there is an external reality that corresponds to the infant's own capacity to create. In other words there is an overlap between what the mother supplies and the child might conceive of. To the observer, the child perceives what the mother actually presents, but this is not the whole truth. The infant perceives the breast only in so far as the breast could be created just there and then. There is no interchange between the mother and infant. Psychologically the infant takes from a breast what is part of the infant, and the mother gives milk to an infant that is part of herself. In psychology, the idea of interchange is based on an illusion in the psychologist. (Winnicott 1971a: 11-12)

In Fig. 10:

A shape is given to the area of illusion to illustrate what I consider to be the main function of the transitional object and of transitional phenomena. The transitional object and the transitional phenomena start each human being off with what will always be important for them, i.e., a neutral area of experience which will not be challenged. (Winnicott 1971a: 12)

Winnicott has assumed that:

...the task of reality acceptance is never completed, that no human being is free from the strain of relating inner and outer reality, and that relief from the strain is provided by an intermediate area of experience... which is not challenged (arts, religion etc.). (Winnicott 1971a: 13)

The assertion that the transitional object is a universal phenomenon has been received and treated with caution. As Green has pointed out:

Winnicott has in fact described not so much an object as a space lending itself to the creation of objects. Here, the line itself becomes a space; the metaphorical boundary dividing internal from external, that either/or in which the object has traditionally been entrapped, expands into the intermediate area and playground of transitional phenomena. (Green 1997: 285)

Marion Milner (1978), in her obituary of Donald Winnicott, remembers their common interest in a drawing of hers which showed the interplay of the edges of two jugs. Winnicott refers to it in a discussion of the paradox of a separation that is a form of union (Winnicott 1971a: 98). The baby comes to make use of a symbol of union and so can benefit from separation when using the transitional object.

In the paper 'Psychoses and Child Care' we find further squiggle drawing diagrams depicting the infant's early emotional development.

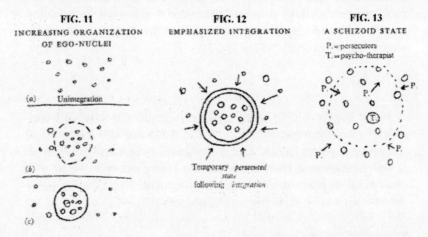

Figs. 11, 12, 13

Fig. 11 demonstrates that, from the infant's point of view, the personality does not start as a completed whole. 'By various means the unity of the individual psyche becomes a fact, at first at moments... and later over long and variable periods of time' (Winnicott 1952: 225). Winnicott has used here Edward Glover's concept of the integration of ego nuclei.

Fig. 12:

...depicts the moments of the gathering together of the bits – dangerous moments for the individual. With respect to the total environmental-individual set-up the integration activity produces an individual in a raw state, a potential paranoiac. The persecutors in the new phenomenon, the outside, become neutralised in ordinary healthy development by the fact of the mother's loving care, which physically (as in holding) and psychologically (as in understanding or empathy, enabling sensitive adaptation), makes the individual's primary isolation a fact. Environmental failure just here starts the individual off with a paranoid potential. This shows clinically so early and so clearly that one can forgive those who (not knowing about infant psychology) explain it in terms of heredity.

In defence against the terrible anxieties of the paranoid state in very early life there is not infrequently organised a state in which the infant lives permanently in his or her own inner world which is not, however, firmly organised. The external persecution... is kept at bay by non-achievement of unit-status. (Winnicott 1952: 226-7)

Fig. 13 shows the experience of a schizoid child's therapy when child and therapist experience being magically controlled by the inner world in which the child lives.

This is a gross exaggeration of a healthy child's ordinary preoccupation during play, but is distinguished from healthy play by the lack of beginning and end of the game, by the degree of magical control, by the lack of organisation of play material according to any one pattern, and by the inexhaustibility of the child. (Winnicott 1952: 227)

The use of squiggle drawings in the diagrams belong to that intermediate area where objective thought is enriched by the experience of subjective personal meaning. They convey Winnicott's understanding of the clinical phenomena he experienced in his treatment of adult borderline patients and also his child patients.

These diagrams, however, must be clearly differentiated from the use of squiggles by Winnicott in his therapeutic consultations with children. In his book *Therapeutic Consultations in Child Psychiatry* (1971b) he mentions how children he saw as part of his paediatric practice had often dreamt of him the night before the consultation. Thus, he had become a subjective object for them. He used this observation and devised a game involving both parties. Winnicott describes how a kind of intimacy develops when he and the child take it in turn to make a squiggle out of the other's formless line on a piece of paper. André Green has described this as:

> ...the spontaneous movement of the hand that allows itself to be guided by the line, a hand which does not act but rather expresses itself, traces a more or less formless line, submitting it to the scrutiny of the other, who, deliberately, transforms it into a meaningful shape. (Green 1997: 293)

On special occasions, Winnicott states, there may evolve a 'sacred' moment when therapist and child mutually understand the special emotional predicament the child has brought to the consultation, *via* a squiggle that may have been completed by either the child or the therapist. As he points out, the squiggle game cannot be copied because the therapist is involved as a person in every case. It is only appropriate to play the game on the first few occasions, that is as long as the therapist remains a subjective object and before the child develops a transference relationship to the therapist as a person.

Winnicott used the squiggle game in his therapeutic consultations with children, then, to provide a space in which the child and the therapist together discover a time-limited mutually meaningful way of communicating and understanding. Only those children capable of using the therapist as a subjective object are suited to the game.

On the other hand, Winnicott used squiggle-shaped *diagrams* to convey his notion of the spatial nature of the environment-individual set-up, and the infant's subjective illusionary experience of the environmental facilitation that takes place in it. Only those readers in whom these visual presentations evoke meaning can use them for additional understanding of Winnicott's propositions.

Green has pointed out that before Winnicott 'there was no psychoanalytic theory of the environment or "set-up", to use Winnicott's own term' (Green 1997: 121). When Winnicott—in 1951, 1952 and 1954—first presented his propositions, he used squiggle-drawing diagrams to communicate in his own personal way with his audience. Masud

Khan, his editor, commented on Winnicott's style of writing and speaking that:

> There is no rhetoric or intimidating jargon in his *écriture*. He wrote as he spoke: simply and to relate. Not to incite convictions or indoctrinate. (Khan 1982: xii)

John Davis, a paediatric colleague and friend of Winnicott, observed that Winnicott was essentially concerned with exploration and with telling people what he had found. 'It is not for arguing', Davis commented, 'it was for taking away and using if you can' (Jacobs 1995: 100).

In the introduction to *Playing and Reality* (1971a) Winnicott stated that the book represented his thinking and his assessment of clinical material, and a development of the basic hypothesis that he had discussed in 1951 in his paper 'Transitional Objects and Transitional Phenomena' (which is re-printed in the book). His explorations centre not so much upon the transitional object itself, but upon the use that is made of it, at first by the infant's creation of it, then by the child's playing and in imaginative living throughout life. Winnicott says that he is reluctant to give examples of transitional phenomena since he fears that they:

> ...can start to pin down specimens and begin a process of classification of an unnatural and arbitrary kind, whereas the thing I am referring to is universal and has infinite variety. (Winnicott 1971a: xii)

The use the infant makes of the transitional object involves paradox. Winnicott repeatedly stated that we do not ask the infant: 'Have you found it or have you created it?' since to resolve the paradox by applying intellectual analysis would destroy its value.

The squiggle-drawing diagrams of the transitional space belong to a similar category: they depict observable phenomena in the shape of what was, for Winnicott, the infant's subjective imaginative experience of them.

THE SIGNIFICANCE OF BION'S CONCEPTS OF P-S↔D AND TRANSFORMATIONS IN 'O': A RECONSIDERATION OF THE RELATIONSHIP BETWEEN THE PARANOID-SCHIZOID AND DEPRESSIVE POSITIONS—AND BEYOND

James S. Grotstein

Introduction

Klein's conceptions of the paranoid-schizoid (P-S) and depressive (D) positions have taken their place amongst the most fundamental and enduring paradigms concerning early infant development.[1] They have become organising 'stations of the cross', so to speak, in the infant's (and the analytic patient's) veritable pilgrimage from the persecutory anxiety of projective disavowal, to the depressive/grieving anxiety of the acceptance of one's life and its ineluctable corollary—the fact of one's *dependency on one's objects*.

In another contribution I have reviewed Klein's Positions in a more detailed theoretical and clinical manner, and have proffered a number of extensions, revisions which I believe are now warranted. In this present contribution, however, I will review and reassess Klein's conceptions of the paranoid-schizoid and depressive positions in a more synoptic way. My aim is to outline some of the modifications I have proposed elsewhere, but with an emphasis on the contributions of W.R. Bion. In my opinion, Bion's works represent a post-modernising expansion and extension of Klein's Positions.

Originally, Bion's conception of the Positions[2] demonstrated a rigorous conformity to Klein's ideas. Later, however, after a series of paradigm shifts in his thinking, he seems to have soared onwards with radical revisions of her notions. The full significance of these shifts—in regard to the Positions as well as to other psychoanalytic conceptions—has been insufficiently appreciated, I believe.

Klein's conception of the Positions: a synopsis

Perhaps one of Klein's most unique contributions to psychoanalytic theory and technique was her concept of the epigenesis of infant development from the perspective of emotional *positions*, which was an innovative advance on Freud and Abraham's notion of *stages* and *phas-*

es.³ The latter were uncompromisingly *linear*, sequential 'way-stations' of development, whereas Klein's concept of the Positions initiated a non-linear gauge of how the infant experienced, and expressed, his or her unconscious anxieties in regard to external and internal part- and whole-objects.

She postulated that in the first three to four months of life the infant was *separate*, in opposition to the orthodox classical belief that the first stage of infancy was characterised by objectless narcissism. The infant was, therefore, ready for object relatedness from the start. Klein postulated further that during this time the infant experiences a cluster of imploding anxieties, originating from outside as well as inside, experienced as *persecutory anxiety* (persecutory, because the infant experiences them as originating outside its psyche). She termed this cluster of anxieties the *paranoid-schizoid* position (Klein 1946, 1952). Interestingly, she formulated this position somewhat later than she formulated its natural successor, the *depressive* position, which—she hypothesised—concerned a later (depressive) infantile cluster of anxieties (Klein 1935).

My aim here is to deconstruct what Klein meant by 'depressive' anxieties. It is reasonably clear what she intended by 'persecutory' anxiety—that is, paranoid terror: painful feelings and urges inchoately forced from outside into the psyche (from the infant's point of view), and accumulating in geometric ratios by attempted projective disidentifications of them. However, the projective disidentification of these painful feelings and urges only causes them to return with added omnipotent force when the object into whom the anxieties were projected is subsequently introjected. The notion of 'depressive' anxiety, however, conveys meanings which are, at the extreme, conflicting and inconsistent.

The problem can be traced as follows. Klein clearly built upon Freud's 'Mourning and Melancholia' (1917) in her formulation of the depressive position. What became increasingly apparent was her failure—in my opinion—to clarify the distinction between *successful mourning* and *failure of mourning* (*melancholia* as depressive illness). We recall that in his seminal metapsychological work, Freud was continuing his exploration of the fate of narcissism in infantile development. The child who has reached the stage of anaclitic object choice⁴ has already evolved from narcissism and is able successfully to mourn the loss of his or her object. The infant or child who is still predominantly narcissistic, however, is *unable* to mourn and therefore, in order to deny the loss, internalises the object and introjectively identifies with it. According to Freud this can occur in two ways: (a) the object is taken in and becomes 'a gradient in the ego', known also as the 'ego ideal' or the superego, or (b) the object is taken into the ego itself. Freud states that, in the case of (a), the ego ideal and the incorporated object with which it is identified exert a maximum of sadism toward the ego, which is identified with the object. This is the internal configuration of melancholia. It formed the master-plan for Fairbairn's (1952a) endopsychic structure, and most evidently for Klein's (1935) original concept of the depressive position.

In her earlier descriptions of the depressive position, Klein refers to phenomena that clearly bespeak clinical, depressive illness (melancholia). This represents the individual's *failure* to be able to mourn. Yet at other times—increasingly more pointedly—she refers to the 'attainment of the depressive position', as a virtual conquest and sublimation of the erstwhile persecutory anxieties of the paranoid-schizoid position—a 'state of grace', as it were. However, she also cautions that the attainment of the depressive position is transient and is not to be taken for granted, because a tendency always lurks in us to regress to the paranoid-schizoid position. Yet despite having stated this, Klein inadvertently impugns and demonises the paranoid-schizoid position, and virtually idealises the depressive position. The important distinction between clinical depressive illness (failed mourning) and successful mourning becomes eclipsed in this polarisation. In her earlier work on the depressive position Klein includes other positions—such as the *manic* and *obsessive positions* (Klein 1933, 1935). The former was subsequently declassified as a position, and emerged instead as a set of defences against experiencing the depressive position. The latter vanished altogether, and simply becoming one of the splitting techniques of the schizoid mechanisms of the paranoid-schizoid position.

I should like to return briefly to what I believe is a key issue in this discussion: the relationship between narcissism and the status of the Positions. Freud, Fairbairn, and early Klein give us to believe that clinical depressive illness constitutes a statement of the narcissist's failure to mourn; he or she becomes melancholic or depressed instead. I understand this to mean that not only does Klein's paranoid-schizoid position represent the continuation of narcissism—albeit in an inchoate manner—but so too does her depressive position and the clinical depressive illness (internalised paranoia) associated with it, albeit at a more advanced, whole-object level.

Perhaps a word on Klein's attitude toward narcissism is needed. We recall that she renounced the notion of *primary* narcissism, although she did allow for the existence of *secondary* narcissism—that is, a condition in which the infant identifies, first projectively and then introjectively, with the object. Pathological narcissism, therefore, would result from the *manic defence* (Klein 1940) in which the infant, in unconscious phantasy, believes that he or she has robbed mother of her goodness and re-appropriated it for him or herself.

Another place in which she acknowledges the effects of narcissism is her conceptualisation of the *schizoid mechanisms* (splitting, projective identification, magic omnipotent denial, and idealisation) all of which act 'narcissistically'—that is, each entails being the centre and putative origin of all events and experiences. Here Klein adhered closely to Freud's principles of psychic reality and psychic determinism. Klein (1933) clearly envisioned that the infant was—from birth—a veritable victim of its alien and unconscious instinctual drives, the most predominant amongst these being the death instinct. As the infant begins to assume its own sense of being a human subject, it also begins to assume—ever so fleetingly—its 'ownership' of its needs and feelings. This inchoate 'ownership' of self, and its emotional 'baggage', allows the infant to feel a sense of *agency* (Stern 1985; Moran 1993).

In summary, Klein seems to have revealed two incompatible attitudes toward the concept of the depressive position, an inconsistency that Likierman (1995) describes as the conflict between the *tragic* and the *moral* aspects of the depressive position. Likierman points out that there is a discrepancy between the way Klein spoke of 'overcoming the depressive position' (by which I take her to mean overcoming the anxieties consistent with the presence of clinical depressive illness—that is, pathological guilt) and—on the other hand—of *achieving* the depressive illness as a sublimated goal. For Likierman, the former view of the depressive position is 'moral', and the latter 'tragic'. She cites the following passages from Klein in order to emphasise her point:

> I have shown here and in my previous paper the deeper reasons for the individual's incapacity to overcome successfully the infantile depressive position. Failure to do so may result in depressive illness. (Klein 1940: 368)

She also quotes Meltzer as addressing this discrepancy:

> I take it that by 'overcoming' the depressive position [Klein] meant learning to tolerate the depressive anxieties about the destruction of the good object. (Meltzer 1978: 10)[5]

Some representative citations from Klein's contributions on the Positions

> In ontogenetic development sadism is overcome when the subject advances to the genital level. The more powerfully this phase sets in, the more capable of object-love the child becomes, and the more able is he to conquer his sadism by means of pity and sympathy. (Klein 1929a: 231)

In this early work, written before she formulated the depressive position, Klein emphasises the importance of the relationship of sadism to the infant's anxiety about objects. She also emphasises that the remedy for this anxiety is the attainment of the genital level, which she will later associate with the attainment of the depressive position.

> The early stages of the Oedipus conflict are dominated by sadism. They take place during a phase of development which is inaugurated by oral sadism (with which urethral, muscular and anal sadism associate themselves) and terminate when the ascendancy of anal sadism comes to an end. (Klein 1930: 249)

In this passage we see a modification—in part—of the ideas expressed previously. Now, even the attainment of the Oedipus complex may be fraught with sadistic anxiety. Moreover, it is interesting to note how Klein still seems dependent on the orthodox/classical phases and stages model. She has already formulated the connection between the emergence of sadism and the formation of the superego,[6] and now the stage is being set for the conception of the depressive position.

> There could be no doubt that the super-ego had been in full operation for some time in my small patients of between two-and-three-quarters and four years of age... Furthermore, my data showed that this early super-ego was immeasurably harsher and more cruel than that of the older child or adult, and that it literally crushed down the feeble ego of the small child. (Klein 1933: 267)

And:

> He thus displaces the source of his anxiety outwards and turns his objects into dangerous ones; but, ultimately, that danger belongs to his own aggressive instincts. For this reason his fear of his objects will always be proportionate to the degree of his own sadistic impulses. (Klein 1933: 270)

> Its [the infant's] belief that in thus attacking its mother's body it has also attacked its father and its brothers and sisters, and, in a wider sense the whole world, is in my experience, one of the underlying causes of its own sense of guilt, and the development of its social and moral feelings in general. (Klein 1933: 273)

It was another thirteen years before Klein formulated the paranoid-schizoid position, but only two years later she formulated the depressive position—although she did hint at a 'paranoiac position' (Klein 1935: 291-292). The paradox of the timing of their respective origins in her thought has contributed to the confusion surrounding which of the two positions is responsible for the mediation of sadism. It is my contention that *both* are, and that this contention is in line with Klein's own thinking. As I shall show, the paranoid-schizoid position mediates primitive sadism in relation to early part-objects, whereas the depressive position concerns the advanced sadism apposite to more nearly whole-objects. Put another way, clinical depressive illness represents the introjective identification with the sadistic object, a phenomenon which I term the *'depressive defence'* and which is analogous to the *manic defence*.

After stating that she wishes to deal with 'depressive states in their relation to paranoia on the one hand and to mania on the other', Klein continues:

> Now, why is it that the process of introjection is so specific for melancholia? I believe that the main difference between incorporation in paranoia and in melancholia is connected with changes in the relation of the subject to the object...In paranoia the characteristic defences are chiefly aimed at annihilating the 'persecutors', while anxiety on the ego's account occupies a prominent place in the picture. As the ego becomes more fully organised,

the internalised imagos will approximate more closely to reality and the ego will identify itself more fully with 'good' objects. The dread of persecution, which was at first felt on the ego's account, now relates to the good object as well and from now on preservation of the good object is regarded as synonymous with the survival of the ego. (Klein 1935: 283)

And:

The paranoiac... has also introjected a whole object and real object, but has not been able to achieve a full identification with it, or, if he has got as far as this, he has not been able to maintain it. (Klein 1935: 291)

Thus we see that the sufferings connected with the depressive position thrust him back to the paranoiac position. Nevertheless, though he has retreated from it, the depressive position has been reached and therefore the liability of depression is always there. (Klein 1935: 292)

The symptoms which derive... from the attacks from bad internal objects and the id against good ones, i.e., an internal warfare in which the ego is identified with the sufferings of the good objects, are typically depressive. (Klein 1935: 293)

In the above quotations, we see Klein developing an association between incorporation and depression, on the one hand, and between projection and paranoia on the other. We also see the first mention of the 'paranoiac position'. What I wish to emphasise, however, is the confusion in which she leaves us concerning the distinction between the infant ego's identification with the good object (true mourning and concern), and another, split-off ego's misidentification with the bad object, leading to *clinical depressive illness* (fraudulent concern and failure to mourn).

There are two other problems with Klein's conception of the depressive position that warrant mention. The first is the problem of regarding the external object as a 'constant', with the infant's psychic determinism as the sole psychoanalytic 'variable'. This reasoning belongs to the deterministic, positivistic orientation of orthodox and classical thinking. Bion, as I shall show, amends this with his post-modern notion of *container/contained* and *maternal dream work* (or *alpha function*). In other words, he provides a model of 'parallel processing' between mother and infant, in terms of the Positions. Put another way, we are now clinically predisposed to consider the infant's formation of his or her *image* of the object as due to: (a) projective identification of aspects of him or herself, and (b) introjective identification with the *real* aspects of the object.

The second problem concerns yet another aspect of the present ambiguity in the status of the depressive position. As Likierman (1995) and Maizels (1996) point out, Klein and her followers sometime speak of 'overcoming the depressive anxieties of the depressive position' and at other times of 'attaining the depressive position' or 'approaching the threshold of the depressive position'. Klein (1940) states:

> In the process of acquiring knowledge, every new piece of experience has to be fitted into the patterns provided by the psychic reality which prevails at the time; whilst the psychic reality of the child is gradually influenced by every step In his progressive knowledge of external reality. Every such step goes along with his more and more firmly establishing his inner 'good' objects, and is used by the ego as a means of *overcoming the depressive position*. (Klein 1940: 314, my italics)

She comes closest to my point of view in another portion of the same paper:

> In short—persecution (by 'bad' objects) and the characteristic defences against it, on one hand, and pining for the loved ('good') object, on the other, constitutes the depressive position. (Klein 1940: 316)

Here, she acknowledges that the depressive position deals with paranoid as well as depressive anxieties. Six years later she postulated the paranoid-schizoid position, assigned to it exclusively paranoid anxieties, and began to refer to 'regression from the depressive position to the paranoid-schizoid position'. In my opinion, Klein was right in 1940. The paranoid anxieties apposite to depressive illness are the syndrome of a failure to mourn *and* the disingenuous (passive/aggressive, perverse) defences against mourning. There always exists an intra-systemic conflict between these two incompatible partners.

The idea of 'regression from D to P-S' is quite another matter, and one which deserves a good deal of rethinking. First of all, does one really 'regress' from D to P-S? I, personally, think not. Freud (1914) had already warned us that one cannot regress back to primary narcissism. When there is a narcissistic regression, it is always to *secondary* narcissism. The principle involved here is 'you can't go home again'. Regression from the mourning which characterises the 'upper depressive position' may take the patient back to the clinical depressive aspects of the 'lower depressive position', but this is a regression back to an aspect of the depressive position that now represents a 'default' status—a disingenuously *altered* depressive position, if you will. I should prefer to call this depressive default the *'depressive position prime'*, thus drawing a distinction analogous to Bion's (1962b) differentiation between beta elements and beta *prime* elements. The former have never been experienced; the latter have been tentatively experienced but rejected from being fully experienced by alpha function. A similar idea pertains, I believe, to the idea of a regression from D to P-S. It is my belief—as stated above—that one can only regress to a new default status, not to the original position. Thus, if a regression does occur from D—or even from upper P-S—then it is back to *D Prime*.[7]

I think a more precise way of thinking about regression from P-S to D is that a level of organisational achievement is abandoned—at a cost—and the cost is depression. Put another way, the infant and/or patient, who seemingly regresses from the depressive position to the paranoid-schizoid position, may actually *default* to a 'Purgatory' position which is part of the clinical depressive illness aspect of the depressive position. My aim thus far has been to show that, in the evolution of the concept of the depressive position, it was progressively disassociated from its original relationship to clinical depressive illness—despite its very name—and became progressively more associated with pining, mourning, reparations, whole-objects, acceptance of psychic reality, and introjection. The crispness of Freud's distinction between mourning and melancholia, each of which properly belongs to the operations of the depressive position, became blurred.

Summary of Klein's position in regard to P-S and D

Klein formulated two important positions of anxiety that occur in the infant—persecutory and depressive. The first is narcissistic, insofar as the infant is concerned for the fate of his/her own ego, whereas in the depressive position it is seemingly concerned for the welfare of its good object, with which it is identified. Projective identification characterises the former position, and introjective identification the latter. The point I should like to make is that there is an in-between state of object-relatedness. This occurs as a 'clinically depressive' continuation of the narcissistically constrained persecutory anxieties of the paranoid-schizoid position into the depressive position, and is tantamount to Freud's concept of melancholia—that is, the introjective identification with persecutory objects so as to control them from within ('depressive defence', or 'internalised manic defence'). It therefore becomes the task of the infant in the depressive position to withdraw his or her introjective identifications with these melancholia-inducing objects, to externalise them, and then to mourn them—by incorporating their essence or legacy, rather than the objects themselves. Here we are reminded of Fairbairn's (1952) theory of introjection. He believed that the infant does not need to introject good objects but only bad ones, in order to control them from within. The good object must be 'let go of', and continuously mourned.

In summary, then, Klein's concept of the paranoid-schizoid position is clear and consistent, whereas her concept of the depressive position—which originally emphasised the presence of clinical depressive illness (introjected paranoia)—came ultimately to represent reparation for sadism in the ongoing protection of the good object. It includes mourning (in the sense of the infant's need to mourn the loss of its omnipotence, and the loss of mother as a part-object possession) but also entails 'depressive' (that is, 'non-mourning') anxieties which are incompatible with the former. Klein's failure to explain the release of melancholic identifications in clinical depressive illness means that the picture of mourning for the object is incomplete.

Further, as the paranoid-schizoid position became ratified through Kleinian usage, a polarised demonisation/idealisation occurred between it and the depressive position. Klein continued to emphasise the prime importance of sadism and the death instinct—and their moorings in P-S—as the most significant etiological agents in mental illness. The sadism apposite to the depressive position, however, was thus displaced onto its counterpart, P-S.

Bion and the positions

As I adumbrated above, I wish to use three of Bion's major theoretical innovations as a means of addressing his direct and indirect modification of Klein's concept of the Positions. These are: (a) container and contained, (b) the reversibility of the relationship between P-S and D (P-S↔D) (to which I would now add P-S↑↓D),[8] and (c) transformations and evolutions in O (T K↔O).

In his earlier works on the psychoanalytic treatment of psychotics, Bion seems to fall into the Kleinian practice of both condemning the paranoid-schizoid position and idealising the depressive position. He also tends to confuse depression with mourning; he does not seem to regard clinical depressive illness as an advanced form of a narcissistic and/or paranoid defence against acknowledging one's dependency on a separate object. I shall cite references that reveal that this propensity in Bion is closely linked to Klein's own views on these matters. I shall also cite some later references, however, which reveal a changing Bion, who—beginning with the notion of container/contained—gains glimpses of phenomena which lie beyond the one-person model of psychoanalysis, and also beyond K (Knowledge), which he identifies with the depressive position. At the same time, owing to his gift for seeing things from *reversible perspectives* (Bion 1962b), he was able to conceive of the *interdependence* of D and P-S, to which he gave the label P-S↔D. This change in his outlook is ultimately best represented in his formulation of transformations and evolutions in O.

Although he did not complete his exploration of this last concept, he did open doors onto the *numinous* and *ineffable* in psychoanalytic thinking, and made possible an understanding of the importance of *intuition* and *intuitionistic science*, as well as incorporating the concept of *infinity*.[9] These evolutions and transformations can be understood mathematically as T K→O and T O→K, which can be combined into T K↔O, and to which I would now add T K↑↓O.

The early Bion is reflected in the following passages:

The capacity to form symbols is dependent on:
(1) The ability to grasp whole objects.
(2) The abandonment of the paranoid-schizoid position.
(3) The bringing together of splits and the ushering in of the depressive position...

> Verbal thought sharpens awareness of psychic reality and therefore of the depression which is linked with destruction and loss of good objects. (Bion 1954: 26)

Here one should note the severity of 'the *abandonment* of the paranoid-schizoid position' and also his confusion between the patient's achievement of verbal thought and the onset of 'depression'. He does not specify whether the putative damage to the object was accepted—that is, regretted and mourned—or denied, ergo leading to depression. On the same page he goes on to state:

> The patient feels that the association between the depressive position and verbal thought is one of cause and effect—itself, a belief based on his capacity to integrate... (Bion 1954: 26)

Again, Bion is highlighting the psychotic patient's hatred of verbal thought, because the latter is associated with the 'integrative' force of the depressive position. Characteristically, Kleinians—including Bion at this time—believe that the psychotic cannot tolerate the integrative agony consequent upon achieving the depressive position, and therefore regresses back to P-S. I would strongly question this assumption. The clinical depressive illness which may appear in its own right, or as a characteristic accompaniment of schizophrenia, represents a *default melancholia within the depressive position*. Bion all but says as much a little later:

> I described the inception of verbal thought as appertaining to the depressive position; but the depression that is proper to this phase is itself something to which the psychotic personality objects and therefore the development of verbal thought comes under attack... I have said that in the even earlier phase, the paranoid-schizoid position, thought processes that should be developing are in fact being destroyed. (Bion 1957a: 60)

Later, Bion withdrew altogether from the concept of the Positions as sequential phases, and conceived of them instead as simultaneously inter-relating. A year later, in 'On Hallucination', he wrote:

> I regard this phase of advance to, and retreat from, the depressive position as critical, not least because the danger of suicide is

liable to obscure the significance of the retreat to the paranoid-schizoid position... (Bion 1958: 81)

Bion addresses the retreat from the depressive position into possible suicide, but he seems not fully to realise that he is describing a retreat from the integrative aspects of the depressive position, in which mourning can take place, to the melancholic default (Purgatory) of the same (depressive) position (that is, 'psychic retreat').

Container/contained (♀♂)

Bion's first major revision of Kleinian theory was his formulation of the concept of the *container and the contained*.[10] In so doing he launched a major paradigm shift in Kleinian theory, and also participated in ushering in the post-modern notion of *intersubjectivity*. Bion had found clinical evidence of an *infantile catastrophe* in psychotic patients. One aspect of this catastrophe was the experience of the infant having been raised by a mother who could not tolerate the infant's projections, and who consequently became internalised by the infant as an 'obstructive object'. Bion gives a first hint of this new concept in his paper 'On Arrogance':

> In some patients the denial to the patient of a normal employment of projective identification precipitates a disaster through the destruction of an important link. Inherent in this disaster is the establishment of a primitive superego which denies the use of projective identification. (Bion 1957b: 92)

He becomes more explicit in his paper 'Attacks on Linking', under the subheading 'Denial of Normal Degrees of Projective Identification':

> Throughout the analysis the patient resorted to projective identification with a persistence suggesting it was a mechanism of which he had never been able sufficiently to avail himself; the analysis afforded him an opportunity for the exercise of a mechanism of which he had been cheated. (Bion 1959: 103)

It was this paper which introduced the *intersubjective* aspects of psychoanalysis into Kleinian theory, and fundamentally altered the

Kleinian conception of projective identification. Bion repeats his new theory of maternal neglect in his next paper, 'A Theory of Thinking':

> If the mother cannot tolerate these projections the infant is reduced to continued projective identification carried out with increasing force and frequency. (Bion 1962a: 115)

Implicit in Bion's thinking is the assumption that, in order for the mother or the analyst to be a container for the contained, he or she must first have achieved the depressive position, in order to be able to be separate from and yet care for the infant or patient. I would consider this the achievement of that aspect of the depressive position in which one has achieved reconciliation with oneself and one's objects and in which one shows respect, mercy, and forgiveness towards them. The mother and analyst must have transcended the melancholic Purgatory default of the depressive position. Ultimately, the infant or patient who has been able to experience containment will be able to internalise the experience and be able to become a tolerant friend to his or her own troubled self (Bion 1962a, 1963)—as well as to the container, during the moments he or she is unable to function as such.

The significance of P-S↔D

One of Bion's first creative reinterpretations of the Positions was to put reciprocal arrows between them: P-S↔D. The idea of fluctuations between the paranoid-schizoid and depressive positions was not new, however. Klein had already described regressions and progressions between them. What Bion did was, first of all, to systematise their inter-relationship as a constant (Bion 1963). This change in paradigm had a number of significant implications. Firstly, it implied that P-S and D were coeval—that is, simultaneous and dialectically interactive—as Ogden (1988) was later to elaborate. I have already criticised the concept of 'regression from D to P-S' as a misnomer for 'regression from D (mourning) to D (depression proper—that is, clinical depressive illness)'. To me, P-S↔D signifies an ongoing dialectical relationship between the always newly generated virginal *beta elements* from the unconscious id, and the depressive position—and not the *beta prime elements*, which have already seen life (so to speak) but have been rejected by the mind.

Another significant implication of Bion's formulation was his de-demonisation—as it were—of the paranoid-schizoid position in its relationship to the analytic subject and, commensurately, his de-idealisation of the depressive position. Although he did not use the term, it is clear that Bion—who understood logic—had applied the principle of *dialectics* to the Positions, and had showed that each was a necessary counterbalance to the other. In post-modern terms, one can see—from Bion's perspective—that the paranoid-schizoid position, particularly given its penchant for splitting, can serve to *deconstruct* the rigidity and staleness that the symbolic representations of the depressive position accrue over time, as they become 'Establishment' preconceptions or assumptions. Thus, P-S—at best—serves as a challenging *guardian* of the freshness and vitality of depressive position achievements, and serves to implement the *principle of distinction* between values and qualities. On the other hand, the operation of the depressive position can counteract the tendency of P-S towards infinite splitting, by acting as a veritable container and condenser. In so doing, the depressive position reveals its functioning according to the principle of *generalisation* or *symmetry*.[11] In *Attention and Interpretation* Bion wrote:

> For this state [the abandoning of memory and desire] I have coined the term 'patience' to distinguish it from 'paranoid-schizoid position', which should be left to describe the *pathological state*[12] for which Melanie Klein uses it... 'Patience' should be retained without 'irritable reaching after fact and reason' until a pattern 'evolves'. This state is analogous to what Melanie Klein has called the depressive position. For this state I use the term 'security'... I consider the experience of oscillation between 'patience' and 'security' to be an indication that valuable work is being achieved. (Bion 1970: 124)

Ultimately in this, and later works, Bion repeatedly states that normal thinking depends fundamentally upon the successful partnership expressed in P-S↔D and $\female\male$ (Bion's algebraic label for container/contained).

Earlier I suggested, following Young, the construction of P-S↑↓D as a complement to Bion's P-S↔D in order to account for the multidimensionality of the concept. In other words, the horizontal and reversible arrows designate the simultaneity and co-existence of P-S and D as parallel and dialectically interactive processes, whilst the vertical reversible arrows designate the level of maturity and developmental sophistication in terms of sequentiality—a concept better known as *regression* and *progression*.

Transformations in O and their significance with regard to the positions

After he had completed his series of clinical papers on psychosis, Bion began to veer in different epistemological directions in order to explore the phenomena of transformation. This exploratory vector seems to have emerged as a continuation of *container/contained*, especially with regard to precisely how the raw sense data of emotional experience in the infant (beta elements, or 'things-in-themselves') become transformed into alpha elements suitable for 'mental digestion' (reception and encoding for memory, dreams, and thinking). At first, the mother performs the transformations of her infant's beta elements into these alpha elements (which Bion writes as: Tm I$\beta \rightarrow \alpha$). The mother is able to accomplish this transformation in the infant because of her state of *reverie*, which enables her to employ her *own* alpha function for this purpose. This model applies not only to the mother/infant interaction, but also to the analytic situation. It is also a model for normal thinking.

Bion was to spend the rest of his professional life attempting to unravel the mysteries of transformation. One first gains a glimpse of this radical change in his 'Commentary' at the end of *Second Thoughts*. This portion of his book explores how and why he had 'second thoughts' concerning the conclusions he had reached during his early, formally Kleinian stage of development, and hints at the new directions he believed should be explored in order to understand the underpinnings of normal and abnormal minds. Bion had begun to commit himself and his future endeavours to the study of *epistemology*—that is, to how the mind learns and evolves.

At the beginning of this new odyssey, he postulated and explored 'alpha function', 'alpha elements', 'beta elements', P-S$\leftrightarrow$D elements, L, H, and K transformations (that is, 'Love', 'Hate' and 'Knowledge'), the analytic object, sense, myth, passion, the grid, and other aspects of this new epistemology. He seemed keen on employing mathematical concepts, because of their rigour and 'freedom from saturation'. In one of his 'imaginative conjectures', he realised that mind had to be separated in its inchoateness from the *thoughts* that it thinks. Bion thus postulated that thoughts ('beta elements', things-in-themselves) originated *without a thinker to think them*, but required a mind for this purpose. His subsequent formulation of L, H, and K *linkages* was an intermediate means of apprehending the *analytic object*. The latter, according to Bion, was suspended between inchoate O and ultimate O, which—mysteriously—are the same. He had also begun to realise that the most fundamental need of every individual is for *truth*—and that this truth ultimately lay beyond knowledge (K) in O.

In *Transformations* (Bion 1965) he ventured even further into the domain of epistemology, this time into the mystical realm of O which he also described as 'Absolute Reality' or 'Ultimate Truth'. He linked O with the *'Godhead'* of the mystics—such as Meister Eckhart. He also believed that O was equivalent to Kant's (1965) 'thing-in-itself', and his own 'beta elements'. The mystical nature of these investigations had far-reaching consequences on his reputation in England and elsewhere. Many contemporary Kleinians have openly made statements such as the following: 'Bion was a genius, perhaps as great as Klein herself—until he got into that mystical rubbish, "O"!'

Bion penetrated the Kleinian veil of logical positivism, and opened up her theories to the post-modern age of relativity, deconstruction, intersubjectivity, chaos, complexity, and indeterminacy. In the midst of this profound paradigm shift, maybe even Bion himself failed sufficiently to realise the importance of what he was illuminating. He had, in effect, transcended the Freudian-Kleinian firmament, and the primal fixity from which their theories derive: the assumption of a constant conjunction between the *instinctual drives* (particularly the death instinct, with regard to Kleinian thinking) and the evolution of *psychic reality*. The latter element has been radically reformulated by the intersubjective trend, handed down through Ferenczi, Fairbairn, Winnicott, Sullivan, Kohut, and so many others. This entailed a new valorisation of external reality as 'the most important' reality. Bion, meanwhile, went in the opposite direction. By sifting through the shards of an all but forgotten religious, philosophical, and mystical legacy of epistemology, he replaced the primacy of the drives with the deeper awesomeness and randomness of the infinity and mystery of O. Virtually simultaneously, Lacan (1977) was formulating his register of the *real*, whilst Matte-Blanco (1975, 1988) was working on his own mathematical-logical formulation of *infinite sets* and *bi-logic*.

Transformations and evolutions to and from O, and their profound significance for psychoanalysis

The concept of O requires some introduction for the 'uninitiated'. It is not uniformly interpreted by Bion scholars, and in this contribution I shall render only my own reading of it.

Bion, closely adhering to Heisenberg and his Principle of Uncertainty, as well as to Einstein and his Principle of Relativity, presupposes that the 'reality' in which we dwell constitutes in effect a *consensual myth*. Put another way, we live in a symbolic rex and reification of our imaginative perception of things. Put yet another way, we live in a world which we ourselves invent—a bell-jar, as it were—but we lose sight of its being self-imagined and co-constructed because others enter with us into cultural *mimesis*, a *folie à deux* which convinces us of the absolute *Otherness* of objects in the world. The fact is, paradoxically, that these objects (human and otherwise) *are* Other, but we do not know that. Our perceptions and, therefore, the conceptions that derive from them, are constrained—*chained*—to our, at first, idiosyncratic and then culturally induced creation and re-creation of the reality we think we behold. Our inescapable *subjectivity* forms an invisible 'contact lens' which we do not realise that we are wearing, and can only begin to intuit when we are in analysis. The mystic, on the other hand, is in resonance with O and experiences things as they *are*, without the filters – 'For now we see through a glass darkly, but then face to face. Now I know in part, but then shall I know even as I am known' (1 Corinthians 13: 10-11).

As we have seen, Bion's concept of P-S↔D implies that the depressive position exists and functions simultaneously with the paranoid-schizoid position from the very beginning. Bion demonstrated this through a dazzling display of 'reversible perspectives': he depathologised projective identification (the chief mechanism of P-S) by drawing attention to how the psychotic patients whom he had treated presented evidence that they were deprived of *normal* use of this mechanism by mothers who were unable to contain their infant's projections. The infant originates 'thoughts-without-a-thinker': Bion's description of the inherent preconceptions which are looking for realisation as experienced conceptions. These are 'beta elements', or 'things-in-themselves', which have not yet been experienced as thoughts. The infant acquires his or her thinking mind by incorporating his or her experience of mother's 'alpha function'—which delays, suspends, detoxifies, and 'translates' the infants raw experience, returning it to him or her as emotional knowledge about him or herself.

Next, Bion used the notion of the L (love), H (hate) and K (knowledge) linkages to the object, by means of which—after alpha functioning is acquired—the infant is able to apprehend the object he or she needs. Bion suggested that human beings 'know' the object through their sensory linkages (L, H, K) but fail to *really* know it because of the fundamental ineffability of its Otherness—its Absolute Truth, its Ultimate Reality. Hitherto, Bion had envisaged mental transformations as akin to the digestion and elimination of food in the digestive tract. According to this model, the raw, sensory data of emotional experience (alpha/beta elements) become mentally digested (transformed) into mental knowledge (K-elements). However, he then began to re-formulate this process in terms of a transformation or evolution from and to O. O was the 'beyond' of K yet, paradoxically, also anteced it, as if there were a cosmic epistemological circle that began and ended with O. O, the thing-in-itself, Kant's 'noumenon', which transcends the phenomenon of sensual experience, constitutes the ineffable template and provenance of the phenomenon.

In other words, Bion asserted that the noumenon, O, ineffably surrounded and mysteriously penetrated the phenomenon, K, without revealing itself because—unlike K—there is no object in O, but only the subject! Bion hereby inaugurated a psychoanalytic version of 'mystical science', leaning heavily on the works of Plato, Kant, Meister Eckhart, Scholem, and Poincaré.

The significance of these transformations between K and O for the concept of the Positions is that P-S (which Bion had already liberated from its 'demonisation' and collaboration with the id) could now be clearly seen as coeval with and complementary to D. P-S could be considered a primitive, mental, 'digital computer', by which the raw data of sensory experience (chaos) could be effectively differentiated into categories such as good/bad, pleasant/unpleasant, me/not me, and so on. Once this data was differentiated (split) or 'pre-digested' by P-S, it could then be sent on to D, where it could be concentrated and condensed into meaningful K elements (symbols) for memories, thoughts and dreams. In other words, P-S *and* D now become complementary 'filters' which transduce the chaotically infinite nature of O into: (a) binary oppositions of 'good' and 'bad' (L and H), and then (b) into separate objects of symbolic knowledge (K)—before they can be re-evolved into O once more.

O itself is situated beyond and before these transformations. It stands athwart all the transformational procedures. The transformation from K to O (T K ↔ O) constitutes—in my opinion—the entry to a new position, the *transcendent* position (see below). Transformations from O to K (P-S or D), on the other hand, constitute *catastrophic change*. Failures of transformations from O to K, meanwhile, constitute *infantile catastrophe*, or the 'black hole'.

The importance of transformations in O for a revised conception of the positions

I should like to discuss the importance of Bion's conception of O in relation to the Positions. The prime movers of psychic determinism—in the Freudian and Kleinian lexicon—are the instinctual drives. Freud imputes the experience of *danger* to their irruption into the ego, and he labels their moorings in the unconscious 'a seething cauldron'. Klein, similarly, empowers the death instinct with ultimate destructive power over our mental lives, from infancy onward. The paranoid-schizoid position represents its furthest thrust, and the depressive position its recessional. When P-S becomes constantly conjoined in psychoanalytic thinking with the effects of the death instinct, it begins to appear as the prime cause of mental illness—and the 'achievement of the depressive position' seems the cure.

The effect of Bion's imaginative conjecture of O (as well as Lacan's register of the 'real', and Matte Blanco's 'infinite sets' and 'bi-logic') is to de-emphasise the toxicity of the drives and of P-S, and to highlight instead the randomness, chaos, unpredictability, infinity, numinousness, ineffability, awfulness, and awesomeness of O. It is, at worst, the absolute, ultimate traumatic state—like Sodom and Gomorrah—or, from a more evolved perspective, it is ultimate serenity. Bion's ideas enable us to understand how P-S, through its capacity to attach unconscious *phantasies* to elements from inchoate O, becomes a first mediating filter for the apprehension of O. Subsequently, D acts as a *symbolic* filter-mediator. Thus, P-S↔D takes on a new meaning. The Positions are dialectically, mutually co-operative transducers of raw feeling which enable stepped-down transformations of O into acceptable, meaningful experiences for the mind to think about, dream about, and to store in memory. Through Bion, the Positions can be freed from their demonism and seen as epistemological transducers of O.

In recent contributions I have discussed Bion's conception of O from other perspectives, and have proffered the idea of the *transcendent position* as a worthy 'container' for O (Grotstein, 1984, 1993, 1997).[13] As I have tried to show, Klein's uneven conception of the Positions assigned too many tasks to the depressive position: the manifestation of overt or cryptic clinical depressive illness *and* of mourning phenomena, including reparation, restoration, and gratitude. In the minds of some writers—Bion, Meltzer, and Maizels principal amongst them—*spiritual values* also appear as a consequence of this position. Synoptically, then, the depressive position represents the acceptance or ownership of one's own 'demon' self, one's contrition for it, and one's ability to find and recognise K. In this position, one metaphorically wears one's sins about one: first as punishment (in the earlier aspect of the depressive position) and then, in the later part, as accepted reminders of the continual presence of one's *shadow self*. The *transcendent position*, I have argued, can be reserved for the emergence of the post-depressive-position self, the one that has *evolved* beyond it, has achieved *negative capability* and is able to forgo memory, desire, and understanding in order to resonate with, evolve into, and become transformed into O; that is, to *'become* O'.

Other papers on the positions

The concept of the Positions has been addressed by other contributors. Brown (1987) has formulated the concept of a *transitional position,* in order to attempt to address what he believes are serious discrepancies in Klein's assertion that the depressive position becomes apparent at three to four months of age. Brown believes that the cognitive requirements implicit in Klein's theory require a more developed mind; thus, his formulation of an intermediary position, the transitional, is an attempt to reconcile Klein and infant cognitive research.

Steiner has studied and treated borderline and other primitive mental disorders, and believes that these patients clinically demonstrate a distinctive, intermediate buffer between P-S and D which is worthy of separation from its counterparts as the *borderline position*.[14] Subsequently, he formulated 'pathological organisations', and held that these dwell in *psychic retreats*, which are analogous to the borderline position.

Ogden (1988, 1989), in his rereading of the works of Bick, Meltzer, and Tustin, and in his own clinical work, hypothesised a position earlier than P-S—the *autistic contiguous position*. This, he suggests, mediates the psychological and psycho-physical phenomena which occur in the apposition of the infant's skin surface against his or her mother's skin. This position forms the developmental foundation of a psychological 'sense-organ' for apprehending the object.

Meira Likierman's (1995) noteworthy contribution has already been mentioned. She too became aware of certain discrepancies in the ongoing conceptualisation of the depressive position by Klein and her followers. She formulates a valuable distinction between the *tragic* and the *moral aspects* of the depressive position. The former relates to the infant's belief that the putative damage it has caused the object is irreparable, and thus evokes despair; whereas in the case of the latter, if enough positive feelings have been accumulated toward the object, the infant becomes *moral* and finds the determination to repair the object, thus predicating *hope*.

Maizels, in an unpublished paper that was written independently and simultaneously with mine (Grotstein 1993), entitled 'Working Through, or Beyond the Depressive Position: Achievements and Defences of the Spiritual Position, and the Heart's Content', addresses virtually the same issues as in my critique of Klein, and arrives at a remarkably similar remedy: a *spiritual position* which is situated beyond the depressive position.

Conclusion

In conclusion, the concept of the Positions constitutes one of the most important and enduring in the entirety of the Kleinian legacy. However, like so many of her other contributions, the Positions were formulated during the hegemony of orthodox psychoanalysis, and consequently bear the stamp of the positivism and determinism which was characteristic of the era. Bion, however, was perhaps the only Kleinian who was truly innovative, in that he dared to challenge some of her ideas whilst basically honouring them.

His first major departure was the notion of container/contained, which brought the post-modern, two-person, intersubjective model to the Kleinian, one-person, psychoanalytic model. As his work progressed, it gradually became apparent that he was interested not in a modernist slant on drive determinism, but on parts of the post-modernist oeuvre: *epistemology* and *meaning*. His concepts of alpha function, L, H and K linkages, and transformations, prefigured his interest in ultimate transformation: evolutions from O. It is my impression that Bion meant by O an intuitive epiphany that transcends P-S↔D. This, I would argue, constitutes the *transcendent position*, the position of *serenity*, without an object.

Notes

[1] See Klein 1935, 1940, 1946.

[2] I follow Bion's custom in his writings by employing the term 'the Positions' to include both the paranoid-schizoid and the depressive positions.

[3] See Freud 1905, Abraham 1948, and Klein 1935, 1940, 1946, 1952.

[4] 'Anaclitic object choice' was later to be called 'object constancy' and 'permanence'. See Fraiberg 1969.

[5] The previous quotations from Klein and Meltzer are cited in Likierman 1995: 148.

[6] See Klein 1927, 1928, 1929b.

[7] It is my impression that my 'D Prime' corresponds to Steiner's 'psychic retreats'. See Steiner 1993.

[8] I am indebted to Dr. Enid Young (personal communication) for the idea and significance of P-S↑↓D, which is discussed in more detail in what follows.

[9] As did Matte-Blanco. See Matte-Blanco 1975, 1988.

[10] See Bion 1959, 1961, 1962a, 1962b.

[11] See Matte-Blanco 1975, 1988; Grotstein 1981.

[12] The italics are mine. Here I wish to demonstrate a relapse on Bion's part in pathologising the paranoid-schizoid position—in effect making it a scapegoat.

[13] See Grotstein 1984, 1993, 1997.

[14] See Steiner 1979, 1987, 1990, 1993.

THREE IN ONE: FAIRBAIRN'S VOLATILE TRINITY[1]

Eleanore Armstrong Perlman

Fairbairn's object relations theory emphasises the significance of interpersonal factors on the development of psychic structure and the genesis of psychopathology. For Fairbairn this stress on the interpersonal is central. The psyche of man is determined by his need for loving, nurturing acceptance. The primary need is relational. Man needs warmth. This constitutes the necessary ground of being. Deprivation (and, later, the threat of deprivation) evokes fear of abandonment, threatening psychic annihilation. The preconditions for individuation and separateness, the goals of mature development, are regulated by the need to maintain tolerable relatedness. The need for parental acceptance becomes a major variable affecting the emergence of an individuated self. The recognition of this was the theoretical shift which inaugurated object relations theory.

The Fairbairnian neonate differs from the Freudian. The Fairbairnian infant is sensual, sentient and reality-oriented in a rudimentary form from birth—possibly even earlier. This emergent, embodied human subject is construing his experience of self and other from the earliest stage.

It is at these earliest stages of the developmental process that the psychic structures—which play such a crucial role in Fairbairn's theories—develop, or (possibly more appropriately) are constructed. The infant is born with innate structures waiting to emerge and do battle.

Fairbairn's object relations theory represents a major break with the Freudian paradigm, which minimised the role of relational factors in the *genesis* of repression and defence. It also differs from other object relations theories, in which the relevant objects are constructed by drives, or instincts.

A theory which takes account of the particularity of crucial environmental deficits differs fundamentally from a theory of internal conflict, based on impersonal warring dualities. There is a Copernican shift in the psychoanalytic paradigm from a solipsistic model of warring instinctual forces to an interactional model. Phenomena that might be adduced as evidence of the impersonal forces of Eros and Thanatos are viewed as derivatives of the frustrated need for loving acceptance. They reflect the vicissitudes of love and hate between the self and other who was the erstwhile ground of one's being and the source of meaning.

If Fairbairn's assumption concerning the nature of man is valid, the role of acceptance by a benign parental object becomes relevant not only to the aetiology of psychopathology but, more importantly, to the aetiology of the basic psychic structures. Both can be traced to early patterns of relationship with the primary caretaker. The adaptation of the parent to the child's emergent need enters the foreground of theory construction.

It is important to emphasise the fundamental step taken by Fairbairn. Most—if not all—psychoanalytic theories will grant some role to environmental factors in the aetiology of psychopathology. Freud, who uses the terms 'constitutional' and 'accidental' wrote:

> No other influences on the course of sexual development can compare in importance with releases of sexuality, waves of repression and sublimation—the two latter being processes of which the inner causes are quite unknown to us. It might be possible to include repressions and sublimations as part of the constitutional disposition, by regarding them as manifestations of it in life; and anyone who does so is justified in asserting that the final shape taken by sexual life is principally the outcome of the innate constitution. No one with perception will, however, dispute that an interplay of factors such as this also leaves room for the modifying effects of accidental events experienced in childhood and later. (Freud 1905: 239-240)

Similarly, in Kleinian theory the role of the mother as container is sometimes emphasised. How this role is carried out may alleviate, or exacerbate, the primary inherent aggression of the infant. But neither in Freud nor Klein is the fundamental psychic structure and its dynamics represented as formed by relational interactions.

For Fairbairn the experience of the interpersonal, in the earliest stage with the mother or her substitute, permeates and suffuses the emergent self. Psychic structures arise from the defensive manoeuvres undertaken by the emergent self to render unsatisfactory experience more tolerable.

In this chapter I will elaborate Fairbairn's account of how the primacy of the need to maintain a satisfactory relationship with the mother, *combined* with the need to separate from the mother, leads to the development of psychic structures. I will also discuss how these structures are organised, the purpose they serve, and their effects on later development.

The need to relate and separate

Like Freud, Fairbairn traces back the preconditions of love to infancy. The infant is initially in a state of primary identification. This state is initially physical; the mother's body and access to her breast is the ground of well-being. As long as this state persists the infant's identity, as yet undifferentiated, is absolutely dependent on her availability. At this stage any frustrating response is experienced as a world gone bad, and thus—given the lack of differentiation—the infant himself is bad. To use a poetic metaphor, he rises or falls with his world. The sensed availability and, later, the attitude of the other is of primary import; it defines the world. The contents of this as yet undifferentiated flow—experienced, perhaps, as a flux—lays down the conditions that affect his emergent subjectivity and his developing capacity to differentiate self and other as separate but interpenetrating, as interactive centres of volition. The earliest contact with the mother is sensual and erotic embodied relationship. This sensual conjunction of two bodies can alternate between passionate excitement, raging frustration, withdrawal from intrusion, taking the mother for granted, and the beatitude of the contented, sleepy suckling. Being held by mother can assuage distress. She is the primary object of comfort and solace. But, just as important, she is also the primary object of his love. She is the gateway through which the infant enters the world.

The role of this early physical responsiveness at the earliest stages is emphasised by Stern:

> The most basic physical language of love is both performed and learned by the fourth and fifth month of life. (Stern 1993: 176)

This love is not simply beatific and tranquil. Passion, in the sense of *excitement*, is also there. Contours are being established. Stern writes of the excitation—envelopes which, one day, will be filled with sensual (sexual) content.

There are two requirements for a successful transition from the state of primary identification—a state of attuned, not-too-sharply-differentiated self-other—to mature dependence, a state of a *separate* self-other.

The first offers the possibility to explore slowly the world that lies outside the initial primary other to whom one has been attached. The second is the slow acquisition of confidence in one's ability to prove effective in one's encounters.

Fairbairn assumes that there is an innate developmental tendency—part of our biological inheritance—to tolerate increasing separation without undue anxiety, if the infant's needs for closeness with the body of the mother are met:

> In a state of nature it would be rare for the infant to be deprived of the shelter of his mother's arms and of ready access to her breast until, in the ordinary course of development, he himself became increasingly disposed to dispense with them. (Fairbairn 1944: 110)

Satisfaction of this primary need for embodied contact enables increasingly confident exploration of the external world. Security provides the basis for toleration of actual physical separation. But this security needs to be grounded on the well-founded expectation of the continuous accepting responsiveness of the mother or her substitute, whenever she is called upon. Such attuned responsiveness to the needs of the infant is the necessary matrix for the emergence of a confident, spontaneous, vigorous embodied self.

For the infant to explore confidently the frightening maze which is the world out there, the mother, like Ariadne, must provide the appropriate thread: loose enough to give scope for wandering, strong enough to be secure enough, so that the infant can return to safety.

This potential haven provides the basis of hope. The world is not an alien place, nor is the infant alienated from the world. In states of tension he can conjure up the image of the responsive mother. He has someone to whom he can turn. This expectation preserves hope. The other, though not there, is nevertheless available, although not yet. Absence is not equivalent to the loss of the mother's love. he is not abandoned. Waiting is finite. There is light at the end of the tunnel.

Continual breaches of the primary need for the responsive acceptance of the mother can stifle the infants ability to explore, to wander, and thus to begin the necessary process of separation. Continual breaches—if too dramatic—can stunt the emergent self.

If the mother is not there for the infant, he is deserted. Because she initially constitutes the infant's world, he is in a desert, without sight of or hope of an oasis. This constitutes the conditions of trauma. The cohesion and even the very existence of the self is jeopardised by cumulative trauma, an experience which by definition cannot be assimilated.

To summarise: for Fairbairn frustration of the infant's desire 'to be loved as a person *and to have his love accepted* is the greatest trauma that a child can experience' (Fairbairn 1941: 39, my emphasis). In fact, both are important. To be loved is to be recognised and valued as a differentiated other. To have one's love accepted is to be acknowledged as a contributor, an active source of value, the bearer of a gift. If this is absent, trauma results. Being subject to such trauma is intolerable. Moreover, any expression by the infant of the unmet need heralds the danger of the repetition of trauma. The trauma is a situation of primitive agony that we can perhaps only access in the adult patient through metaphor. Some patients produce images of intolerable howling in the desert, or of a volcano of feeling sweeping away everything in its path; but in these cases the predicament is that of an adult, capable of symbolic representation.

How is the infant to cope with the threat of being subjected to such potential trauma? Flight from the mother in external reality is impossible, so it becomes internal: a flight from a holistic, integrated impression of the mother and of the self. Fairbairn concentrates on the techniques utilised by the infant to render tolerable the intolerable. His thesis is that the roots of all later psychopathology are to be found in the strategies adopted to render an intolerable situation tolerable.

Defensive techniques and the creation of psychic structures

Fairbairn considers three stages in the process of building a defensive structure to protect the infant from the intolerable threat of trauma: *internalisation, splitting,* and *repression.* Before considering these in detail it is necessary to secure a good grasp of the concept of an internal object, derived from a process of internalisation.

An internal object is a representation of an outside object, or some aspect of the outside object. However, unlike the kind of representation involved in a thought, a memory, or an image, the representation produced by the process of internalisation is much more substantial and significant. For Fairbairn, an 'internal object' may be defined as:

an endopsychic structure other than an ego structure, with which an ego structure has a relationship comparable to a relationship with a person in external life. (Fairbairn 1994: 112)

However, Fairbairn's internal objects owe:

their ultimate origin to a process of introjection, and as constituting internal structural representatives of emotionally significant aspects of persons upon whom the subject depended in early life. (Fairbairn 1994: 112)

Moreover, this relationship can—and often, in order to succeed, *must*—be able to overwhelm the relationship in external life. As we shall see, it is a substitute created by the psyche exactly for this purpose.

I shall turn now to the development of defensive structures.

Internalisation

The first step taken to avoid the intolerable situation of being confronted by the ambivalent response or the lack of an appropriate response from the mother is internalisation:

With a view to controlling the unsatisfying object, he employs the defensive process of internalisation to remove it from outer reality, where it eludes his control, to the sphere of inner reality, where it offers prospects of being more amenable to control in the role of internal object. (Fairbairn 1951: 172)

The child internalises the pre-ambivalent object which is in some measure both satisfying and unsatisfying (Fairbairn 1951: 178). It is clear from Fairbairn that what is internalised at this stage is the relationship with the whole object—in this case, the mother with all her contradictory and confusing features.

Fairbairn stresses the defensive use of internalisation. A defence always has a protective function. The protective function of internalisation in this case is to preserve the external image of the mother as a safe person to whom the infant can safely turn in external reality. The relationship between the ego and this new internalised object constitutes a separate constellation in the mind. However the internalised mother is still desired and still frustrates. She tantalises and is thus exciting, but—in as much as she frustrates—she is rejecting. If the mother is too frustrating, given the infant's absolute need of her—she becomes infinitely desirable *and* infinitely frustrating. This gives rise to rejective anger. Not only is his desire exacerbated, so is his rejective rage and hatred. But because the mother constitutes the conditions of hope, an acceptable representation of an accepting mother is essential for the maintenance of the self. So, this first method of protection does not solve the problem, because the main body of the object is internalised, and 'both the over-exciting and the over-frustrating elements in the internal (ambivalent) object are unacceptable to the original ego' (Fairbairn 1944: 135).

The ego is confronted with the internalised ambivalent object, which remains both the alluring all-bountiful source of goodness, and the depriving punitive withholder. This duality constitutes as great a difficulty within the inner world as it did externally. The danger of loss has merely been transferred to an internal theatre.

Splitting

The next step in the process of developing a defensive structure is to cope with the internalised object. This is achieved by the process of splitting.

The internalised whole object is split into an acceptable good object, and the unacceptable frustrating but rejective bad object. The latter is further split into two parts which, when combined, produce the condition for trauma: the exciting and rejective aspects. The over-exciting and over-frustrating elements of the internal object are split off in order to leave the nucleus of the original object shorn of its 'bad' features. It becomes a desexualised, ideal object, which the ego may be able to cope with more easily as a substitute for the external object. By splitting the object, then, the ego has been able to reconstitute an object that it can safely love.

However, this poses yet another problem. For Fairbairn, as for Freud, the ego is the mediator between the inner psychic world and the world of outer reality. The whole purpose of the defensive structure now being erected by the infant is to cope with an outside world that has become intolerable. If the ego became attached to all the internal objects constructed by the process of splitting it would be confronted by all the dilemmas and frustrations encountered in the whole unsplit internalised object. In effect, the inner world mirrors the outer, and could not affect the relationships there.

To resolve this problem, Fairbairn argues that alongside the splitting of the internalised object there is also a splitting of the ego into three parts, corresponding to the three aspects of the split object. He calls these: the *central ego*, the *libidinal ego*, and the *anti-libidinal ego*. Each of these becomes libidinally attached to one of the internal objects. The central ego—which is also that aspect of the ego which mediates between the inner and outer world—becomes libidinally attached to the *ideal object*, which has been shorn of all its bad elements. The libidinal ego becomes attached to the *exciting object*, and the anti-libidinal ego to the *rejective object*. These sub-selves, with their respective objects, constitute separate dynamic structures of volition. They are constellations characterised by different affects. They are dynamic structures of a self that has become split in relation to the splitting of the internalised object.

Now that the central object is attached to the ideal object, it can externalise this ideal object onto the original object in outer reality, converting it also into a good object. Shorn of its frustrating and alluring features it is rendered an acceptable object that the child can safely love and project onto the external other.

If this process could be maintained the defensive structure would be complete and successful. The infant's relationship with the outside object could also be maintained as good via the mediation of the central ego's attachment to the internal ideal object. But this structure is constantly under threat. For it to function successfully, the central ego must be protected from being polluted and inundated by those elements that have been split off.

Repression

For Fairbairn, repression is the mechanism used by the central ego to maintain its libidinal attachment to the ideal object and thus maintain the external object as good. To avoid the re-merger of the split-off objects with the good object, the central ego represses the split parts of itself—the libidinal and anti-libidinal egos—which are attached to the exciting and rejecting objects.

> Repression is primarily exercised, not against impulses which have come to appear painful or 'bad' (as in Freud's final view) or

even against painful memories (as in Freud's earlier view), but against internalised objects which have come to be treated as bad... but also against parts of the 'ego' which seek relationships with these internal objects. (Fairbairn 1944: 89)

By repressing those parts of the ego that have been split off and have become attached to the split-off bad objects, the central ego is repressing the objects themselves. Repression is a defence against relationships with bad objects. This is necessary because only by this means can the central ego maintain its link between the internal ideal object—created by splitting—and the external object. This permits an acceptable (or at least survivable) relationship with the external object. As long as the repression is successful the child has a supportive and protective parent in external reality. This relationship contains the satisfactory elements of the real relationship. The central ego has a foothold in the interpersonal world.

Fairbairn wrote that—for Freud—repression originates as a means of reducing the expression of libido towards the parent of the opposite sex, and as a means of reducing aggression towards the parent of the same sex—in the setting of the Oedipus situation. However, for Fairbairn:

both direct and indirect repression originate in infancy before the emergence of the Oedipus situation; and indirect repression is a special technique adopted by the child to reduce the expression of both libido and aggression towards his mother at a stage when she is his only significant object and he is almost wholly dependent on her. (Fairbairn 1951: 174)

Thus even repression, the most fundamental notion in psychoanalytic theory, is for Fairbairn a defensive construction, arising from the initial frustrating relationship.

A diagrammatic representation

Some readers might find helpful a diagrammatic representation of the processes involved. This is supplied in the right-hand side of Figure 1 (overleaf), in the column labelled 'Model 2'. The steps (a) - (e) show the process from primary identification to the creation of the repressed endopsychic structures.

66 *Three in One: Fairbairn's Volatile Trinity*

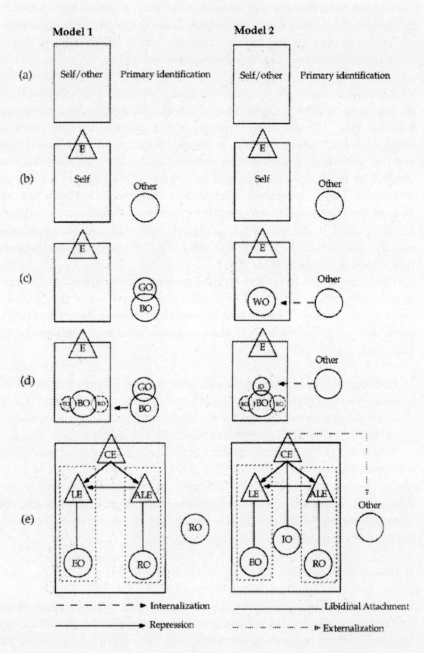

Figure 1

Step (a) represents a non-differentiated state of self-other. The self-experience is as yet permeated and suffused by the other. In step (b) the self and other separate. The ego emerges and a relationship with the other is not only possible but, given the helpless state of the infant, necessary and vital for survival. It is at this stage that the relationship with the other can become traumatic. If this threatens, the defensive structures begin to develop. In step (c) internalisation occurs. The whole external object is internalised and an internal object is created (WO). A libidinal attachment to this internal object does not solve the problem, because the internal object is just a representation of the external object—with all its frustrating and exciting features. The next step (d) is to split the internal object into an ideal object (IO) and a bad object. In step (e) the splitting process is completed. The bad object, split off from the good object, is in turn split into its exciting element (EO) and its rejecting element (RO). At the same time the ego is also split into three parts: the central ego (CE), the libidinal ego (LE), and the anti-libidinal ego (ALE). Each of these becomes libidinally attached to one of the internal objects. As we have seen, the central ego attaches to the good or ideal object. It is through this attachment that the central ego can relate to the external object and maintain it as acceptable by externalising its attachment to the internal ideal object.

The arrows in step (e) show the necessary process of repression maintaining the defensive structure. The central ego represses the two split-off elements of the ego, and in effect represses the relationships with the bad objects.[2] This ensures that only the relationship with the good object is externalised onto the external object.

However, internalisation and splitting do not—after all—eliminate the bad aspects of the real object that provoke and will later evoke trauma. It simply transfers them to the internal theatre. The dramatis personae of this internal world are created, recreated and amended in the light of ongoing experience.

The process of internalisation, splitting and repression is continuous. These processes may serve as a defensive structure for the infant, but they do not change the reality of the continuing relationship with the problematic external other. As new and potentially traumatic interactions occur, the process must be—and is—repeated, in order to maintain the libidinal attachment of the central ego to the continuously created ideal object. This permits the central ego to maintain the outside other as good, in spite of the actual interaction.

Fairbairn's self-other or self-object configurations are thus to be regarded as dynamic structures, not merely as self-representations. These dynamic structures, with their respective dynamic objects, mediate the affective life of the individual. They are continuously created and re-created.

We see that the Fairbairnian model is based on the need of a child to have a secure sense that he is loved for himself. For this, an acceptable relationship with a benign primary care-giver is necessary. If the care-taking is too frustrating, the pristine self takes on the primary task of creating that caretaker for itself. It is for this purpose that during this process the endopsychic structures are created.

As Sutherland writes, Fairbairn's basic endopsychic situation sets up an inner world (Sutherland 1994). It is created to make good deficiencies in the outer world, whenever the outer world threatens the emergence of an identity that is capable of acting within it. It is the relationship with the ideal object which compensates for emotional deficit.

If the repression is successful, the interaction can be maintained in a dynamic equilibrium. But this is a fragile situation. The repressed relationships are lurking, *sotto voce*. The dynamic equilibrium can be easily disturbed, either by a failure of repression, or by an increase in the traumatic input too great to be coped with by repression. These obdurate, persistent sub-systems may threaten the relationship of the central ego with the ideal object. Further strategies may be required.

The breakdown of repression

With the breakdown of repression the defensive structure, so carefully constructed, collapses like a house of cards. The exciting and rejective objects—scrupulously kept apart by the structure—re-merge and, in the process, engulf the ideal object. At the same time the two split-off parts of the ego—the libidinal and anti-libidinal—tend to re-merge with the central ego.

Faced with the loss of his internal and external good object, the outer darkness of abandonment—'where there is wailing and gnashing of teeth'—becomes a psychic reality for the infant. The infant—or, later, the adult—may enter a 'black hole', seeing only 'nothingness' or—even worse—rejecting hatred in the eye of the other. This primitive agony of despair may lead to a disintegration of the central ego. Grief or mourning for the lost object is not a psychological option at this level of psychic dependence.

The central ego, a fragile construct, based on an acceptance of the values of the idealised object, can easily be overwhelmed by reactivated relationships with bad objects:

> When such an escape of bad objects occurs, the patient finds himself confronted with terrifying situations which have hitherto been unconscious. External situations then acquire for him the significance of repressed relationships with bad objects.
> (Fairbairn 1943: 76)

Inner reality is superimposed upon outer reality.

Such an individual is in danger of re-experiencing the malign dyadic situation of infantile ambivalence, a situation of murderous intensity, an emotional Hungerford.[3] The benign and just Godhead can be polluted by the return of the demonic; the Virgin Mary adulterated by an unrepentant and provocative Mary Magdalene. Aggressive impulses, if not constrained, can destroy objects in external reality.

But in this situation need for the other is merely intensified. The individual can be overwhelmed by desperate longings for the body of the mother. These longings may be highly eroticised. Conscious incestuous fantasies may break through the weakened repression barrier. Desperate measures are necessary to preserve the self and both the internal and external other from annihilation.

The central self requires a narrative to cope with this threat of disintegration. Moreover, it must construct a narrative that will maintain the other as good at any cost. The process chosen might be sketched out at the subjective level as follows: *If you are bad I would reject you, but I can't, because I need you. If I am good, how can you be bad to me? The reason you are bad to me is because I am bad.* The solution, then, is to take on board the burden of the badness.

Unable to blame the external object, lest this leads to a resurrection of the bad object, the only recourse is to label the self as bad. Guilt comes into operation and confusional doubt is repudiated. The cost may be high, but:

> It is better to be a sinner in a world ruled by God than to live in a world ruled by the devil. A sinner in a world ruled by God may be bad: but there is always a sense of security to be derived from the fact that the world around is good—'God's in His heaven—

All's right with the world!'; and in any case there is always a hope of redemption. (Fairbairn 1943: 67)

Hope is preserved. The libidinal ego can permeate consciousness on the condition that it accepts the badness: 'God have mercy on me, a sinner, beset by the temptations of the flesh'. To question the goodness of God is the ultimate sin, the sin of the heretic who establishes his own autonomy. For this the individual is not yet ready; for this he requires a differentiated self.

We see that Fairbairn's account of repression is a two-step process. Primary repression creates the ideal object by splitting the over-exciting and rejective elements from the internalised object. This is accompanied by a splitting of the ego, thus allowing each ego element a relationship with part-objects (see the diagram). Ego relationships are compartmentalised and kept separate by repression. This split preserves the exciting object and the central ego from contamination by disgust or hatred. Failure in primary repression would lead to the ideal object (and therefore the external object) becoming a tantalising persecutor. Such a breakdown would strengthen the rejective hatred of the anti-libidinal ego: *I hate you because you are rejecting me. You are bad.* Rendered unacceptable the good object is lost.

If primary repression fails, the ideal object degenerates. The rejecting object is unconditionally bad from the point of view of the anti-libidinal ego. The rejective hatred could overwhelm the central ego and be transferred onto the external object. At this stage we encounter secondary repression. All aspects of the internal object, the good and the bad, are converted into a single idealised object—at the cost of converting the self into a bad object. By repressing the good aspects of the self the object is maintained as good. The now *idealised* object can be externalised onto the outside other by the central ego.

This process is akin to cleaning the family silver; the tarnish that spoiled the silver is removed by an internal process and the satisfactory aspects of the object are preserved. However, if the central ego takes on the burden of badness, then the accepted object is sanctified. Rendered sacrosanct, it is not an 'ideal object' but an *idealised* object.

I want to take the Fairbairnian account a bit further. Taking on the burden of badness preserves the other as a good object, but does not solve the problem of the need for acceptance. To get what I need, I have to become good in your eyes. I need to be acknowledged as the beloved son or daughter in whom you are well pleased. I take on your values as the condition of my self-esteem. If this fails, however, the subsequent disappointment may lead to the threatening re-integration of persecutory figures, which is intolerable. So I try even harder, modelling myself on that which I think will secure your acceptance. I put the 'you' over the 'I'. Submission becomes a good, the role of 'your most humble servant' becomes a worthwhile sacrifice to secure your approval. The values of the other are seen as good from the standpoint of the central ego, and are put over the self—a super-ego ideal.

Taking on the burden of the badness masks the impotent predicament of the unbalanced power-relationship entailed by monopoly dependence. The conscious self takes on the values of the other. The rejective or punitive parent is justified. The parent becomes at least morally good. Hope for the responsiveness of a 'good' other is maintained.

Ferenczi wrote that the immature self can only cope with assault by identification with the aggressor (Ferenczi 1949: 162). The ego submits to the values of the other. Justice is restored. Self-value is permeated by the rejective other. The self joins the ranks of the *unter-mensch*. Self-acceptance is formed by the construed values of the other. But, more important for my purpose, such an acceptance of the values of the other preserves hope of redemption. Attempting to construe an identity in terms of what pleases the other offers hope of acceptance. It provides a goal to strive for and the hope of ultimately attaining the desired response from the other.

Internal objects and internalisation

Internal objects play a role in many versions of object-relations theories. The use of similar terminology can cover-up major differences in the assumed endopsychic structures and the processes creating such structures.

An internal object can arise by two separate processes. It can be created *ab nuovo* by the operations of pre-existing ego elements; or, inherently, through innate object images which are externalised onto outside objects. Theories which adopt the latter approach tend to minimise the role of the external world and the environment on the development of endopsychic structures. How the environment responds to the workings of these structures may be considered important to the outcome, but tends not to be considered as a major factor in the creation of the structures.

'Internalisation' is a process, not a state. It is a process of bringing in from the outside. The object arising from the process of internalisation is the transformation of that which has been brought in from the outside, not a new creation. Internal objects of this type represent elements which actually exist in the external object that has been internalised. Objects created by this process, and the endopsychic structures created to deal with them, are both dependent on the outside objects. Theories in which the internal objects are transformations of that which has been internalised—rather than new creations, or inherent pre-existing elements with which one is born—stress the role of environment in the development of endopsychic structures, not just in the outcome.

Although Fairbairn's theory is clearly of the latter kind, he is often not clear when it comes to stressing the relevant distinction. Moreover, Fairbairn changed his own theoretical structure quite fundamentally, but without—at least explicitly—recognising the importance of the change. This can lead to confusion in the interpretation of Fairbairn, and a muddling-up of fundamentally different theories.

The process of the creation of internal objects—described in the last section and depicted in the diagram in the column labelled 'Model 2'—represents Fairbairn's revised version of an earlier model (Fairbairn 1951). In this earlier model the process was substantially different. It is shown in the column of the diagram marked 'Model 1'. The first two steps are the same, but then the structure changes. In step (c) the external object is split externally into a good and a bad object. In step (d) the bad object is internalised and again split into the rejecting and exciting objects. At the same time the ego is split into its three parts (as in 'Model 2').

Fairbairn's argument for this position is that:

> it is always 'bad objects' that are internalised in the first instance, since it is difficult to find any adequate motive for the internalisation of objects which are satisfying and 'good'. Thus it would be a pointless procedure on the part of the infant to internalise the breast of the mother with whom he already had a perfect relationship... It is only later that good objects are internalised to defend the child's ego against bad objects which have been internalised already; *and the super-ego is a good object of this nature.*
> (Fairbairn 1944: 93, my emphasis)

But at this stage in the development of his theory, the super-ego is an internal object created by the ego-structure. It is not an internalised object transformed by the ego structure. At this stage no 'good' element of the outside object has been internalised.

In his justification of the change in models Fairbairn is concerned with the possible criticism of why a good object should be internalised—as in 'Model 2'—given his previous claims. In this discussion he again confuses internalisation as a process and an internal object (the super-ego) as a creation (Fairbairn 1951: 134). His ultimate justification for the internalisation of the whole object is based on his new view that splitting occurs after internalisation, not before. The whole, pre-ambivalent object is neither wholly good nor wholly bad. The internalisation of this whole object is:

> explained on the grounds that it presents itself as unsatisfying in some measure as well as in some measure satisfying. On this assumption ambivalence will be a state arising in the original unsplit ego in relation, not to the external object, but to an internalised pre-ambivalent object. (Fairbairn 1951: 135)

It is this ambivalence that leads to the internal splitting of the good and bad objects described above.

We see that the resulting structure is fundamentally different. As in 'Model 2' the libidinal ego and the anti-libidinal ego attach themselves to the exciting and rejecting object (called 'the internal saboteur'), but the central ego is not libidinally attached to an internal good object because this aspect of the external object been internalised in this model. Moreover, because of this there is also no externalisation of an internal object onto the external object. This is not surprising, the reason being that in this structure the external object remains good because its parts have been split off, and only these have been internalised. The outside object has been purified, cleansed of its bad elements. These are internalised in the hope of coping with them by repression.

Moreover, within this structure it is logically necessary that the super-ego—which arises after the breakdown of repression that results in the moral defence—can only be created *ab nuovo*. It is an internal object which must be constructed. In this model there is no internalised good object which can be transformed into something which plays the role of a super-ego.

In his later theory, Fairbairn found no need for the super-ego construct. All the functions of the Freudian super-ego could be explained—he believed—more simply. As he put it:

> the anti-libidinal ego, the rejecting object and the ideal object are all independent structures playing different roles in the economy of the psyche, they are all included by Freud in the comprehensive concept of 'the super-ego'. (Fairbairn 1954: 108)

With the breakdown of repression the internalised split objects remerge and, as we saw above, the whole object becomes transformed into an idealised object externalised onto the outside other. However, the breakdown of repression has another consequence. Formerly repression kept apart the split object, by keeping the split egos apart. As long as repression worked these could continue their libidinal attachment to their objects without impinging on the central ego. With the breakdown of repression the object becomes idealised and the egos merge. The libidinal attachment of the anti-libidinal ego to the rejecting object is no longer possible, or must be transformed. Its hate and fear of the rejecting object, which has now been transformed into part of the idealised object, must go somewhere else. An idealised object cannot be tarnished by hate. With the moral defence the central ego has accepted the burden of the badness. It now becomes the target of the anti-libidinal ego, and self-hatred ensues.

Let me stress again an important point: for clarity of exposition I have described the evolution of the Fairbairnian psychic structure as a chronological process unfolding over time. However it should be conceived of as a dynamic, fluid structure which can change from one state to another, and back again, depending on the particular environmental stimuli and the degree of breakdown of repression. Moreover, repression and defence can work at various levels of the unconscious simultaneously.

Conclusion

Fairbairn, working in the relative isolation of Edinburgh, which at that time was considered a psychoanalytic wilderness, slowly and often painfully developed a fundamentally new conceptualisation of psychoanalytic theory. He recognised quite explicitly his disagreements with the Freudian paradigm and replaced it with a new structure. This did not arise like a Phoenix from the ashes, ready to take flight. Throughout his working life his theory was modified and sometimes drastically changed. But the fundamental theme of the relational nature and the relational needs of human beings runs through all his work. Psychic structures are developed in order to cope with these needs; the ways in which these structures develop, and the forms which they take, are affected by how well these needs are met.

The Freudian psyche is structured in terms of impersonal instincts and energies. The Oedipal phase, itself inherently ordained, leads to the tri-partite psychic structure of ego, id and super-ego. The ego, beset and beleaguered by anxiety and guilt, is buffeted by alien impulses of sexuality and aggression. It has the function of mediating and negotiating the relationship with external reality, whilst coping with its internal battles. The concept of inherent structural conflict is basic. The ego inhabits a house (the psyche), but it is a house divided.

Freudian clinical theory assumes that these 'psychic structures' become manifest in the transference relationship. They acquire representational form in terms of self-and-other transference configurations over time in the content of the relational setting provided by the analyst. The clinical enterprise is to interpret, and therefore:

> to elucidate the nature, origins and multiple (conscious and unconscious) functions of the representational structures which thematise the transference relationship. (Stolorow 1994: 316)

For Fairbairn, in contrast, the psychic structure is erected within the framework of a primary dyadic relationship. It is constructed as a defence mechanism to maintain the inherent relational needs of the infant. Its changing shape is affected both by the environmental responses to these needs, and by the power of repression—itself a construct of the psyche. The Fairbairnian model offers an alternative framework to the Freudian in terms of an elaborate interplay between dynamic ego structures and their respective objects, aided and abetted by secondary manoeuvres. Symptomatology arises from the complex interplay of these dynamic structures. Symptoms are the product of the personality as a whole. Hysterical, paranoid, obsessional and phobic conditions are specific techniques for regulating internal object relationships established in early life. They function as homeostatic regulators defending the central ego against the re-activation of relationships with bad objects. They are manoeuvres fending off the return of the repressed.

The clinical enterprise is to breach the closed internal system so painfully constructed. Psychoanalytic treatment:

> resolves itself into a struggle on the part of the patient to press-gang his relationship with the analyst into the closed system of the inner world through the agency of transference, and a determination on the part of the analyst to effect a breach in this closed system and provide conditions under which, in the setting of the therapeutic relationship, the patient may be induced to accept an open system of outer reality. (Fairbairn 1958: 385

The significance of the inter-personal relationship, and its role in the development of psychic structure, have to be recognised in the psychoanalytic encounter.

Notes

[1] I would like to thank Dr. John Padel, for helping to develop my interest in Fairbairn, and for his thoughtful comments on this paper.

[2] Fairbairn also argues that the anti-libidinal ego also represses the libidinal ego, which is why there is a 'repression' arrow here (indirect repression). This is not, however, crucial for the analysis.

[3] In 1987 a man in Hungerford, England, who had lived innocuously with his mother, went on a random killing spree. The first victim was a young mother picnicking with her children. The last victims were his own mother and himself.

THE FLOW OF NARCISSISTIC ENERGIES: KOHUT'S DIAGRAM IN *THE ANALYSIS OF THE SELF*

Phil Mollon

Set within the context of his model of narcissism, Kohut's diagram (Figure 1, below) represents a common form of narcissistic disturbance. He uses it to portray a situation in which the child's performance has been used by the mother narcissistically, in order to support her own grandiosity. At the same time, the child's need for recognition of his/her independent strivings has been neglected by the mother. This results in a paradoxical state of affairs, in which overt grandiosity coexists with low self-esteem, shame, and other indications of impaired narcissism.

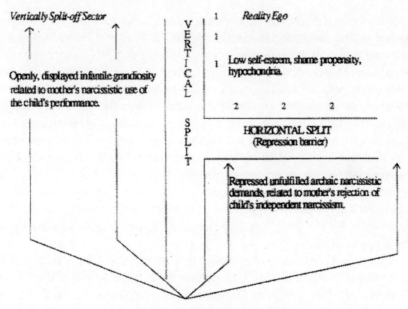

Figure 1. (Kohut 1971: 185)

To understand the diagram requires consideration of a number of unique concepts introduced by Kohut. These include: the notion of the separate line of development for narcissism; the grandiose self (and 'idealised parent imago'); the selfobject; transmuting internalisation and the development of structure; and the concept of structural deficit. Of particular significance are, firstly, Kohut's emphasis upon *psychoeconomic* trauma—that is, disturbance due to the *quantities* of narcissistic excitement—and, secondly, his account of the absolute dependence of development upon the adequate empathic responsiveness of the care-giving environment.

At the time of the publication of *The Analysis of the Self* (1971), Kohut placed his model of narcissism within a classical, essentially Freudian and ego-psychological framework. However, in his later writings (Kohut 1977, 1984) he presented a much broader 'self psychology' which he intended as an all-embracing, new theory for psychoanalysis. This wider and more radical theory is not addressed in detail in the following discussion. The full span of Kohut's writings are considered in reviews such as Ornstein (1978) and Mollon (1986a).

The line of development of narcissism

Kohut's crucial postulate of a separate line of development for narcissism was first presented in his 1966 paper, 'Forms and Transformations of Narcissism'. It takes Freud's 'On Narcissism' (1914) as its point of departure. Kohut followed Freud in viewing the earliest stage as one of *autoerotism* and an unintegrated body-image; this then develops into the stage of *narcissism*, in which the infant takes the self as its object. Libido resides in the self, producing a natural early grandiosity and illusion of perfection in the self. Kohut also accepted Freud's suggestion that narcissistic illusions may be preserved by the infant through locating perfection in an object, usually a parent. This projected ideal becomes gradually re-internalised to form the ego-ideal. However, where Kohut crucially departed from Freud was in his suggestion that narcissism did not give way to object-love, but continued along its *own* developmental line.

This radical shift in conceptualisation meant that it became possible to consider healthy as well as pathological forms of narcissism. In analysis—Kohut proposed—narcissistic strivings needed to be released from repression, experienced in relation to the analyst, accepted by the ego and integrated into the personality—just as would infantile object-relational strivings. Kohut believed that this point of view allowed a more understanding and essentially more *analytic* approach to narcissism. He felt that the earlier, Freudian position tended to lead to implicit exhortations to the patient to give up his/her narcissism and move towards object-love. The contrast between the analytic stances arising from these alternative points of view is illustrated most vividly in Kohut's paper 'The Two Analyses of Mr. Z' (1979).

Kohut postulated that the line of development of narcissism bifurcated into the 'grandiose self', on the one hand, and—on the other—into the image of the idealised, or omnipotent, parent. In the position of the grandiose self the child could feel: 'I am perfect'. Through basking in the reflected glory of the idealised other, the child could feel: 'You are perfect, and I am part of you'.

By referring to the 'grandiose self' as a 'normal' position in childhood, Kohut meant only that a child has a need to display his/her mind-body-self, and for this to be responded to with interest and empathy. For example, a patient who appeared to have received very little empathic mirroring in her childhood began, after some years of analysis, to bring her paintings to show the analyst. She did so against a background of great anxiety that this display might be rejected, mocked, criticised or ignored. In so doing she was bringing into the analytic relationship the natural needs—which every child has—to show her paintings and other creations to someone who will be interested. The 'idealised parent imago' similarly refers to something very ordinary in childhood—the child's wish to participate in, and feel held and protected by, a parent's strength and importance. For example, a man whose father had died when he was six (resulting in a shattering collapse of idealisation) had the comforting thought, on walking past the prestigious clinic where his therapy took place, 'That's where my therapist works!'—a clear derivative of the typical childhood thought: 'That's where my father works'. Through perceiving the clinic and the therapist as embodying admirable and reassuring qualities he could feel that he was participating in these himself.

In normal development, as these positions and narcissistic strivings evoke appropriate empathic responses from care-givers, they progress into more mature derivatives of narcissism. The strivings of the grandiose self give way to realistic ambitions, whilst the idealised other becomes the inner ego-ideal. Kohut sometimes wrote of our being *driven* by our ambitions and *led* by our ideals. He also believed that wisdom, humour and creativity depend upon transformations of infantile narcissism into more mature forms. Thwarting of narcissistic needs leads to their intensification and suffusion with aggression, as well as regression to earlier forms. Regression along the lines of narcissism might result in infantile and pathological forms of narcissism.

In the domain of the grandiose self, these might include: haughty grandiosity, imperious behaviour, or affected speech and gestures. In the domain of the idealised other, it might involve trancelike religious feelings, or hypomanic excitement. Where there is regression to the stage of autoerotic fragmentation of the self, pathological forms of narcissism might entail hypochondria about physical and mental health, self-stimulation, or perverse fantasies and activities. These regressions might typically be triggered by *narcissistic injuries*, such as slights and misunderstandings, failures of empathy by others, or failure by idealised others to live up to the idealisation. In analysis, the pattern of these regressions can usefully be explored in relation to the analyst.

Kohut viewed perverse sexual fantasies and behaviours as sexualised statements concerning narcissistic injuries. For example, a child's chronic failure to elicit appropriate recognition of the natural, phase-appropriate exhibitionistic display of his/her body-self might result later in a more crudely sexualised wish to display the body or sexual parts of the body.

At this stage of his theorising, presumably in order to maintain some continuity with more classical psychoanalytic theory, Kohut referred to 'narcissistic libido', which he contrasted with 'object libido'. He wrote as if he envisaged this as a kind of mental energy, flowing along certain channels and capable of becoming blocked and diverted, or of flooding the psyche. It is difficult to ascertain how literally Kohut viewed this energic metaphor. Certainly the notion of narcissistic libido and—indeed—the whole idea of the flow of narcissistic energies (as represented in Figure 1) had disappeared by the time of his next book (1977). By this time he had begun to present a new model of the mind, based on the central notion of the 'bipolar self'. What seems most likely, however, is that Kohut, being a highly sophisticated theoretician, was fully aware of the purely metaphorical nature of these energic concepts, but felt that they captured something of the *introspective experience* of narcissistic strivings. Certainly he considered that the domain of psychoanalytic enquiry was limited to that which is available through introspection and empathy (Kohut 1959). A concept of two forms of mental energy—narcissistic and object relational—taken in a literal biological or a literal physical sense is clearly outside the bounds of this domain, since we do not have direct introspective access to the biochemical phenomena of our bodies.

The concept of the selfobject

Kohut's development of the concepts represented in Figure 1 began with his observations of certain transference-like conditions (the 'narcissistic transferences'), in which the analysand's psychological functioning and sense of well-being appeared dependent upon the analyst's consistent and accurate empathic attunement. When this was disrupted, the analysand's state of mind would deteriorate along the line of narcissistic regression, as described above.

Kohut recognised that the analyst was not functioning in these states as a separate object invested with object libido—that is, desired as an incestuous object or feared as a rival in love. Instead, the analyst was needed in order to provide certain *functions* necessary for the analysand's mental equilibrium:

> [T]he analyst, though cognitively acknowledged as separate and autonomous, is nevertheless important only within the context of the analysand's narcissistic needs and is appealed to and otherwise reacted to only insofar as he is felt to fulfil or frustrate the patient's demands for an echo, approval, and confirmation of his grandiosity and exhibitionism. (Kohut 1971: 204)

Because the analyst's empathic responses are needed to maintain the patient's mental equilibrium and sense of well-being, this responsiveness forms a kind of system with the patient's own mind. It is these *functions* performed by the analyst's empathy to which Kohut gives the term 'selfobject', thereby indicating that they take place *between* the self and the object. The selfobject is not an object, cathected with love or hate. Rather, it is an other person *experienced in terms of their functions* in the maintenance of narcissistic equilibrium.

Transmuting internalisation and the development of psychic structure

Kohut often referred to 'psychic structure', but his use of the term was rather distinct. By it he meant that, gradually, in the course of development or during analysis, the child or analysand becomes able to perform for him/herself some of the functions originally provided by the selfobject. This *internalisation of function* is what he meant by 'structure'.

The development of structure takes place, according to Kohut, by means of repeated internalisations of function, in response to the parent's or analyst's failure as selfobject. If these empathic failures are small and manageable, the child or analysand can use these as a spur to growth and can take over these functions. Repeated 'microtraumas' of this kind do not lead to massive internalisation (Goldberg 1983), which would result in an 'internal object' (as described, for example, in Fairbairn 1952), but to the internalisation of *function*—a process Kohut termed 'transmuting internalisation'.

People whose narcissistic development has not proceeded well, and who are thus particularly vulnerable where the selfobject is concerned, may be said to be suffering from a *structural deficit*. The concept of 'deficit' in Kohut's psychology derives from his concept of the selfobject and his view that the functions of empathic responsiveness from others are absolutely necessary for adequate development in the narcissistic realm. A narcissistic disorder cannot, in Kohut's scheme, be regarded as a purely intrapsychic conflict; there has been a failure—on the part of the principal care-givers—to provide certain necessary *functions*. Kohut believed, moreover, that human beings never outgrow their need for selfobjects; we all require empathy from others, although the form of this need may alter as we mature.

One of the results of the availability of adequate selfobjects in childhood is that narcissistic needs are met appropriately, at the right time, and therefore do not have to be warded off. They do not acquire added intensity and urgency, as they would if frustrated. This means that the narcissistic sector of the personality is integrated and matures with the rest. Kohut views this process (in relation to 'narcissistic libido') as analogous to the sublimation of sexual libido (as described by Freud), and the neutralisation of the aggressive drive (as described by the ego psychologists). The availability of selfobjects in childhood thus leads to the establishment of inner structure which 'neutralises' narcissism, preventing its emergence in crude infantile forms and channelling it into more mature forms. The potential re-emergence of 'unneutralised' crude narcissistic desires may be highly threatening to a person's psychological equilibrium.

Psychoeconomic trauma

Another feature of Kohut's account is his observation that an absence of adequate selfobject experiences in the childhood of patients may result in a deficiency of structures for 'self-soothing'. Such people are, therefore, 'thin-skinned', easily hurt and offended, prone to overwhelming shame, and their fears and worries tend to expand, becoming boundless and catastrophic. Kohut notes that these patients are subject to recurrent traumatic states, both in analysis and daily life. He comments:

> At such times the focus of the analysis shifts temporarily to a near-exclusive consideration of the overburdenedness of the psyche, i.e. to a consideration of the existing psychoeconomic imbalance. (Kohut 1971: 230)

Patients with narcissistic disturbance are excessively prone to feelings of shame. Kohut gives the example of exaggerated shame reactions to the memory of committing a *faux pas*:

> His mind returns again and again to the painful moment, in the attempt to eradicate the reality of the incident by magical means, i.e. to undo it. Simultaneously the patient may angrily wish to do away with himself in order to wipe out the tormenting memory in this fashion. (Kohut 1971: 231)

He emphasises the importance of the analyst's tolerance of the patient's repeated recounting of the painful event:

> For long periods the analyst must participate empathically in the psychic imbalance from which the patient suffers; he must show understanding for the patient's painful embarrassment and for his anger that the act that has been committed cannot be undone. (Kohut 1971: 231)

Kohut points out that often the traumatic states may be precipitated by events within the analysis. Paradoxically, it may be precisely those interpretations which are empathic and correct that give rise to psychoeconomic trauma. Although these effects might superficially give the impression of a negative therapeutic reaction, due to unconscious guilt or envy, this is not the case. Kohut gives an example of a patient who, in talking about his restless loneliness, mentioned that his mother had seemed to dislike her own body and would recoil from physical closeness. The analyst had commented that the patient's restlessness seemed to relate to his never having learned to experience himself as 'loving, loveable and touchable'. The patient responded with excitement, declaring 'Crash! Bang! You hit it!', and shortly afterwards became tearful. The following day he arrived in a dishevelled, excited and disturbed state, reporting that he had been unable to sleep. He also mentioned grossly sexual fantasies about his (female) analyst, dreams of eating breasts, and a variety of bizarre images and fantasies. Kohut explains this as follows:

> In essence the patient's traumatic state was due to the fact that he had reacted with overstimulation and excitement to the analyst's correct interpretation. His vulnerable psyche could not handle the satisfaction of a need (or the fulfilment of a wish) that had existed since childhood: the correct empathic response of an all-important figure in his environment. (Kohut 1971: 234)

Kohut advises that the most helpful response to these traumatic states is for the analyst to explain to the patient that the understanding attained in the previous session, and the fulfilment of the wish for (empathic) understanding, had been overexciting.

Kohut's explanation of narcissistic anxieties is always set, essentially, in terms of psychoeconomic threat: the destabilising potential of narcissistic energies, sensations and images which have not been moderated, harnessed, socialised and integrated into the ego through the transmuting crucible of selfobject experiences. He writes:

> The danger against which the ego defends itself by keeping the archaic grandiose self dissociated and/or in repression is the dedifferentiating influx of unneutralised narcissistic libido (towards which the threatened ego reacts with anxious excitement) and the intrusion of archaic images of a fragmented body self (which the ego elaborates in the form of hypochondriacal preoccupations). (Kohut 1971: 152)

Thus Kohut describes the central anxiety in the narcissistic disorders as the fear of the disorganising intrusion of early forms of narcissism and their energies. Within this spectrum he specifies four particular anxieties: (1) the fear of the loss of the reality self through ecstatic merger with the idealised parent imago (or quasi-religious regressions involving a sense of merger with God); (2) the fear of loss of contact with reality through grandiose excitements; (3) shame and self-consciousness; (4) hypochondriacal anxieties.

An important point regarding narcissistic anxieties is that they often possess a *vague* quality, making them difficult to perceive with clarity. Kohut contrasts this with Oedipal anxieties in which—for example—there is a fear of being killed or mutilated by an adversary of superior strength. Even where Oedipal anxieties are expressed in regressive pre-Oedipal imagery, the movement of the analytic material will be towards the elaboration of a *specific* fear. In the case of narcissistic anxieties, however, the longer the analytic work proceeds, the vaguer the content may appear to become. Kohut observes:

> The patient may ultimately speak of vague physical pressures and tensions, or of fears of loss of contact, of contentless, stimulating anxious excitement, etc., and he may begin to talk about childhood moments of being alone, of not quite feeling alive, and the like. (Kohut 1971: 154)

The inherent vagueness of narcissistic anxieties may have meant that prior to the provision of Kohut's conceptual lens, it was not possible for most analysts to grasp these.

Horizontal and vertical splits

Kohut describes two groups of patients in which a failed integration of the grandiose self formed the basis of the disturbance. The groups differ according to the prevalence of *repression* or *dissociation*, which Kohut described—respectively—as 'horizontal' and 'vertical' splits in the mind (see Figure 1, above).

In the first group, the grandiose self exists primarily in a repressed state. This repression might be described as a 'horizontal' split (between consciousness and unconsciousness). The reality ego is thereby deprived of narcissistic nutriment from 'deeper' sources of narcissistic energy, resulting in symptoms of 'narcissistic deficiency', such as diminished self-confidence, vague depressions, absence of zest for work, and lack of initiative.

In the second group, the psychological situation is similar to the first, in that there may be a repressed grandiose self beneath a horizontal split, giving rise to the symptoms described above. However, this mental structure is complicated by the coexistence of an unmodified grandiose self, present *alongside* the reality ego, but kept apart from it by a 'vertical' split. Here Kohut is describing the defence of *dissociation* which (since the mid-1980s) is commonly discussed in connection with severe trauma-based dissociative disorders, such as multiple personality disorder (Mollon 1996). This dissociated grandiose self—which may be present in consciousness—is derived from the mother's narcissistic investment in her child. The mother might have been greatly admiring of her child, but only so long as he/she was fulfilling the mother's own narcissistic aspirations, and not necessarily if the child was pursuing an independent agenda. In this way the child's authentic, grandiose self might have become quite neglected and rejected. The overt grandiosity, based upon the mother's narcissism, may give rise to attitudes of arrogance, vanity, boastfulness, and intemperate assertiveness. These overtly grandiose attitudes would coexist or alternate with symptoms of narcissistic depletion—such as low self-esteem, lethargy, and vague depression. Consequently, the person's overtly expressed attitudes might seem quite inconsistent.

Kohut saw dissociation—or 'vertical splitting'—as particularly characteristic of narcissistic disorders. He wrote:

> In the narcissistic personality disturbances (including especially certain perversions) we are not dealing with the isolation of circumscribed contents from one another, or with the isolation of ideation from affects, but with the side-by-side existence of disparate personality attitudes with different goal structures, different pleasure aims, different moral and aesthetic values. (Kohut 1971: 183)

The function of the analyst in bringing about therapeutic progress

The analyst's task is not to gratify the patient's narcissistic demands, nor to educate the grandiose sector of the psyche, nor to exhort the patient to give up his/her narcissism. Instead the analyst's stance is one of 'acceptance which stresses the phase-appropriateness of these demands within the context of the transference revival of an archaic state' (Kohut 1971: 179).

As a result of this accepting stance, patients in whom there is a combination of vertical and horizontal splits begin to encounter their repressed narcissistic needs:

The patient will then come face to face with formerly unrecognised defences which had protected him against the discovery that, despite the seemingly self-assured assertion of narcissistic claims by one sector of his psyche, the most centrally significant sector of his personality is deprived of the influx of self-esteem-sustaining narcissistic libido. (Kohut 1971: 179)

Kohut gives the example of 'case J', a man who—for some time into the analysis—displayed only a flagrant grandiosity and exhibitionism. During one session he mentioned, casually, that after shaving in the mornings he would carefully rinse his razor and clean the sink before washing and drying his face. Kohut noted that although the account itself seemed irrelevant, it was presented in a slightly arrogant and tense fashion. In retrospect, this became the first indication of the presence of a hidden area of the patient's personality. Gradually they came to understand that the patient's *overt* vanity and arrogance was linked to his mother's acclaim for various performances in which he was shown off for the advancement of *her* self-esteem:

> [This] noisily displayed grandiose-exhibitionistic sector of his personality had occupied throughout his life the conscious centre of the psychic stage. Yet it was not fully real to him, provided no lasting satisfaction, and remained split off from the coexisting, more centrally located sector of his psyche in which he experienced those vague depressions coupled with shame and hypochondria that had motivated him to seek psychoanalytic help. (Kohut 1971: 180-181)

The shaving habit, in which performance of fastidious washing of his razor and the basin took precedence over attendance to his face, was an endopsychic replica of his need for his mother's acceptance of his displayed body-self and her rejection of this. Kohut notes that:

> Gradually, and against strong resistances (motivated by deep shame, fear of overstimulation, fear of traumatic disappointment), the narcissistic transference began to centre around his need to have his body-mind-self confirmed by the analyst's admiring acceptance. (Kohut 1971: 182)

Kohut and the patient came to understand that a crucial fear for the patient was that the analyst might value the patient only as a vehicle for the analyst's own aggrandisement, and would reject the patient if he displayed his own initiative in relation to his body and mind. The patient gradually became aware of his hitherto repressed yearning for acceptance of his 'archaic, unmodified grandiose-exhibitionistic body-self' (Kohut 1971: 182), a yearning which had been hidden by the noisy display of narcissistic demands expressed through a vertically split-off sector of his personality. As these wishes were worked through and integrated, the patient was able to arrive at a position where—as he humorously put it—he could 'prefer my face to the razor' (Kohut 1971: 183).

It is surely a remarkable and subtle insight by Kohut that openly displayed grandiosity may be essentially false, in that it does not relate truly to the patient's deeper core but is derived from narcissistic use of the patient by a parent—and that hidden behind this is a more authentic need to display and to be admired. During the 1970s Kohut's theory was often compared and contrasted with the work of Kernberg. However, a close reading of Kernberg (for example, Kernberg 1974) will reveal that although he adopted Kohut's term 'the grandiose self', he refers only to conscious grandiosity, and was describing the state of affairs represented only by the left side of Figure 1—the vertically split-off sector containing overt grandiosity, related to the mother's narcissistic use of the child's performance.

Kohut advises that the first stage of analytic work in these conditions is directed at undoing the vertical split (at the points marked '1' in Figure 1), so that the reality ego is able to know and control the formerly uncurbed narcissism which finds expression in the split-off sector. There is a significant sentence in Kohut's note explaining his diagram, which suggests a point that is not made particularly explicit in the rest of the text:

> The narcissistic energies which are thus prevented from finding expression in the vertically split-off sector (left side of the diagram) now reinforce the narcissistic pressure against the repression barrier (right side of the diagram). (Kohut 1971: 185)

It is as if Kohut is saying that the narcissistic energies leak away through the vertical split, leaving the main personality depleted. He implies that the mother's narcissistic use of the child hijacks (rather than nurtures) the child's narcissistic energies, leaving a rupture in the psyche through which there is continual leakage. Analytic work at the vertical split heals the rupture and stems the leak. Work can then take place at the horizontal split (at the points marked '2' in Figure 1), where the now enhanced energic pressure pushes the repressed, true narcissistic wishes through the repression barrier.

According to Kohut, the correct analytic stance is one in which the infantile narcissistic needs are activated and brought into consciousness whilst not gratified on an infantile level. The analytic work, of transference interpretations and genetic reconstructions, prevents regressive evasion of the narcissistic needs either through re-repression (horizontal split) or through re-exclusion (vertical split). This stance allows the narcissistic energies to proceed in only one direction, toward maturation and integration into the reality-oriented ego. The positive benefits of this are an increase in realistic self-esteem, enjoyment of success, the harnessing of fantasies of achievement into realistic plans, as well as the development of qualities such as humour, empathy, wisdom and creativity.

The place of Kohut's model in relation to other psychoanalytic models and theories

Kohut's theory of narcissism, as outlined in 1971, is unique. He views narcissistic anxieties and tensions not as the result of conflict in relation to the superego, or the ego ideal, or the external world of other people. Instead he explains these anxieties as due to the threatening intrusion of unmodified ('unneutralised') infantile narcissistic strivings which would overwhelm the ego—a psychoeconomic trauma. This formulation is possible because of Kohut's insight that narcissism has its own line of development. The therapeutic aim can thus be seen in terms of the transformation of narcissism from primitive into more mature forms. This transformation depends absolutely on the transmuting availability of selfobjects; the patient *cannot* transform his/her narcissism without this external help. Thus Kohut's is not a model of purely intrapsychic disturbance, but embraces the notion of a child in an environment which forms a *system* with the child's mind. Later, some of Kohut's followers (Stolorow, Atwood and Brandchaft 1994) developed these ideas and presented their 'intersubjective approach' which sought to dispel the 'myth of the isolated mind'.

Kohut's model of narcissism has its roots partly in Freud's 'On Narcissism', but his emphasis upon the role of the environmental response to the child places him in the tradition of Hartmann and other American ego psychologists who described the ego developing within an 'average expectable environment'. (see, for example, Hartmann 1958.) In terms of British psychoanalytic writing, the theorist to whom he is closest is Winnicott, who similarly wrote with great sensitivity on the subtle aspects of the mother's response to the child, which he described as the 'facilitating environment' (Winnicott 1990). Like Kohut, Winnicott understood how the child's own innate blueprint for development might be derailed by pressures to perform for the mother's gratification, resulting in a false self. However, whilst there are thirteen citations and eleven references to Hartmann in Kohut's book of 1971, there are only two citations of Winnicott and one reference. Kohut's work has to be understood against an American historical context.

One other British theorist in the Kleinian tradition—superficially very different, but with important points of contact with Kohut—is Bion. His model of the mother's response to the crying infant has much in common with Kohut's concept of the selfobject (Mollon 1986b). According to Bion (for example, Bion 1977) the baby's scream of distress embodies a fantasy of projectively expelling the 'bad thing' (hunger, cold, fear, etc.). The mother, through her thoughtful and receptive attentiveness (her empathy), figures out what is causing the distress and responds appropriately, thus returning the projection in a modified, detoxified form. The projected 'screamed out' object is caught and returned as *thought*. Thus Bion regarded projective identification not merely as a phantasy (as Klein had described it) but as an interaction which forms the basis of thinking and communication. Bion was describing the mother not as a love object, but as the provider of *functions* necessary to support her infant's developing psyche. According to Bion, the mother's failure to receive, think about and detoxify the infant's emotions—perhaps even adding her own anxiety—results in the infant being deprived of meaningful communication and left with 'nameless dread'. Perhaps this 'nameless dread' has something in common with the state of fragmentation of the mind-body-self, and resulting hypochondriacal anxiety, which Kohut describes as the earliest position on the line of development of narcissism. For Kohut, regression to the fragmented mind-body-self is precipitated by empathic failures in the selfobject realm.

When compared with other models of narcissistic disturbance, Kohut's can be seen to embrace far more phenomena than that of any other theorist (Mollon 1993: 103). Not surprisingly, therefore, his work became the doorway onto the radically new formulation of psychoanalysis known as 'self psychology'. This became part of the broad trend towards intersubjective and relational perspectives which began to transform the American psychoanalytic landscape. By the end of his life and his last book (1984), Kohut had completed his personal transmutation of classical psychoanalysis.

HOW TO SQUARE THE MEDICINE WHEEL: JUNG'S USE OF THE MANDALA AS A SCHEMA OF THE PSYCHE

Michael Whan

[T]he physician must have exact knowledge of man and recognise him in the mirror of the four elements, in which the whole microcosm reveals itself.—Paracelsus.

From subject to microcosm

As an image of the psyche, the mandala in Jung's psychology highlights the enigma of psychic self-representation. In his last major text, *Mysterium Coniunctionis*, Jung observes:

> The mandala symbolises, by its central point, the ultimate unity of all archetypes as well as of the multiplicity of the phenomenal world, and is therefore the empirical equivalent of the metaphysical concept of the *unus mundus*. The alchemical equivalent is... in particular the Microcosm. (Jung 1955-56: 661)

This chapter will concentrate on drawing out the full significance and implications of these remarks.

In Jungian psychology the mandala holds various modes of *interiority* in tension. The tension arises from the way in which the subjective arises from a radical separation or polarisation, between the 'subject' as inner being, and the world and its things as exteriority. Yet, conversely, the notion of psyche as *microcosm* – also conveyed by the mandala – suggests an intrinsic identity or analogy between psychic man and the world, a fundamental concord.[1]

In his many writings on mandala symbolism, Jung works with *both* conceptions – sometimes in the language of the modern introspective subject, at other times in alchemical, Hermetic, Christian, Gnostic or Cabalistic terms. On the subject of the mandala, then, Jung employs the language of a historical polyglot, drawing upon antiquity, the Middle

Ages, the Renaissance, Western Modernity, as well as Tibetan Buddhism and Tantric yoga.

Metaphorically, the circularity of the mandala embodies a form of *movement* privileged within Jungian psychology – that of involuted or inner spiralling, the *opus circulatorium*[2] of the alchemists. For Jung, alchemical work provided a fitting metaphor for the psychotherapeutic process and its setting. Alchemy involves a closed, cyclical operation in which the *materia* is refined, through heating, evaporation, cooling, and condensation. Similarly, the work of psychotherapy expresses itself in the form of a transference of emotions, through fantasising and dreaming, reflection and psychological insight. For Jung, psychotherapy can be metaphorically likened to these operations. The ethic of confidentiality and containment within the psychotherapeutic setting is similar to the hermetic sealing of the alchemical vessel. The engendering of affectivity in the transference corresponds to the process of 'heating'; 'evaporation' suggests the fantasies and dreams which arise in connection with the emotional 'heat' of the transference; the 'cooling' process is figured in the reflectiveness of association, amplification, and the discussion of psychic contents; 'condensation' expresses itself in the psychological insights that result. Jung regards this differentiating, inner-circling movement as the essence of the dynamic of individuation.[3] In his commentary on an ancient Chinese alchemical text, *The Secret of the Golden Flower*, Jung describes this process as 'movement in a circle around oneself'. In the course of this convolutional process many sides of the personality are touched upon, the 'poles of light and dark are made to rotate' (Jung 1929: 38), signifying finally 'nothing less than self-knowledge by means of self-brooding' (Jung 1929: 39). This inner circulation is incubatory, yet disrupts the ego-centricity of consciousness. Instead, the paradoxical tensions of psychic wholeness come to the fore – the *complexio oppositorum*[4] of psychic experience, or what Jung describes otherwise as the relativisation of the ego-complex.

Jung's conception of the mandalic nature of the psyche, and of its circumambulatory way of moving, finds many cultural and historical echoes in Western as well as Eastern traditions. To take but one instance, the Neoplatonist Plotinus wrote in his *Enneads*:

> Every soul that knows its history is aware, also, that its movement, unthwarted is that not that of an outgoing line; its natural course may be likened to that in which a circle turns not upon

some external but on its own centre, the point to which it owes its rise. (Plotinus 1981: VI, 9, 8)

Plotinus asks of this inner-centring, soulful rotation: 'Is then this "centre" of our souls the Principle for which we are seeking?' He answers himself:

[W]e must admit a principle in which all these centres coincide: it will be a centre by analogy with the centre of the circle we know... not a centre in the sense of a geometric figure but in that its primal nature (wholeness) is within it and about it, and that owes its origin to what is whole. (Plotinus 1981: VI, 9, 8)

Hence, in Neoplatonism, self-knowledge – the 'soul that knows its history', its 'primal nature' – entails insight into the soul's primordially inscribed *circular* movement.

Jung's account of the phenomenology of the mandala reveals a problem concerning the conflict between the subjectivist and microcosmic interpretations of the nature of the psyche. Perhaps this reflects the tension between Jung's own extraordinary depth of imagination and experience, and the strictures of psychological theorising. At the heart of the matter, however, lies the question of the psyche's concealedness, its existence as an *unknown* factor which depth psychology attempts to grasp through the concept of the 'unconscious'.

For Jung, the unconscious is 'not this thing or that; it is the Unknown as it immediately affects us' (Jung 1957). This question of concealment, the hidden, lies also at the heart of the mandala symbol and its interpretation.

The mandala, suggests Jung, 'expresses the essence of a certain kind of *attitude*' (Jung 1936a: 247). Unlike conscious intentionality, this attitude displays 'no definable aim and no visible purpose'. Rather, it points towards something 'shrouded in "metaphysical" darkness' (Jung 1936a: 247). Jung approaches this primordial concealment of the depths of the psyche under the influence of the metaphysics of *subjectivity*. It could be argued that this approach is a consequence of Jung's Protestant inheritance. He identifies the mandala as a symbol of the 'self', a term which he questions as soon as he utters it: 'It is easy enough to say "self", but exactly what have we said?' (Jung 1936a: 247). When Jung attempts to comment further on what he means – that is, on the self as the *totality* of conscious and unconscious psyche – he comes up against the enigma of the psychic unknown, the logical difficulty of the unconscious:

> In so far as the unconscious exists it is not definable; its existence is a mere postulate and nothing whatever can be predicated as to its possible contents... Consequently the 'self' is a pure borderline concept similar to Kant's *Ding an sich*... Since we cannot possibly know the boundaries of something unknown to us, it follows that we are not in a position to set any bounds to the self... these limits... lie in the unconscious. We may be able to indicate the limits of consciousness, but the unconscious is simply the unknown psyche and for that reason illimitable because indeterminable. (Jung 1936a: 247)

However, to conceive of the self as a borderline concept, epistemologically close to Kant's 'thing in itself', throws up the fundamental internal dilemmas of Jung's psychology. One area of difficulty, for instance, arises from his claim to be an 'empiricist first and last', and from declaring his psychology 'scientific'.[5] Evidently, the '"metaphysical" darkness' Jung attempts to address psychologically cannot be approached empirically. Empirical thought denies Jung's psychology precisely the thing in which his own psychic life was so rich and vivid. A positivistic approach to the psyche holds Jung back from that 'ontological' type of thinking which is capable of addressing a deeper meaning of concealment (*letheia*).[6] It is this which Jung attains through his imagination and intuition. A psychology which operates wholly within empiricism predicates itself logically on the notion that what is hidden in the psyche cannot be thought.

Our understanding of the unknown psyche, then, its unrevealed depths, depends mostly upon the language of knowing and not-knowing; we apprehend psychic reality entirely in terms of whether it is *conscious* or *unconscious*.[7] Psychoanalysis understands *concealedness* exclusively through its concept of the unconscious – that is to say, as a product of repression and dissemblance. Thus it formulates the unconscious in two, interwoven senses: firstly, in the sense of that which is hidden as opposed to that which is disclosed; and secondly, in the sense of distortion or disfigurement.[8] Being unconscious means – in psychoanalysis – being *repressed*, as, for instance, in the bifurcation of dream experience into manifest and latent content, due to a *deformation* by the dreamwork's mechanisms of displacement, condensation, pictorial representation, and secondary revision. Interpreting all forms of the hidden through its agonistic concept of the unconscious, then, psychoanalysis necessarily focuses in the analytic session upon so-called 'resistance' and 'dissemblance', because these are the only kinds of concealment it is able to recognise. Consequently, disclosure, insight, and that which remains concealed are understood as matters of wholly human activity, rather than as that which *befalls* beings – human or otherwise – or as that which belongs to the very nature and truth of being as un-concealment (*a-letheia*).[9]

As I have intimated, Jung's conception of the psyche as the unknown cannot be reduced entirely to concealedness as repressive strife, nor to dissemblance – although these are part of its meaning. It also includes the notion of concealment as sheltering, conserving, bestowing through self-withdrawal what is essential, holding sway as *mystery* (rather than mystification), as the unbeknown.[10] As a symbol of the psychic microcosm, then, the mandala coaxes psychological thought beyond subjectivism, towards a realisation that the psyche is primarily engaged with being-in-the-world.

The mandala in Jung's life and work

The mandala as microcosmic image served Jung as a foundational myth – in his work and in his life. Its numinosity, its overwhelming value and meaning, extending to the heart of healing and psychic experience, came from a source deeper than human subjectivity. Jung perceived this underlying agency as *nature itself*. Quoting Jakob Böhme, he asserted that the mandala points symbolically to a 'Centre of Nature' (Jung 1950: 592).

Jung saw the mandala as an attempt on nature's part at 'self-healing', springing from an 'instinctual impulse', transforming neurotic fixation and one-sidedness through the healing movement of circumambulation. In this way, the roots of the mandala as a 'natural symbol' reach down into the world itself, into the *macrocosmic* ground. As with much else, this primordial image entered the stream of Jung's psychology through his own fantasy and dream-life.

In his autobiography *Memories, Dreams, Reflections* he records a mandala dream from childhood. It occurred at a time when Jung was becoming deeply interested in the natural world, and when what he called his 'No. 1 personality' and 'No. 2 personality' were struggling over a choice of profession. In the dream the mandala presents itself –

significantly – in the form of a strange creature which Jung encounters in a forest:

> In the darkest place I saw a circular pool, surrounded by dense undergrowth. Half immersed in the water lay the strangest and most wonderful creature: a round animal, shimmering in opalescent hues, and consisting of innumerable little cells, or of organs shaped like tentacles. It was a giant radiolarian, measuring about three feet across. It seemed to me incredibly wonderful that this magnificent creature should be lying there undisturbed, in the hidden place, in this clear, deep water. It aroused in me an intense desire for knowledge, so that I awoke with a bearing heart. (Jung 1963: 85)

Mandalic shape, nature, hiddenness, depth, and the 'desire for knowledge' all combine in this fateful dream. Along with an earlier dream, it was this which prompted Jung to study the natural sciences. Indeed, Jung's evident passion for nature resonates in an almost Emersonian way. In an essay entitled 'Circles', the American philosopher Ralph Waldo Emerson envisaged this particular form as nature's 'primary figure'. He suggests it forms part of our fundamental symbolic interpretation of the world:

> It is the highest emblem in the cipher of the world... We are all our life time reading the copious sense of this first of forms. (Emerson 1995: 136)

In the circle Emerson discovers nature's infinite and boundless depth:

> Our life is an apprenticeship to the truth, that around every circle another can be drawn; that there is no end in nature, but every end is a beginning; that there is always another dawn risen on mid-noon, and under every deep a lower deep opens. (Emerson 1995: 136)

For both Emerson and Jung, then, nature teaches us the finitude and provisionality of consciousness and knowledge. As Emerson puts it:

> The natural world may be conceived as a system of concentric circles, and we now and then detect in nature slight dislocations which apprise us that this surface on which we now stand is not fixed, but sliding. (Emerson 1995: 145)

The mandala can be understood, from the perspective of Jungian psychology, as a symbol of psychic interiority (microcosm) and also, as in the Eastern traditions, of the totality of the universe (macrocosm).

The next reference to a mandala figure in Jung's life occurs during his training as a physician, in his dissertation: 'On the Psychology of So-Called Occult Phenomena'. This work is a study of Jung's mediumistic cousin – Hélène Preiswerk – who is referred to in the text as 'S.W.' Jung had attended a number of her seances, and sought to give a psychological account of the spiritualistic happenings he had witnessed.

Jung noted that Hélène, over a certain period, had conveyed revelations from spirits concerning forces in the world and beyond. After a time, when all had become silent, she gave Jung instructions to draw a diagram.[11] This represented a 'mystic system' which Hélène explained as follows:

> The forces are arranged in seven circles. Outside these are three more containing unknown forces midway between force and matter. Matter is found in seven outer circles surrounding the ten inner ones. In the centre stands the Primary Force; this is the original cause of creation and is a spiritual force. (Jung 1902: 66)

Recognition of the psychological value of this mandala lay in the future for Jung. At the time of the incident Jung contented himself with the recollection that he and others had spoken in Hélène's presence about forces of repulsion and attraction, gravity as a form of motion, the conservation of energy, and the various forms of energy. All of this Jung connected with Kant's cosmogony, in his writings concerning the rotation of the earth and the theory and natural history of the heavens (Jung 1902: 66). Thus Jung understood Hélène's 'system' as compiled from what she had absorbed during the discussions.

Whether or not Hélène's 'mystic system' held any greater interest for Jung later, with the benefit of his conception of the mandala, is debatable. However, the concentric microcosmic and macrocosmic structure of Hélène's system is noteworthy. 'Matter' appears in its outer circles, whilst the centre contains the spiritual principle, the 'Primary Force'. The relations between the various parts of the system operate through combinations and oppositions. In Jungian terms, the diagram can be seen as an attempt to project an image of the psyche and its workings – envisaged in terms of conjunctions and separations – both in itself and in relationship to material nature.

Further mandala motifs appear in the watershed text *Wanderlungen und Symbole der Libido* (1911-12). This was the work which Jung began whilst still under the influence of Freud, but which marked the break between them. In this study, Jung discusses a variety of images: dream cities, sun-wheels, crosses and mystic roses. Nonetheless, only once he had revised the text in 1952, giving it the title (in the English translation) *Symbols of Transformation*, did he retrospectively treat these images as mandala symbols.[12]

In the period which followed the separation from Freud, Jung suffered a great psychic upheaval, which included intensely vivid fantasies, emotional turbulence, and visions. Indeed at one point, after an apocalyptic visionary episode, he felt 'menaced by a psychosis' (Jung 1963: 176). Gradually, however, he developed a means of relating to the diverse imaginal figures and events occurring in his psyche: he wrote about them, painted them, entered into dialogue with them, and allowed himself to go down into the fantasies. In this way he sought to distil the images hidden in his emotions, and hence find their meanings.

During the period 1918-1919, whilst acting as *Commandant de la Region Anglaise des Internes de Guerre*, Jung, each morning, sketched a small, circular drawing. He viewed these as 'cryptograms' which corresponded to his 'inner situation' (Jung 1963: 195-196). In *Memories, Dreams, Reflections* he expresses his idea of the mandala in Faustian terms, as 'Formation, Transformation, Eternal Mind's eternal recreation' (Jung 1963: 196).[13] Between 1918 and 1920 Jung came to the realisation that:

> the goal of psychic development is the self. There is no linear evolution; there is only a circumambulation of the self. (Jung 1963: 196)

As we have seen, it is this very movement which the mandala describes – the labyrinthine path of individuation. In the following passage from his autobiography, Jung also relates his mandala drawings to the metaphor of the microcosm.

> I had the distinct feeling that they were something central, and in time I acquired through them a living conception of the self. The self, I thought, was like the monad which I am, and which is my world. The mandala represents this monad, and corresponds to the microcosmic nature of the psyche. (Jung 1963: 196)

Jung's reference to the 'monad' and the psyche's 'microcosmic nature' may suggest an underlying allusion to Leibniz, whose philosophy belonged to a tradition of thought in which the concepts of microcosm and macrocosm continued to exert an influence. In order to assert a fundamental sense of unity in all things, Leibniz developed a principle of pre-established harmony between the monad and the universal whole. This Leibnizian notion of harmony between the individual and the universe is related to the notion of correspondence between the microcosm and macrocosm.[14] It reappears in Jung's theories on the nature of matter and the psyche, and on the relationship between physics and psychology.

In 1927 and 1928 Jung painted two important mandalas. To the first, dedicated to Hermann Sigg, a recently deceased friend, he gave the title 'Window on Eternity'. The title highlights the temporal dimension of mandala phenomenology. Taken in the context of friendship, loss, life and death which surrounds the production of the painting, the mandala becomes a symbolic portal located on 'this side' of time, and opening onto the timeless. This was a theme elaborated by Jung's colleague, Marie-Louise von Franz, in her work on mandala symbology and notions of time.[15]

Jung mentions that the painting was occasioned by a dream, in which he and others were making their way through the dark, wintry, winding streets of the city of Liverpool. In the dream the city was arranged radially around a small island in a circular pool:

> On it stood a single tree, a magnolia, in a shower of reddish blossoms. It was as though the tree stood in the sunlight and were at the same time the source of light. (Jung 1963: 198)

The dream was accompanied by a sense of *finality*:

I saw that here the goal had been revealed... Through this dream
I understood that the self is the principle and archetype of orientation and meaning. Therein lies its healing function... Out of it
emerged the first inkling of my personal myth. (Jung 1963: 198-199)

Whilst painting the second mandala of this period – entitled 'The Castle' – Jung received from the sinologist Richard Wilhelm a copy of a Taoist-alchemical treatise, *The Secret of the Golden Flower*. This occurrence put an end to Jung's feelings of isolation; he used the text as a means of defining and confirming his ideas on the mandala as a symbol of the circumambulatory movement of the psyche.

As Jung knew well – from his own experience, and from that of his patients – the mandala usually appears in periods of crisis: 'in conditions of psychic dissociation or disorientation' (Jung 1955: 714). From this perspective, then, the mandala has an apotropaic function, a monocentric or 'integrative' meaning, and counters states of confusion and mental travail. The mandala fulfils this function through the 'central point to which everything is related, or by a concentric arrangement of the disordered multiplicity and of contradictory and irreconcilable elements' (Jung 1955: 714).

Several thinkers in the field of Jungian and archetypal psychology have taken up this aspect of the mandala and used it to reflect critically on Jung's psychology. Hillman points out that Jung discovered the mandala towards the end of his period of psychic upheaval. Is there then, Hillman asks, a *defensive* stance in Jung's use of the mandala against the experience of falling apart?[16]

At the time of his discovery of the psychological meaning of the mandala Jung was also at work on what would later be published as *Psychological Types*. With its four- and eightfold structure, Jung's typology of personalities can be read as a conceptual mandala. It too entails a defensive, ambivalent function.

On Jung's theory of psychological types, Hillman ventures that:

> it belongs to the rhetoric of the archetypal perspective of fourness to present itself as a systematic whole, a mandala with an internal logic by means of which the system defends itself as all-encompassing... an entire *Weltbild* of oppositions and energies held together by its mandala form. (Hillman 1980: 19)

In another subtle and persuasive critique, Noel addresses the defensive logic of the mandala which, he suggests, epitomises certain facets of Jung's style of theorising. Noel charts the development of the mandala in Jung's life and work alongside his encounter with the anima and his reactions to modern art.[17] Jung recounted how – in the process of writing down his fantasies following the break with Freud – he heard a woman's voice tell him that what he was doing was 'art': 'I recognised it as the voice of a patient, a talented psychopath who had a strong transference to me. She had become a living figure within my mind' (Jung 1963: 185). He felt great resistance to the claims of the voice, and replied: 'No, it is not art! On the contrary, it is nature' (Jung 1963: 186).

Gradually, he began to understand this inner feminine voice as a primitive soul, the anima-image that plays an archetypal role in man's unconscious life. The disruptive effect of the anima upon the harmony of mandalic order was demonstrated graphically when Jung received a letter from the woman who carried his anima projection, in which she reiterated her assertions concerning the artistic merits of Jung's fantasies. He was irritated by the hubristic and potentially seductive effects of this claim, which resulted in a mood of inner disharmony. From this feeling 'proceeded, the following day, a changed mandala: part of the periphery had burst open and the symmetry was destroyed' (Jung 1963: 195). The anima figure had transgressed the mandalic boundary, rupturing its enclosure.

Jung's resistance against the persuasions of his anima involved, by the same token, a struggle against his own 'aestheticising tendency' (Jung 1963: 188). Noel explores in some detail a number of Jung's mandala paintings, including one previously unpublished – 'The Baynes Mandala'. Behind the symmetry and harmony, Noel uncovers a de-centring psychic background, containing triangular and alchemistic fragments, cabalistic shards, an 'imagery of fragmentation' (Noel 1995: 87). The end of the period of Jung's 'dark night' was marked by two events, which again demonstrate the connection between the mandala symbol and the anima experience. Firstly, Jung broke off relations with the woman who declaimed the artistry of his fantasy life, and felt – as a consequence – that he had begun to understand the symbolism of his mandalas (Jung 1963: 195-196). Secondly, he decided to give up his 'aestheticising tendency' and to choose instead 'scientific comprehension'. Noel, in his essay, asks whether Jung's 'sense of self with its bias in favour of mandalic harmony served to distance him from the pandaemonium of anima's unconscious contents' (Noel 1995: 75, 83) – that is, whether Jung *used* the mandala as a way of protecting ego-consciousness against the upwelling of fantasy and affect.

Though Jung recognised its apotropaic function, by envisaging the mandala as *nature's* attempt at self-healing, he placed it at a deeper level than that of an ego-defence. Indeed, by conceiving it is as a product of nature, the mandala came to play a key role in Jung's study of *alchemy*.

The mandala and alchemy

Jung's interest in alchemy had two sources. Firstly, he interpreted alchemy as an antecedent of contemporary depth psychology. The alchemists, Jung believed, projected the contents of the unconscious onto matter – into nature – in much the same way as the patient and the psychotherapist project onto one another through transference and countertransference. Alchemical language, for Jung, was metaphorical rather than literal. Through the paraphernalia of alchemy, Jung asserted, the alchemists worked on their own psyches. The labour of the alchemical transmutation expressed symbolically what Jung understood psychologically as the *individuation* process: the *opus* of inner differentiation and transformation.

The second source of Jung's interest was that – through alchemy – he could explore the meaning of nature, as it is mirrored in the psyche, and of the psyche's place in nature. In this respect, the role of the mandala in the alchemical setting held a particular psychological value because, as a symbol of the microcosm, it alluded to nature as the macrocosm in which the microcosmic psyche was contained. It intimated a form of interiority *related to* – rather than closed off from – nature. Stated more strongly, it indicated symbolically and conceptually *the interiority of nature*.[18]

Jung interpreted the mandala patterns he found in Gnosticism and alchemy in terms of the transformational and circular movement of the psychic energy of the self. In ancient philosophy, existence was conceived as cyclical: birth, life, death and re-birth. The followers of Parmenides, for instance, held that absolute being was spherical. In Plato's Timaeus a double mandala appears: the first, a timeless sphere, the second finite and temporal. The mandala form makes a reappearance in Neoplatonic philosophy.[19]

According to von Franz, the early models of matter and the alchemical *opus* were mandala-shaped. The *Rosarium Philosophorum* – a major alchemical text – cites the pseudo-Aristotelian saying:

> When thou shalt have obtained water from earth, air from water, fire from air, and earth from fire, then possessest thou our Art fully and completely. (Cited von Franz 1974: 182-183)

This is a description of the circular movement of the elements and the analogous pattern between the soul, the logos and the cosmos. The mandala as microcosm also appears in connection with one of the key imaginal figures in alchemical discourse – *Mercurius*. This figure from the alchemical imagination made a deep impression upon Jung's thought. He described this duplex, autonomous, chthonic spirit of the Hermetic mystery as the archetype of the unconscious.[20]

Hermes-Mercurius symbolised, in alchemy, the transforming substance, and was also associated with both roundness and squareness. The square has a symbolic meaning in terms of the fourfold aspects of nature: earth and air, fire and water. Nature's totality was thus represented by the number four. Jung, in a discussion of the alchemical *lapis* (that is, the goal of alchemy, known otherwise as the 'philosopher's stone'), observes the link between Mercurius and the mandala form:

> In the stone sleeps the spirit *Mercurius*, the 'circle of the moon'... the *rotundum* of alchemy is identical with Mercurius, the 'round and square'. (Jung 1950a: 541, 549)

In *Mysterium Coniunctionis* Jung quotes John Dee, the Elizabethan occult philosopher, in order to emphasise the symbolic meaning of the Mercurius figure as a microcosm:

> 'that other Mercurius' who appears in the course of the work is the 'Mercurius of the philosophers', that most renowned Microcosm... (cited in Jung 1955-56: 545)

Elsewhere he notes:

> He [Mercurius] is also the microcosm, or even 'the heart of the microcosm', or he has the microcosm 'in himself, where are also

the four elements and the *quinta essentia* [the quintessence]... (cited in Jung 1948: 268)

The self-concealment of depth psychology

Mandala symbolism, like alchemical language, offered Jung a figural means of depicting the psyche. To Jung's mind, depth psychology—namely, the psychology of the unconscious—remained in itself fundamentally problematical. Perhaps it is this *aporetic* character of depth psychology that lies behind Jung's diagrammatic employment of a mandala form in his London seminars of 1935 (known also as the 'Tavistock Lectures').

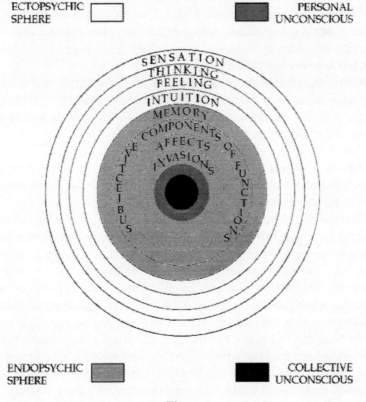

Figure 1.

It might be argued that although this diagram apparently describes the psyche, thus providing a schema—a founding image—for Jung's psychology, its *mandalic* form implicitly alludes to the nature of the problem with depth psychology itself. Viewed as a symbolic microcosm, this diagram cannot be understood *positivistically*. There is an ambiguity here: should one treat the diagram as an abstract *concept* (schema) or as a *symbol* (microcosm)? If the former, then it is simply an abstraction, a device, serving the purpose of conceptual description. If the latter, then depth psychology's epistemology—its' way of knowing'—is itself figural, symbolic. In this case the depth psychologist can never straightforwardly interpret the psyche's symbolic language; the psychological language of interpretation is already and ineluctably symbolic, metaphorical. Every psychological statement concerning the unconscious must speak in a way that can never fully objectify its hiddenness, but can only deal with its symbolic traces. Depth psychology casts a peculiar mirror-image, rather like the figure in the Magritte painting entitled *Reproduction Prohibited*, in which a man gazes at his reflection in a mirror, but sees only himself from behind. 'Reflection', here, has become perplexing, enigmatic.

Writing in a letter about his 'descent to the greatest depth in oneself', Jung refers to a 'parable on the mandala' (Jung 1973: 311). In this curious tale he allegorises the dilemma of the depth psychologist attempting to schematise the psyche:

> There was once a queer old man who lived in a cave, where he had sought refuge from the noise of the villages. He was reputed to be a sorcerer, and therefore he had disciples who hoped to learn the art of sorcery from him. But he himself was not thinking of any such thing. He was seeking only to know what it was that he did not know, but which, he felt certain, was always happening. After meditating for a very long time on that which is beyond meditation, he saw no other way of escape from his predicament than to take a piece of red chalk and draw all kinds of diagrams on the wall of his cave, in order to find out what that which he did not know might look like. After many attempts he hit on the circle. 'That's right', he felt, 'and now for a quadrangle inside it!' – which made it better still. His disciples were curious; but all they could make out was that the old man was up to something, and they would have given anything to know what he was doing. But when they asked him: 'What are you doing

there?' he made no reply. Then they discovered the diagrams on the wall and said: 'That's it!' – and they all imitated the diagrams. But in so doing they turned the whole process upside down, without noticing it: they anticipated the result in the hope of making the process repeat itself which had led to that result. This is how it happened then and how it still happens today. (Jung 1950b: 233)

Like the alchemists with their arcane geometry, Jung, in this 'Just-so' story, characterises psychological theorising as an attempt *to square the circle*. He highlights a difficult problem – the predicament of *transmissibility*. If the mandala symbol – as an autonomous image produced by the psyche – is put to use as a *schema* of the psyche, then what happens as it passes from being a symbol into the register of abstraction. How can it be passed on, without falling into the deadening grasp of imitation and self-parody? Does the mandala lose its symbolic resonance – becoming, in Jung's terms, merely a 'sign'? Does symbology give way to semiotics? Can the symbol survive the training institute?

In the opening commentary of his London seminars, Jung examines the way in which psychology necessarily stands across its own path, due to this problem of self-reflection and self-representation. The depth psychologist, suggests Jung, must follow the winding course of psychology to its innermost, where it folds back upon itself. To 'think psychologically', then, means to enter the round of this subtle and perplexing movement.

Jung begins by doubting whether psychology has yet fully beheld the meaning of itself. If this is the case, then psychology is still in the process of becoming psychology. It has yet to grasp the enormity of its own undertaking, 'the perplexing and distressingly complicated nature of its subject-matter: the psyche itself' (Jung 1935: 6). If the psyche is the proper 'object' of psychology, then it also comprises its 'subject'. Hence the depth psychologist has still to realise the 'menace of so formidably vicious a circle' (Jung 1935: 6). In depth psychology there is no Archimedean or methodological point beyond the psyche from which one could wholly 'objectively' perceive it. We are already and always in the midst of things psychological. The psyche is ever upon us:

> We should never forget that in any psychological discussion we are not saying anything *about* the psyche, but that the psyche is always speaking about *itself*. (Jung 1954: 483)

In his seminar, Jung defined psychology in a twofold sense, as a 'science of consciousness', and as a 'science of the products of what we call the unknown psyche' (Jung 1935: 8). The predicament of depth psychology arises because the unconscious cannot be directly known. Instead, it can be expressed only 'by consciousness and in terms of consciousness' (Jung 1935: 8). Even a psychological consciousness must, therefore, fall under a 'hermeneutics of suspicion'[21] for it views the unknown psyche as its own negative or counter-image, as the *un*-conscious. All we say about the psyche should recognise this 'ultimate critique' (Jung 1935: 8). Psychological language is, inherently, an 'as if' statement. Jung's assertion points to a tautology, a hermeneutic circle – namely, the question of how to approach the *circulatio*, the circumambulation of the psychological work.

In Jung's theory, the quintessential circular movement expresses itself as a form of thinking, a metalogic which combines contradictions, overcomes antinomies, delineates paradoxes and enigmas.

In a commentary on one of his own mandala paintings, Jung declares: 'It [the mandala] portrays the antinomies of the microcosm within the macrocosmic world and its antinomies' (Jaffe 1979: 75). Psychology, the *logos* of the psyche, moves within the hermeneutic circle:

> The symbol is not a sign that veils something everybody knows… it represents an attempt to elucidate, by means of analogy, something that still belongs entirely to the domain of the unknown. (Jung 1966: 494)

Jung's technique of *amplification* consists of 'successive additions of other analogies to the analogy given in the symbol', thereby enriching 'the individual symbol' until the 'outcome is an infinitely complex and varied picture' (Jung 1966: 495). Using amplification, we feed the imaginal psyche with further images, spreading beyond the personal to the cultural and historical psyche. This movement unfolds in a labyrinthine rather than a linear way:

The life-line constructed by the hermeneutic method... does not follow lines that are straight, nor lines whose course can be foreseen... 'All truth is tortuous,' said Nietzsche. (Jung 1966: 501)

Heidegger himself provides a strikingly uroboric image[22] of hermeneutic or originary thinking:

The principle of the ground – the ground of the principle... Here something turns around itself... curls itself up in itself without... closing itself, but rather unlocking itself... Here is a ring, a living ring, something like a snake. Something catches itself with its own tail. Here there is a beginning which is already completion. (Schofer 1972: 285)

Despite his hostility towards Heidegger, Jung himself could not have poeticised more hermetically.

A dilemma emerges, then. Although Jung asserts the 'empirical phenomenological approach' of his psychology, which thus falls 'within the framework of natural science', it simultaneously departs from it. Depth psychology simply names 'the unknown by the more unknown', because it is itself rooted ineluctably in the psychic.

As 'pure' psychology its principle of exploration is *ignotum per ignotius* ['naming the unknown by the more unknown'], for it can reconstruct the observed process only in the same medium from which that process is itself constituted. (Jung 1946: 162)

The meaning of theory twists critically. Each so-called 'reconstruction' takes a deconstructive turn:

Every psychic process, so far as it can be observed as such, is essentially *theoria*, that is to say, it is a *presentation*; and its reconstruction – or 're-presentation' – is at best only a variant of the same presentation. (Jung 1946: 162)

In the uroboric shadow of his psychological praxis, Jung throws representational thought and language – indeed, even his own use of them – into question.

Jung's concentric diagram condenses heterogeneous layers of interiority. As he explains his mandalic model of the psyche, he appears to talk his way from the 'outer' to the 'inner', from the subjective (the 'ectopsychic sphere' and the 'personal unconscious') to the microcosmic (the 'endopsychic sphere' and the 'collective unconscious'). The so-called 'ectopsychic' aspect corresponds to a subjective consciousness standing over and against the world as object. The four functions of *sensation, thinking, feeling,* and *intuition* are employed in the apprehension of the 'facts and data' entering from the 'environment'—that is, 'the external facts given... by the function of my senses' (Jung 1935: 20). These functional, 'empirical' layers of the psychic are therefore concerned—according to Jung—with the 'external' world. They fit in with a Cartesian, Kantian notion of the mind. The innermost core of the diagram is the 'collective unconscious', which Jung here portrays at the very centre of the psyche. As 'collective' it is also the most archetypal or universal aspect. In this latter sense, it corresponds to the psyche as a microcosm. The innermost ('collective unconscious') of the individual psyche is related to the whole, the totality of the macrocosmic universe.

He then turns to his theory of psychological types, which he bases upon the varying degrees to which individuals rely upon the functions of *sensation, thinking, intuition* and *feeling*. Jung structures this typology in terms of a fourfold polarity of dominant, inferior, and the two auxiliary functions. Ego-consciousness, in Jung's typological model of the psyche, tends to utilise one of the four functions. Further, depending on the attitude-type of the individual, this will take a more or less introverted or extraverted form. Thus, for example, an introverted personality may have *intuition* as its conscious ('dominant') function. According to Jung's oppositional structure of the functions, the most unconscious ('inferior') function will be—in this case—*sensation*, with *thinking* or *feeling* as the auxiliary functions. The latter can be more or less developed, combining with the dominant function to form—let us say—*intuitive feeling*. Access to the inferior function is through one or other of the auxiliary functions—in this example, a connection between *thinking* and *sensation*. The inferior function inhabits the deepest levels of the unconscious, manifesting itself symbolically as an 'archaic personality', an 'open wound', which is the threshold through which the unconscious enters ego-consciousness as—for instance—a dream, fantasy, affect, or sensation.

This fourfold model of personality types is an illustration of Jung's mandalic conception of the psyche as a whole. The genesis of this mandalic conception must be understood within the context of Jung's problematisation of depth psychology. Jung radically questioned the modern notion of consciousness, and turned psychology upon itself in order to break from the cult of consciousness which is so deeply embedded in the occidental – especially the Protestant – mentality. 'Our true religion,' argued Jung, 'is a monotheism of consciousness' (Wilhelm & Jung 1965: 111).

The typology of personality types, Jung states, originated from his need to define how his psychological approach differed from those of Freud and Adler. Through it, he sought to account for: 'the various aspects of consciousness, the various attitudes the conscious mind might take toward the world, and thus [constitute] a psychology of consciousness' (Jung 1920: v). Jung developed a critical metapsychology which interrogates different psychological theories and provides a critique of our ways of knowing and experiencing.[23] In this way, then, Jung attempted to find a strategy for listening to the other, to the heterogeneity of psychological discourse:

> The typological system I have proposed is an attempt... to provide an explanatory basis and theoretical framework for the boundless diversity... in the formation of psychological concepts. (Jung 1936b: 987)

Under sway of a monotheistic consciousness, psychology itself suffers the selfsame pathology which – for Jung – afflicts the neurotic mind: *one-sidedness*. In his London seminars, Jung remarked that psychology may take a pathological turn:

> Medical psychology, therefore, should be careful not to become morbid itself. One-sidedness and restriction of horizon are well-known neurotic peculiarities. (Jung 1935: 5).

Depth psychology is a maieutics, a midwifery of the soul, and proceeds by way of dialogue. In Jung's psychotherapeutic approach to the psyche, the patient and psychotherapist can never directly 'know' the *ultimate* nature of that with which they are dealing. Rather, they circumambulate its meanings, by way of association and amplification—that is to say, by way of indirection and mediation. As distinct from the psychoanalytic approach—in which the content of a fantasy may be 'objectively' paraphrased—the Jungian psychotherapeutic dialogue is itself no less metaphorical or symbolic than the fantasy upon which it comments.

In his later, alchemical studies, Jung adds an archetypal and microcosmic meaning to his typology. In *Mysterium Coniunctionis* he interprets the ancient four divisions of the alchemical opus[24] as a symbolic process corresponding to transformations through the elements, from earth to fire. This alchemical idea led Jung to propose that:

> one's given personality could be represented by a continuous circle, whereas the conscious personality would be a circle divided up in a definite way, and this generally turns out to be a quaternity. (Jung 1955-56: 261)

Significantly, he suggests that the quaternity archetypically prefigures 'what we today call the schema of functions' (Jung 1955-56: 261).[25] Already, in his book *Psychological Types*, Jung had referred to an ancient symbolic typology, the origins of which lay in Hellenistic syncretism, and which – he asserted – was a precursor of his own theory of functional types. In this ancient conception, humankind is classified into three forms: '*hylikoi, psychikoi,* and *pneumatikoi* – material, psychic, and spiritual beings' (Jung 1936b: 964).[26] To this Hellenistic trio, Hillman adds a fourth – the noetic, *nous* ('of the intellect') – and proposes that this antique typology reveals the archetypal imagination at work in Jung's own typological schema. That is, Hillman suggests Jung's psychological typology itself reflects an archetypal form of ordering things in terms of a *fourfold*. Jung's typology is—then—simply a contemporary manifestation of what appeared (in ancient conceptions) as a fourfold schema of human nature. Thus Jung's model is an archetypal fantasy, appearing in the same light in which depth psychology today might regard the antique theory of the 'four humours' which produce the human personality. If—as Jung and Hillman indicate—'four' is an archetypally symbolic number, then its appearance in Jung's fourfold typology of the human personality is suggestive—analogically—of the ancient concept of human nature as a microcosm, reflecting the four elements (earth, water, fire, and air) of the cosmos, the macrocosm.

Jung also provides us with an account of the various levels of conscious and unconscious subjectivity – memory, subjective response, the shadow, the body, and affectivity. Reaching the internal limits of the psyche, 'subjectivity' gives way to 'otherness'. We reach the psyche's de-centred, animistic, disassociated core, which Jung likens to the so-called 'primitive' mind. Jung refers at this point to the *personifying activity* of the psyche, and offers as examples: 'the devil or an incubus or a spirit going into man, or of his soul leaving him, one of his separate souls' (Jung 1935: 43). The idea that a person might lose their soul is another illustration of this primitive level of psychic functioning.

At the innermost concentric circle of his conceptual mandala, Jung locates the collective unconscious which – paradoxically – embodies also the psyche's most *worldly* root. This is the sphere of the archetypes, the psyche's impersonal, inner infinity, that 'ultimate kernel which cannot be made conscious at all' (Jung 1935: 92). It is archaic, and contains the primordial images and mythological motifs which determine the characteristics of psychic life. In an earlier lecture, Jung traced the history of the idea of an impersonal unconscious through Von Hartmann, Schopenhauer, C.G. Carus, Hegel, Schelling (the 'eternally unconscious'), Kant, and Leibniz ('*petites perceptions*').

Contrasting this notion with the relativity of consciousness, Jung links the collective unconscious with Schelling's 'absolute ground of consciousness' (Jung 1932: 1223). In doing so he exposes the founding paradox and self-contradiction of depth psychology: *the collective unconscious is known by consciousness, but only as 'the unknowable'*. As 'absolute ground' it cannot be immediately and reflectively grasped by the conscious mind, which apprehends it only negatively.

Schelling, with his notion of the 'absolute ground', also conceived of the subject as emerging from the primacy of unconscious activity. For Schelling, the absolute unconscious subject-object was *nature* (Bowie 1993: 58). As such, nature itself embraces a contradiction: it is that which lies between itself as both 'subject' and 'object', and out of which self-consciousness emerges. The mandala, accordingly, traces symbolically the identity and non-identity of the conscious and the unconscious, the 'absolute ground' of psychic wholeness. At its innermost – the collective unconscious – 'subject' and 'object' coalesce as the hidden identity of the psyche as microcosm and the world as macrocosm.

An exchange between Jung and Dr. Eric Graham Howe – one of the members of the eminent audience at the London seminars – appears to suggest this same view of the relationship between the psyche and the world. Howe criticises Jung's diagram of the psyche as misleading, employing Jung's own psychological theory in his argument:

> I would criticise if I may the whole diagrammatic system of Jung because he is giving you a three-dimensional presentation of a four-dimensional system, a static presentation of something that is functionally moving. (Jung 1935: 115)

Jung agrees; a dynamic psychology needs 'the time factor' to avoid a static conception of the psyche. Howe proceeds to develop a mandalic geometry of the psyche:

> You and I do not regard the shape of the ego as a straight line. We would be prepared to regard the sphere as a true shape of the self in four dimensions, of which one is the three-dimensional outline. If so, will you answer a question: What is the scope of that self which in four dimensions is a moving sphere? (Jung 1935: 117)

Immediately, however, Howe responds to his own question:

> The universe itself, which includes your concept of the collective racial unconscious... How big is this sphere, which is the four-dimensional self? I could not help giving the answer and saying it is the same bigness as the universe. (Jung 1935: 117-119)

Jung answers Howe by acknowledging a reciprocity, a circular transaction between the psyche and the world but – in doing so – does not conflate the two. Speaking in terms of introjection and projection, Jung proposes that the 'image of the world is a projection of the world of the self, as the latter is the introjection of the world' (Jung 1935: 120).

Elsewhere in his work, Jung refers to the 'interpenetrating mysteries' of life and the psyche, in which the soul and the world are indeterminably created out of each other (Jung 1918: 23). Perhaps, with this notion, Jung is attempting to construct a depth psychology which goes beyond subjectivism, and in which the mandala features as a privileged symbol of the psyche, conceived as microcosm.

Notes

[1] See Jung 1955-56: 761.

[2] In alchemy the *circulatorium* is a glass vessel in which the liquid is rotated, ascending and descending alternately. For Jung, it represented the 'circularity' of the individuation process,

in which the various contraries and elements of the psyche are related and drawn together, a deep 'rounding' of the individual's personality.

3 Jung defines *individuation* as 'a process of *differentiation*, having for its goal the development of the individual personality' (Jung 1921: 759).

4 *Complexio oppositorium*: this term, 'the complex of opposites', corresponds, for Jung, to the symbolic unification of the contraries of the psyche. In other words, it is a symbol representing the central archetype—'the Self'.

5 See Giegerich 1987.

6 The Greek word *'lethe'* denotes 'a forgetting, forgetfulness'. In his many writings on the Western notion of truth, Heidegger employs the Greek word *'aletheia'* (un-concealment) to portray truth as a revealing and concealing (*a-letheia*). *Letheia* thus signifies the concealment (forgetfulness, untruth) of truth, out of which things are brought into *un*concealment.

7 See Holt 1992.

8 See Strambaugh 1992.

9 See Heidegger 1992: 61-65.

10 See Heidegger 1992: 61-65; Strambaugh 1992: 7-20.

11 This is reproduced as 'Figure 2' in Jung 1902: 66.

12 See Jung 1973: vi.

13 Jung is quoting Goethe's *Faust*, Part Two. Goethe 1959: 78.

14 See Allers 1944: 324.

15 See von Franz 1974, 1992.

16 See Hillman et al. 1960: 157-158. See also Fordham 1985: 14; Redfern 1985: 48, 122.

17 See Noel 1995.

18 See Maclean 1989; *Biblioteca Philosophica Hermetica* (n.d.); Klossowski de Rola 1988.

19 See von Franz 1974.

20 See Jung 1948.

21 The phrase 'a hermeneutics of suspicion' is taken from the work of Paul Ricoeur (1965). It denotes an iconoclastic style of interpretation in which everything interpreted is put in question, put under suspicion, in the light of a basic principle of reality. For example: in Freudian psychoanalysis this reality is infantile sexuality; in Marxism, the fundamental economic order of society. Everything interpretable is reduced back to this basic reality, which amounts to disclosing 'the truth'.

22 The *Uroboros* is an archetypal symbolic image of a serpent coiled in a circle and eating its own tail. It served as an emblem of alchemy, representing Mercurius and the process of transmutation. Feeding upon itself, the uroboric serpent symbolised unity. Jung understood it psychologically as a symbol for the integration and assimilation of the opposite—that is, of the Shadow. My application of the adjective 'uroboric' to Heidegger is intended to highlight the way this image underlies the circularity of hermeneutic thinking. For instance, it is the nature of a question that it already—in some sense—contains its own answer. This motif of the circularity of thought is certainly not peculiar to Jung. As demonstrated here, it is found also in the works of Heidegger—and in others, such as Hegel. It belongs to the problems raised by the hermeneutic approach and—indeed—by all notions of understanding. See Schofer 1972.

23 See Hillman 1980: 24.

24 The four divisions or stages of transmutation in alchemy: (1) the *nigredo* or blackening—this is often symbolised by images of death and melancholy; (2) the *albedo* or whitening—in this stage, following on from the blackening, there is a process of cleansing or purification;

(3) the *citrinas* or yellowing—a transitional stage between the whitening and the culmination of the transmutation; (4) the *rubedo* or reddening—the achievement or perfection of the goal of the alchemical *opus*.

[25] See Hillman 1980: 20-23.

[26] *Hylikoi* ('hylic', material); *psychikoi* (psychic, soulful); *pneumatikoi* (spiritual).

TURNING A TELESCOPE ON THE SOUL: FREUD'S INTERPRETATION OF THE STRUCTURE OF THE PSYCHE

Sharon Morris

Introduction

> Suppose I have a picture-puzzle, a rebus, in front of me... But obviously we can only form a proper judgement of the rebus if we put aside criticisms such as these of the whole composition and its parts and if, instead, we try to replace each separate element by a syllable or word that can be presented by that element in some way or other... A dream is a picture-puzzle of this sort and our predecessors in the field of dream-interpretation have made the mistake of treating the rebus as a pictorial composition: and as such it has seemed to them nonsensical and worthless. (Freud 1900: 278)

The Interpretation of Dreams is a radical and innovative work because, in it, Freud takes seriously the playfulness of the soul. Dreams—like visions, hallucinations and symptoms—reveal unconscious processes, but only in the mischievous disguise of the rebus, or picture-puzzle.

Dreams—asserts Freud—should no longer be interpreted according to a collective code or cultural lexicon, but should be understood as signs along the 'royal road' to the understanding of ourselves. Unravelling the meaning of the dream by applying the same method he had used for unravelling the symptoms of hysteria, Freud locates the dream upon a *chain* of associations which extends back to our earliest memories, a chain composed of images and words. The links holding the chain together are the tropes of language: metaphor and catachresis, metonymy and synecdoche, homonyms and puns, figuration, dramatisation, and so on. When we wake from a dream, we are left with only our visual memories and our associated verbal description of it. The immediate account of the dream Freud calls *manifest content*. Further associations to it form the *latent content*. Thus dreams—in a sense—represent both that which we know, and that which we do not. Through describing and analysing the processes of dream formation and interpretation, Freud states that his aim is to 'deduce from these processes the nature of the psychical forces by whose concurrent or mutually opposing action dreams are generated (Freud 1900: 1).

In the process of offering an explanation for the strange and puzzling qualities of the dream, Freud produces a diagram of the structure of the psyche, using a 'telescope' as an analogy. The aim of this essay is to look at the strengths and weaknesses of the 'telescope' as a viable metaphor. In order to do this, I will compare the 'telescope' of 1900 with an earlier schema, worked out by Freud in the course of his correspondence with a colleague, the ear, nose and throat specialist, Fliess, during 1895 and 1896. Posthumously published as 'Project for a Scientific Psychology' (1954), in this work Freud gives an account of the psyche as a system of sign-relations, signs which can be interpreted as referring both to 'psychical' structure and the neuronal networks of the brain. This attempt to bring together 'verbal language' and 'neuronal structure' as types of signs introduces the concepts of 'translation' and 'transference', which are central to the later model of the 'telescope'. In the 'Project', Freud also gives us an account of how the ego is formed (through a differentiation of neuronal structure) which, although not repeated in the 'telescope' of 1900, underpins his later thinking.

In conclusion, I will briefly introduce an even earlier semiotic, graphical schema. This dates from 1891, and attempts to represent how language relates to perceptions (Freud 1915: 209-216). It was from his observations upon different forms of aphasia that Freud developed this theory of how we acquire speech, and it is evident that this work provides the foundation for his later theory of 'speech-signs' which appears in both the 'Project' and 'the telescope'.

Turning a telescope on dreams

Through following dreams from their manifest to their latent content, Freud raises fundamental questions as to why dreams are constructed in this way.

> The dream-thoughts and the dream-content are presented to us like two versions of the same subject-matter in two different languages. Or, more properly, the dream-content seems like a transcript of the dream-thoughts into another mode of expression, whose characters and syntactical laws it is our business to dis-

cover by comparing the original and the translation. (Freud 1900: 277)

'*Zeichen*' in the original German—here given as 'characters'[1]—can also be translated as 'sign'. This opens up the possibility that Freud is thinking of the psyche in *semiotic* terms. Signs can obey laws different from the syntax of speech; they can encompass pictorial representation as well as representation through words. As Freud goes on to comment, the dream-content is expressed: 'as it were in a pictographic script' (Freud 1900: 277). Dreams, then, are only *analogous* to writing. Yet Freud writes of the relation between the dream-content and its interpretation as a 'translation'. How can we understand this as an act of 'translation' if syntax is not preserved?

Dreams, in their unintelligibility, appear beyond our control and knowledge. They are 'other'. They *happen* to us: 'we are just as ready to say *"mir hat geträumt"* ["I had a dream", literally "a dream came to me"] as *"ich habe geträumt"* ["I dreamt"]' (Freud 1900: 48). It is this feeling which was captured by the philosopher and physicist Fechner, in his comment that: '*the scene of action of dreams is different from that of waking ideational life*' (Freud 1900: 48). In order to grasp this conceptually, Freud constructs a parallel between '*psychical locality*' and '*spatial location*', but without implying a necessary relation between mental and physical events, or tying this in with the anatomy of the brain. Freud sets out to explain the radical incompatibility between dreams and verbal language, and it is in order to help his own theorising that he develops a graphic representation of the structure of the psyche—as a 'telescope'.

The 'telescope' analogy is introduced in the chapter on 'Regression' in the last section of *The Interpretation of Dreams*, at a point where Freud has already described and analysed the form and construction of many dreams. From these analyses he learns the representational laws of dreaming: the motivation of dreams is unconscious 'wish-fulfilment', and illicit wishes are represented in visual forms in order to evade censorship. By thinking of a dream as a rebus, a picture-puzzle, Freud isolates two specific forms of representation: 'condensation' and 'displacement'. 'Condensation' is a superimposition of ideas and images which allows a vast amount of psychical material to be represented simultaneously. 'Displacement', on the other hand, entails a transference of psychic intensity from the central elements of the dream onto ideas and images of lesser importance, amounting—in effect—to a disguise of the truth.

But why should Freud choose the 'telescope' as a graphical analogy of the structure of the psyche?

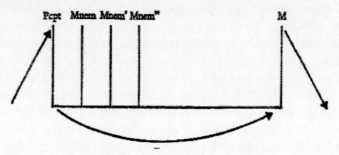

Diagram 1. (Freud 1900: 538)

The telescope is an optical system, which conducts light through a series of lenses and mirrors to produce an image on the retina. The parallel being drawn by Freud is that the psyche also mediates sensory—in this case visual—inputs from the external world. The 'lenses', then, represent the psyche's systems of perception and memory. Even towards the conclusion of *The Interpretation of Dreams*, although Freud has acknowledged some of the limitations of the 'telescope' model, he asserts:

> But we are justified in assuming the existence of the systems (which are not in any way psychical entities themselves and can never be accessible to our psychical perception) like the lenses of the telescope, which cast the image. And, if we pursue this analogy, we may compare the censorship between two systems to the refraction which takes place when a ray of light passes into a new medium. (Freud 1900: 611)

Refraction—the way glass bends and splits up light—also represents, therefore, the relation between the unconscious realm of the dream-processes and the syntax of speech. Like any form of metaphor, analogies introduce ways of thinking about reality which are *specific*, and can only make explicit a particular *part* of reality. The price paid for their heuristic value, in one respect, may be their capacity to mislead or to obscure another aspect of the reality they seek to represent.

The main feature of the telescope is that it represents *direction* within an apparatus. As light is conducted one way through the system of lenses, so sensations move through the psychic structure—perception, memory, cognition, recognition, and so on. Also underpinning the telescope analogy is another premise—that the 'model' for every psychical function is a *reflex* process (Freud 1900: 538). Obeying the overall action of a reflex, the 'telescope' receives input at one end ('Pcpt'), eventually discharging energy through the motor end ('M'). The overall system strives to maintain a *constant* level of energy—the 'constancy principle'. Too much energy is experienced as 'unpleasure' (Freud 1900: 565). Indeed, this linkage of the experience of 'pleasure' and 'unpleasure' with the quantity of psychical energy in the apparatus is a fundamental premise of both the 'telescope' model of 1900 and—as we shall see later—the schema of the 1895 'Project'.

In the normal course of the day, perceptions enter the apparatus in the direction of the arrow. The first system (Pcpt) remains open to receiving perceptions, but the subsequent, mnemic series (Mnem, Mnem', etc.) retains these perceptions as an alteration of the system itself. Perception and memory are, therefore, mutually exclusive. The first of these mnemic systems retains a record of perceptions according to *simultaneity in time*. Later systems, Freud suggests, record other kind of relations, such as *similarity, contiguity* and so on. On the question of *what* is actually being recorded, Freud writes that:

> A trace is left in our psychical apparatus of the perceptions which impinge upon it. This we may describe as a 'memory-trace': and to the function relating to it we give the name of 'memory'. (Freud 1900: 538)

From his analyses of dreams, Freud had already concluded that inadmissible thoughts and unconscious wishes are excluded from gaining consciousness by a critical agency. This is represented by Freud in Diagram 2, below, as a *screen*—another 'lens' of the 'telescope'—between the unconscious system (*Ucs.*) and the system of consciousness (*Cs.*). The system *Cs.* acts like an organ of perception turned on the internal systems of the psyche. Intermediate between the two is the system *Pcs.*, or the 'preconscious', which determines whether *Ucs.* images may become conscious. The 'telescope' analogy has thus successfully represented the two *psychical localities* of Fechner, as two separate domains of the apparatus.

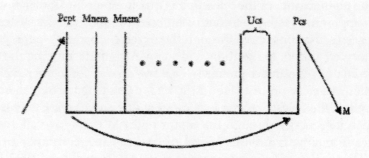

Diagram 2. (Freud 1900: 541)

However, there is a paradox in the structure of the apparatus, which emerges if one examines Freud's classification of dreams. Freud's analyses include two dreams: the *'Autodidasker'* dream (Freud 1900: 298-302), and the dream of the 'burning child' (Freud 1900: 509-511).

The dream of the *Autodidasker* consists of two parts. First of all, the actual word *'Autodidasker'* and, secondly, a fantasy from the day before it was dreamt. Freud fantasised that when he next saw Prof. N. he should tell him: 'The patient about whose condition I consulted you recently is in fact only suffering from a neurosis, just as you suspected.'

Freud analyses the word *'Autodidasker'* as a neologism combining the word *'Autor'* ('author') and *'Autodidakt'* ('self-taught') and the name 'Lasker'. 'Lasker' Freud associates with 'Lassalle', a founder of the German Social Democratic movement. Apart from the homonymic relation between the names, Freud points out that both Lasker and Lassalle were of Jewish origin. *'Autor'* Freud associates with giving his wife several books by J.J. David, a friend of Freud's brother, and a man who shared his birthplace with Freud. One of the books contains an account of how a man wastes his talents, as a result of which Freud's wife voices her concern that their children may also waste their talents.

One of the underlying meanings of the dream is Freud's fear that what actually brings about men's downfall is women. Lasker died of syphilis, and Lassalle died in a duel over a woman. Freud then summarises these thoughts in the phrase *'Cherchez la femme'*, which leads him to think of his unmarried brother *Alexander*—'almost the same sound as an anagram of "Lasker"' (Freud 1900: 300). Freud then associates his wish that Alexander should have a happy domestic life, with the brief account of Zola's happy domesticity in his novel *L'oeuvre*. Zola appears as the character 'Sandoz' which, Freud points out, is close to an inverted anagram of 'Zola', the construction of this neologism being similar to '*Autodidasker*'. The construction by the dream of '*Autodidasker*' is thus a process of condensation, applying not to memory-images, but to words.

The fantasy involving Prof. N. reminds Freud of a shameful incident in which he, Freud, doubted his own diagnosis of neurosis in a patient. Freud consulted Prof. N., and expected him to confirm that there was a physiological basis to the illness. However, Prof. N. affirmed that it was indeed a neurosis, an opinion which seemed confirmed when the patient later revealed his sexual history. Freud interprets this in terms of wish-fulfilment: 'To be wrong was, however, just what I *did* wish. I wanted to be wrong in my fears, or, more precisely, I wanted my wife, whose fears I had adopted in the dream-thoughts, to be wrong' (Freud 1900: 301). Freud's own fears, then, are displaced—in the dream—onto those of his wife.

However, Freud leaves out of the account a *sexual* interpretation of his own wishes. Downfall through sexual temptation surely applies to Freud himself. Like Lasker and Lassalle, Freud is of Jewish origin, so his fear may be that he himself might waste his talents through his association with women.

The interpretation of the '*Autodidasker*' dream, then, exhibits the effect of *Ucs*. primary processes, primarily upon words and ideas. The dream is a rebus of words and syllables, playing with anagrams and rhymes to reveal unconscious truths. With respect to this dream, then, the 'telescope' analogy provides an account of the effect of primary processes on thought, and helps identify where 'censorship' has taken place.

Dreams like that of the 'burning child', however, require a further explanation of the sensuality of their imagery (Freud 1900: 509-511). Following the death of his young son, a father dreamt: 'that *his child was standing beside his bed, caught him by the arm and whispered to him reproachfully: "Father, don't you see I'm burning?"*' (Freud 1900: 509). The father awoke and rushed next door, to find that a candle had fallen onto his son's corpse. Apart from the light—and perhaps the smell of burning—impinging on the father's dream, Freud adds that the contents of the dream must have been overdetermined—that is, they must carry another association to an earlier memory. Perhaps—Freud suggests—the child's '*I'm burning*' related to a previous fever, and '*Father don't you see*' could be a displacement from an equally charged emotional experience. The dream attempts to fulfil the father's wish that his son was still alive. This dream is much less complex and equivocal than the '*Autodidasker*' dream; it consists of far fewer elements, but its key quality is the intensity of its visualisation.

Freud's hypothesis is that dreams like 'the burning child' have a '*regressive*' character. Somehow, they activate *perceptual* images. This hallucinatory quality implies, therefore, that energy runs *backwards* through the apparatus to the *Pcpt.* system.

> Intentional recollection and other constituent processes of our normal thinking involve a retrogressive movement in the psychical apparatus from a complex ideational act back to the raw material of the memory-traces underlying it. In the waking state, however, this backward movement never extends beyond the mnemic images; it does not succeed in producing a hallucinatory revival of the *perceptual* images. Why is it otherwise in dreams? (Freud 1900: 543)

One answer to this question appears to challenge the validity of the telescope analogy. The waking 'telescope' sequence suggests there is a successive divestment of intensity, from the '*perceptual* images' of the *Pcpt.* system, to the 'mnemic-images' of the *Ucs.*, and then to the 'traces' of the *Pcs*. But when perceptual images in dreams such as 'the burning child' become conscious, not only does this entail that energy is flowing backwards through the 'telescope', against the general flow of information, it also implies a *different* topography. In the drawing of the 'telescope' (Diagrams 1 and 2) the *Pcpt.* and *Cs.* systems are at *opposite* ends. Now, it seems, we need a representation in which they are shown as *directly* connected.

Looking backwards through the telescope

The 'telescope' analogy not only illustrates Freud's ideas on the 'shape' of the psyche, it also clarifies his theory of wish-fulfilment:

> But all this has not brought us a step nearer to solving the riddle of why it is that the unconscious has nothing else to offer during sleep but the motive force for the fulfilment of a wish. The answer to this question must throw light upon the psychical nature of wishes, and I propose to give the answer by reference

to our schematic picture of the psychical apparatus. (Freud 1900: 565)

Freud's theory of wish-fulfilment presumes that the infant first of all experiences pleasure from its mother through being fed, held, and so on. In response to its bodily needs the baby seeks satisfaction and repetition of pleasure. So what are the processes in the psyche which underpin this process? Freud hypothesises that when the baby feels hungry, this hunger is represented by a 'memory-trace'. This starts a search through the memory systems until the associated 'mnemic-image' of hunger re-invokes the *perception* itself—for example, of the breast. This process is repeated until the perception matches the 'memory-trace' associated with the need. The baby's aim, then, is somehow to get the desired response from its mother *in its perception*:

> An impulse of this kind is what we call a wish; and the shortest path to the fulfilment of the wish is a path leading direct from the excitation produced by the need to a complete cathexis of the perception... Thus the aim of this first psychical activity was to produce a 'perceptual identity'—a repetition of the perception which was linked with the satisfaction of the need. (Freud 1900: 566)[2]

The 'telescope' analogy emphasises the primary importance of wish-fulfilment as the template for subsequent processes, such as *cognition*:

> Thought is after all nothing but a substitute for a hallucinatory wish; and it is self-evident that dreams must be wish-fulfilments, since nothing but a wish can set our mental apparatus at work. (Freud 1900: 567)

Freud goes on to describe how infantile scenes of wish-fulfilment, or their reproduction as phantasies, act as 'models' for dream-content. However, in the light of this, to what extent and how often is the psyche's 'normal' direction the same as that of the 'telescope' model? In response to our unconscious motivations and deepest needs, are we not most often looking through the 'wrong-end' of the telescope?

Freud is clear that the value of the 'telescope' analogy is the specific insight it allows into 'regression', which other notations or descriptions would have found difficult to facilitate:

> And it is at this point that that picture begins to repay us for having constructed it. For an examination of it, without any further reflection, reveals a further characteristic of dream-formation. If we regard the process of dreaming as a regression occurring in our hypothetical mental apparatus, we at once arrive at the explanation of the empirically established facts that all logical relations belonging to the dream-thoughts disappear during the dream-activity or can only find expression with difficulty. According to our schematic picture, these relations are contained not in the *first Mnem.* systems but in *later* ones; and in case of regression they would necessarily lose any means of expression except in perceptual images. *In regression the fabric of the dream-thoughts is resolved into its raw material.* (Freud 1900: 543)

Dreams emerge from the nightscape of the soul. Regression is made easy during sleep because we are no longer taking in new perceptions and sensations, and neither are we able to act on our wishes. The *Pcs.* obeys its own wish to sleep, and so the censoring effect is also weakened. However, Freud also proposes that the wishes of the *Ucs.* are seductive and that during sleep they exercise an attraction of their own. This 'attraction' between 'mnemic images' involves a 'transference' of energy from *Ucs.* memories to more recent ideas, thoughts and feelings: 'On this view a dream might be described as *a substitute for an infantile scene modified by being transferred on to a recent experience*' (Freud 1900: 546).

But what does 'transference' mean here? As we have seen in his interpretation of the dreams '*Autodidasker*' and 'the burning child', Freud uses two relational structures to represent psychical overdetermination—displacement and condensation: '*a transference and displacement of psychical intensities* occurs in the process of dream-formation' (Freud 1900: 546). Displacement, then, accounts for the difference between the centre of the dream's latent content and the centre of the manifest content. It may occasion a complete inversion of psychical and sensory values, so that the most arid imagery is linked to the most sensual and seductive part of dream. Thus it is the energy of the 'mnemic-image' that has been transferred.

Condensation—on the other hand—literally produces a reduction in the volume of dream thoughts, by forming intermediary structures which may refer to both recent and early memories. In his account of the dream 'Botanical Monograph', Freud describes condensation of images as producing:

> [A]n intermediate common entity' between two experiences of the previous day: it was taken over unaltered from the indifferent impression and was linked with the psychical significant event by copious connections. (Freud 1900: 282)

Freud compares this process to the *superimposition* of images, as on a photographic plate. Corresponding condensation of words produces neologisms, homonyms and puns, jokes and slips of the tongue, and contradictions not tolerated by the logic of the *Pcs*. Successive transference of energy from the 'mnemic-images' of the *Ucs.*, then, results in ideas of great density:

> And since this process is repeated several times, the intensity of a whole train of thought may eventually be concentrated in a single ideational element. Here we have the fact of 'compression' or 'condensation' which has become familiar in the dream-work. (Freud 1900: 595)

The repetition of this process might produce an idea such as a word picked out in bold—for example, **'*trimethylamin*'** in Freud's dream of 'Irma's injection' (Freud 1900: 595). Condensation, then, is an efficient way of discharging large amounts of *Ucs.* energy.

As described earlier, in the 'telescope' model 'censorship' is drawn as a screen or lens between the *Ucs.* and *Cs.* Freud described wish-fulfilment as hallucinatory, a matching of a 'mnemic-trace' of need with the perception of the thing needed. The baby, therefore, has to have a good command of secondary processes in order to attract its mother and enjoy the pleasures of satisfying that need. But what happens if the early experiences were *not* pleasurable? Freud suggests that in response to *unpleasure*, the associated mnemic image is dropped and the pathway to perception avoided. This process Freud describes as the 'prototype' of *psychical repression*:

Among these wishful impulses derived from infancy, which can neither be destroyed nor inhibited, there are some whose fulfilment would be a contradiction of the purposive ideas of secondary thinking. The fulfilment of these wishes would no longer generate an affect of pleasure but of unpleasure; and *it is precisely this transformation of affect which constitutes the essence of what we term 'repression'*. (Freud 1900: 604)

What underpins this account of repression is the idea that the potent energy of *Ucs.* 'mnemic-images' has to be reduced according to the principle of energy constancy (Freud 1900: 565). Originally experienced as pleasurable, in later development these images clash with social strictures, generating unpleasurable feelings of shame, guilt and so on. Somehow, *Ucs.* energy has to be 'fixed' or 'bound'. Freud proposes that a second system *'binds'* the energy of the first system during the process of searching through memories, in order that thinking does not involve the whole of the memory systems. In this way, thinking can avoid the release of unpleasure.

So, if thinking—a *Pcs.* process—can effectively bind the energy of some associations of 'mnemic-images', then it can succeed in diverting attention away from *Ucs.* wishes and be of use in restricting outbursts of emotion:

The system *Pcs.* not merely bars access to consciousness, it also controls access to the power of voluntary movement and has at its disposal for distribution a mobile cathectic energy, a part of which is familiar to us in the form of attention. (Freud 1900: 615)

Becoming conscious is connected with the application of a particular psychical function, that of attention—a function which, as it seems, is only available in a specific quantity, and this may have been diverted from the train of thought in question on to some other purpose. (Freud 1900: 593)[3]

The process leads Freud to assert that one of the central aims of psychotherapy is precisely this binding of energy:

Its [psychotherapy's] task is to make it possible for the unconscious processes to be dealt with finally and be forgotten. For the fading of memories and the emotional weakness of impressions which are no longer recent, which we are inclined to regard as self-evident and to explain as a primary effect of time upon mental memory-traces, are in reality secondary modifications which are only brought about by laborious work. What performs the work is the preconscious, and *psychotherapy can pursue no other course than to bring the Ucs. under the domain of the Pcs.* (Freud 1900: 578)

Attention may often prove effective at 'binding', but Freud concludes that there is always a danger that reflective thought processes, whilst rifling through memories, become associated with particularly intense early 'mnemic-images' from the *Ucs*. As a result thinking may lose the logic of the *Pcs.* and disintegrate according to the tropes of primary processes.

Ideally, thinking through a train of ideas is brought to a head by the discernment of identity between mnemic-images or traces, on the model of identity between perceptions and mnemic-traces, as described in Freud's account of wish-fulfilment.

[Thus] if a train of thought is initially rejected (consciously, perhaps) by a judgement that it is wrong or that it is useless for the immediate intellectual purposes in view, the result may be that this train of thought will proceed, unobserved by consciousness, until the onset of sleep. (Freud 1900: 593)

'Judgement' is, therefore, based on an act of *comparison*—somewhere in the psychical systems. Freud does not explain any further this act of 'judgement' in his 'telescope' account of the processes of thought. However, in the 'Project' of 1895 'judgement' is described as an *Ucs.* process which seeks identity between sign-relations or mnemic-images. (As we shall see later in this essay, 'judgement' lies at the very heart of wish-fulfilment, thinking, and the formation of the ego.)

Thought, like any psychical process, has to acquire 'quality' in order to gain consciousness. Taking into account the risk of regression through the apparatus to the *Pcpt.* systems, Freud theorises that thoughts become conscious through their association with *verbal* memories:

For this purpose the *Pcs.* system needed to have qualities of its own which could attract consciousness; and it seems highly probable that it obtained them by linking the preconscious processes with the mnemic system of indications[4] of speech, a system not without quality. (Freud 1900: 574)

Attachment to 'speech-signs' lends reality to thought, which then succeeds in gaining consciousness. However, the energy of the 'mnemic-images' is always relative. Consequently, normal thought can never be totally immune from the dangers of 'transference' from intense mnemic-images, and subsequent regression through the apparatus. In other words: some memories are too much to bear.

Of course, Freud was acutely aware of the limitations of analogies, and repeatedly warned his readers of the danger of taking any theoretical construction too literally. The merits of the 'telescope' model are only relative to other graphical and verbal descriptions. As much as Freud stresses the heuristic value of the 'telescope', he also warns the reader not to take it seriously:

> Analogies of this kind are only intended to assist us in our attempt to make the complications of mental functioning intelligible by dissecting the function and assigning its different constituents to different component parts of the apparatus. (Freud 1900: 536)

Having criticised the 'telescope' for its inherent representation of psychical locality as *spatial* locality, Freud is also led to abandon this model because of the way it represents what is a hierarchical order as a serial order:

> So let us try to correct some conceptions which might be misleading so long as we looked upon the two systems in the most literal and crudest sense as two localities in the mental apparatus—conceptions which have left their traces in the expressions 'to repress' and 'to force a way through'... What we have in mind here is not the forming of a second thought situated in a new place, like a transcription which continues to exist alongside the original; and the notion of forcing a way into consciousness must be kept carefully free from any idea of a change of locality... Let us replace these metaphors [*Gleichnisse*][5] by something that seems to correspond better to the real state of affairs, and let us say instead that some particular mental grouping has had a

cathexis of energy attached to it or withdrawn from it, so that the structure in question has come under the sway of a particular agency or been withdrawn from it. What we are doing here is once again to replace a topographical way of representing things by a dynamic one. What we regard as mobile is not psychical structure itself but its innervation. (Freud 1900: 610)

Strictly speaking, there is no need for the hypothesis that the psychical systems are actually arranged in a *spatial* order. It would be sufficient if a fixed order were established by the fact that in a given psychical process the excitation passes through the systems in a particular *temporal* sequence. (Freud 1900: 537)

The topography of the 'telescope' is thus replaced by an account of how *energy* affects the structure of the psyche. The term 'innervation' attempts to describe a corresponding alteration in the nervous structure.[6] Replacing seriality with a hierarchical ordering of the psychical systems allows Freud to articulate 'regression' not only as a retrogressive flow of energy, but also in temporal and formal terms. 'Temporal regression' describes a return to the earliest memories. 'Formal regression' accounts for how *Pcs.* 'memory-traces' become *Ucs.* 'mnemic-images'.

As the first of the two quotations above stresses, Freud does not wish to imply that the lenses of the 'telescope' represent 'separate transcriptions' of a phenomenon.[7] I would suggest that one way out of this dilemma would be to assume that these are the *same* signs—in both the *Ucs.* and *Pcs.*. It is only the equivocation of their signification, and how they are perceived by consciousness *Cs.*, which characterises the difference.

Freud comments that *'interpretation of dreams is the royal road to a knowledge of the unconscious activities of the mind'* (Freud 1900: 608). The 'telescope' analogy was chosen by Freud because of its capacity to represent *direction*. However, when heading along a road we can drive both ways, and expect that the road will turn and branch, adjoin pathways, or become a motorway. We sometimes might enjoy the extraordinary strangeness of driving on the *wrong* side of the road, or getting caught in the illogicality of roundabouts. We may even have to conclude that rules at junctions remain forever mysterious—and the subject of much road-rage...

In the hope of moving beyond some of the limitations of the 'telescope' analogue, I shall now turn to the schema of the psyche described by Freud in the 'Project for a Scientific Psychology' (1895), bearing in mind that although some particular roads turn out to be 'dead ends', the road network itself is vast...

Mindful of signs

In a series of letters to his friend and colleague, Wilhelm Fliess, in which they speculated upon the enigmas of life, Freud sketched another visual schema in an attempt to describe the structure of the psyche. Playing with ideas gained from his training as a neurophysiologist, Freud tried to marry a neuronal theory of the brain with a semiotic theory of mental structure, attempting to avoid the twin pitfalls of reductionism and parallelism. 'Reductionism' implies that the physical can account entirely for the mental; 'parallelism', meanwhile, implies a strict one-to-one correlation between physical and mental events. As Freud had written earlier, in his monograph on aphasia:

> This leads us to suppose that the physiological correlate of the presentation—i.e. the modification that originates from the excited nerve fibre with its termination at the centre—is something simple too, which can be localised at a particular point. To draw a parallel of this kind is of course entirely unjustifiable; the characteristics of the modification must be established on their own account and independently of their psychological counterpart. (Freud 1915: 206-208)

Freud goes on to emphasise that the parallel exists not as one-to-one correspondence of events, but at the level of *process*:

> It is probable that the chain of physiological events in the nervous system does not stand in causal connection with the psychical events... Accordingly, the psychical is a process parallel to the physiological—a 'dependent concomitant'. (Freud 1915: 206)

As we have seen, the aim of the 'telescope' was to demonstrate psychical locality through the analogy of spatial locality. The statement above, however, points to the complexities involved in 'locating' processes. The best way to conceive the schema of the 'Project' is as

Freud's attempt to bring together two different theories of representation: the *neuronal* representation of pathways of energy, and the *semiotic* representation of the sign systems of memory. The precise relation between mental and physical processes—however—is left open to question.

Addressing the question of *what* is represented in the perceptual and memory systems, the 'Project' schema attempts to differentiate between 'mnemic-images' to build a more complex semiotic theory. Instead of uniform 'mnemic images' we encounter 'signs of perception' (*'Wahrnehmungszeichen'*), 'memory pictures' (*'Erinnerungsbild'*), 'pictures of movement' (*'Bewegungsbild'*), 'signs' (*'Zeichen'*) of quality and of reality, and 'signs of speech' (*'Sprachszeichen'*) which convey the quality of verbal memories, and which make a reappearance in the 'telescope' model.

The structure of neuronal networks which corresponds with these semiotic distinctions is divided according to the proposed mental functions of perception and memory. Freud postulates that there are two levels of neuronal structure, which he terms the 'ϕ' of perception, and the 'ψ' of memory. In the 'telescope' all the psychical systems are referred to as ψ systems. Here, in the 'Project' schema, the difference between ϕ and ψ is accounted for by their respective ability to conduct an electric impulse, quantifiable as the 'resistance' or 'facilitation' of neuronal contacts. Topologically, ψ interfaces directly with the body, while ϕ mediates between the body and external reality. Therefore, the ϕ systems act as the sense organs.

As in the 'telescope' analogy, this schema of the apparatus as a whole obeys the principle of constancy of energy. The energy input into the perceptual system ϕ is 'transferred'[8] as a specific quantity, 'Q', through the network of neurones. Memory is explained as a system of preferential connections built up through repetition or habit, bringing about a permanent change in the highly resistant neuronal structure of ψ. This inner system ψ is, therefore, in a different state of 'bound energy', or 'Qn', innervated in proportion to resistance.

However, the schema also requires that energy, Q, possesses 'quality', as opposed to its being merely a registration of quantity. Although 'quality' is related to the periodicity or wavelength of the energy, Freud's choice of terminology also suggests an indication of the *phenomenological* character of experience. It is this question which leads Freud to introduce another system of neurones, 'ω', located *between* ϕ and ψ. In this imagined topography, then, perceptions enter the psyche via the sense organs of φ, energising the neuronal network. A transference of energy takes place from φ to ψ, which results in a registration of the difference between them—of 'quality'—in ω. Both perceptions (at their origin in the system φ) and their residual perceptual characteristics are able to gain the attention of consciousness. However, signs of the *quality* of perception—or 'reality signs' (*'Realitätszeichen'*)—provide indications of the external world. This is in contrast to signs that originate from the memory ψ systems, and which gain perceptual quality only through a backward flow (*Rückströmung*) through the system. (Freud 1950b: 460).

In the 'Project', then, Freud represents the flow of energy through the psychical systems as *relations between signs*. His basic premise is that the overall system functions according to the pleasure principle. As in the 'telescope' model, excessive build-up of energy is associated with unpleasure, whilst the dissipation of excess is pleasurable. Since perceptions enter the psychic systems of φ with a level of energy exceeding the capacity of ψ, Freud proposes a psychical function of 'attention', which inhibits the immediate motor-discharge of the energised neurones of perception. It is this process of 'attention' which is responsible for binding the energy Q into Qn, thus ensuring that only a relatively small amount of energy is then conducted into ψ. This dissipation of energy from φ to ψ generates complexity, according to a mathematical principle reminiscent of Fechner's Law (Freud 1954: 376). 'Attention'—as an inhibitor and deflector of excess energy—enables and protects both the preliminary act of judgement in wish-fulfilment, and judgement in the subsequent cognition of perceptual complexes.[9] 'Attention' also enables a *deflection* of pain, during trauma or extreme conditions. The binding effect of 'attention' lies at the heart of Freud's 1895 conception of the formation of the ego, which he views as the product of a differentiation in the neuronal structure:

> Thus we have unexpectedly arrived at the most obscure of problems—the origin of the 'ego', a complex of neurones which hold fast to their cathexis, and which thus constitute, for short periods of time, a complex with a constant level... The 'experience of satisfaction' brings this nucleus into association with a perception (the wishful image) and the report of a movement (the reflex portion of the specific action). The education and development of this original ego takes place in states in which there is a repetition of the craving, in states of *expectation*. The ego learns first

that it must not cathect the motor images (with consequent discharge), until certain conditions have been fulfilled on the perceptual side. It learns further that it must not cathect the wishful idea beyond a certain degree, because, if it does, it will deceive itself in a hallucinatory manner. If, however, it respects these two restrictions and turns its attention to the new perceptions, it has a prospect of attaining the desired satisfaction. (Freud 1954: 426)

Wish-fulfilment is described in the 'telescope' model, but here we are able to see how the very formation of the ego itself is founded on the search for pleasurable sensations, which in turn is brought about through the deflective and binding effects of 'attention'. The task of the ego—Freud suggests—is to learn not to cathect immediately the mnemic-images of wishes generated in ψ, but to delay the experience of discharging the energy until the right perceptual complex has been brought about in the real world. The ego has to *focus attention*—in other words—in order to bind the energy of the mnemic-images, preventing them from associating themselves with perceptions and thus becoming hallucinatory.[10]

Wish-fulfilment as the matching of energised memories with new perceptions involves an act of comparative 'judgement'. Since these acts of comparison intrinsic to 'judgement' take place, at first, entirely *within* the memory systems of the psyche, it is possible to understand how the psyche generates fallacies of hallucination. As we have seen, in order to avoid 'regression' the ego must bind the energy of mnemic images so that the perceptual cortex is cathected instead. This produces the shift towards the demands of reality, as opposed to the generation of pleasurable but purely internal memories:

Thus judgement is a ψ-process which is only made possible by the inhibition exercised by the ego and which is brought about by the difference between the wishful cathexis of a memory and a similar perceptual cathexis. It follows from this that when these two cathexes coincide, the fact will be a biological signal[11] for ending the activity of thinking and for initiating discharge. (Freud 1954: 390-391)

'Judgement' between perceptual-signs and memory-pictures stops only when 'identity' has been attained, which somehow constitutes a biological '*signal*'—distinct, in Freud's semiotics, from a sign. The 1895 schema provides two accounts of the act of judgement attempting to bridge the physiological and the semiotic.[12] Similarly, Freud also anchors 'logical thinking' in the biological. Logical errors consist in ignoring the biological rules of thought:

> These rules lay down where it is that the cathexis of attention is to be directed on each occasion, and when the thought-process is to come to a stop. They are protected by threats of unpleasure, they are arrived at from experience and can be directly transposed into the rules of logic. (Freud 1954: 443)

Freud does not elaborate upon this thesis of the relationship between logic and 'biological rules', but he does go on to point out that:

> The intellectual unpleasure of a contradiction, which brings critical thought to a stop, is nothing other than the unpleasure stored up for protection of the biological rules, which is stirred up by the incorrect thought-process. (Freud 1954: 443)

This entails ignoring the 'signal' which brings to a halt the process of judgement, operating under the cathexis of attention.

Freud's account of judgement, as it takes place within the complexes of neurones, is represented by an act of comparison between the perceptual neurones (a+b), and those of the cathected or energised memory complex (a+c). Identity is the occurrence of 'a' in perception, and of 'a' of memory.

> If we compare the W ['*Wahrnehmung*', perceptual] -complex with other W-complexes, we are able to analyse it into two portions: a neurone 'a' which on the whole remains the same and a neurone 'b' which on the whole varies. Language later applies the term 'judgement' to this process of analysis, and discovers the resemblance which exists between the nucleus of the ego on the one hand and between the changing cathexes in the pallium and the inconstant portion of the perceptual complex on the other; language describes neurone *a* as a 'thing' [*das Ding*] and neurone *b* as its activity or attribute—in short, as its 'predicate'. (Freud 1954: 390; 1950b: 412-413)

This quotation suggests that in the 'Project' Freud takes the subject-predicate division of language as the fundamental relational structure between signs, even in the Ψ systems of the *Ucs*. What, then, is the ontological status of the thing—'*das Ding*'—to which attributes are predicated? Is Freud thinking within the Aristotelian notion of *substance*? Or is 'the thing' to be understood only in terms of *language*? The same question is reformulated in his account of the act of judgement.

At the heart of the act of judgement is the ability to pick out the recurrence of 'a' within the different neuronal complexes. But is this an assertion of identity *de re*—that is, of the thing-in-itself—or *de dicto*—that is, of the linguistic structure which *refers* to the thing? Absolute identity is not possible, it seems, because one neurone may 'stand in' for a complex. Thus, how are we to understand *what* is being compared? One way of answering this question is to take 'a' (the 'constant' to which the variable is attributed) as a 'class concept'. In this case, 'a' signifies what *kind* of object is being perceived—a crucial component of early cognition and recognition of mother, family, and so on.

In the section of the 'Project' on remembering and judgement, Freud hypothesises as to how the infant perceives a 'fellow human-being':

> The theoretical interest taken in it is then further explained by the fact that an object *of a similar kind* was the subject's first satisfying object (and also his first hostile object) as well as his sole assisting force. For this reason it is on his fellow-creatures that a human being first learns to cognise.[13] The perceptual complexes arising from this fellow-creature will in part be new and non-comparable—for instance, its features (in the visual sphere); but other visual perceptions (for instance, the movements of its hands) will coincide in the subject with his own memory of quite similar visual impressions of his own body—a memory with which will be associated memories of movements experienced by himself. The same will be the case with other perceptions of the object; thus, for instance, if the object screams, a memory of the subject's own screaming will be aroused and will consequently revive his own experiences of pain. Thus the complex of a fellow-creature falls into two portions. One of these gives the impression of being a constant structure and remains as a coherent 'thing'; while the other can be *understood* by the activity of memory—that is, can be traced back to information about the subject's own body. (Freud 1954: 393-394)

Here I have quoted a substantial section because it gives us a remarkable insight into how Freud conceived of the developing sense of an 'other' from the point of view of the growing subject. Pain of the other is understood from its association with our own internal body-images, both the mnemic-images and associated motor-images of our own movements. *Self-perception*, then, becomes the guarantor of the feelings and existence of someone else. It is striking that new knowledge is referred constantly to what is already known. Freud develops this further in his account of learning as *mimicry*, including speech:

> In consequence of the impulse to *imitate* which emerges during the process of judging, it is possible to find a report of a movement [of one's own] attaching to this sound-image. So that this class of memories too can now become conscious. It remains to associate *deliberately produced* sounds with perceptions. (Freud 1954: 423)

In terms of psychical processes, the mnemic systems provide the template for *later* thought processes. For example, the role of judgement in wish-fulfilment provides the 'model' for later judgement occurring in thought.

Freud's account of cognising another 'fellow-creature' depends on being able to recognise that the other belongs to the same 'kind' as oneself. This confronts us with the same problem we encountered earlier: how do we recognise the constant without having an *a priori* apprehension of identity and difference? How can we then recognise that the structure of the complex remains as a coherent 'thing'?

It is important to realise that Freud is not saying that the subject-predicate division is 'inherent' in the neuronal structure but, rather, that the differentiation between 'that which is constant' and 'that which is variable' is *later called* the subject-predicate division. It *becomes* the structure of difference which supports and enables language. The 'Project', then, provides us with the means of understanding the categorical division between the primary processes of the *Ucs.*, and the syntax of language that is the domain of the *Pcs*.—as later represented in the 'telescope' analogy. The seriality of the 'telescope' model aimed to represent the two 'psychical localities' of *Ucs.* and *Pcs.* but also, unfortunately, reified the relationship between speech and the primary processes as a schism. The 'Project', in contrast, enables us to understand their interdependence.

Speaking of signs

'Speech signs' feature in the 'telescope' model as the means by which thoughts may become conscious (Freud 1900: 574). Because Freud views the acquisition of speech as imitative, based in physical bodily experience, speech and motor-signs are—therefore—intimately connected:

> These [speech-associations, *'Sprachassoziation'*] consist in the linking of ψ-neurones with neurones which are employed by auditory images [*'Klangvorstellungen'*] and are themselves intimately associated with motor speech-images [*'motorischen Sprachbildern'*]. These speech associations have the advantage over others of possessing two further characteristics; they are circumscribed (*i.e.*, are few in number) and exclusive. The excitation proceeds from the auditory image [*'Klangbild'*] to the verbal image [*'Wortbild'*], and thence to discharge. (Freud 1954: 421-422; 1950b: 443-444)

The means by which speech-signs signify verbal memories is here, in the 'Project', rooted in the physical sensations of the body. The distinction between signs which are 'pictures' (*'Bildern'*) and those which are 'presentations' (*'Vorstellungen'*) suggests different types of signs with different significatory possibilities. Although Freud does not really explain this taxonomy of signs in any greater detail, the 'Project' suggests that although signs may be hierarchically ordered, they are distinguished by their possible chains of association. For instance: signs which embody the primary processes of condensation and displacement, may also signify the tropes of verbal language—such as metaphor and synecdoche.

Speech-signs, associated with memories of innervated motor-images through the act of speaking, give rise to consciousness—otherwise, consciousness could only be gained by regression to perception.[14] As Freud remarks:

> *Thus, thought which is accompanied by the cathexis of indications of thought-reality or of indications of speech is the highest and most secure form of cognitive thought-process.* (Freud 1954: 431)

Freeing our ego from the confusions of wish-fulfilment protects us from the unpleasure of a delusional world. However, Freud adds that it is always possible that other neurones in the neighbourhood of the thought processes may be drawn into an association with the train of ideas. In Freud's quantitative schema of the psyche, disturbance in thinking may be brought about by transference of energy from excessively excited wishful mnemic-images onto other signs. It is the ego's faculty of 'attention' which makes it possible to distinguish between memory and perception, according to the quality of the signs. This is because quality is (quantitatively) the amount of energy that has to be inhibited or 'bound' by the ego: 'whereas indications of quality derived from outside make their appearance *whatever* the intensity of cathexis, those derived from Ψ only do if the intensities are large' (Freud 1954: 388).

The 'Project' provides a distinction between primary and secondary processes based upon the ego's inhibitory faculty of attention:

> Wishful cathexis carried to the point of hallucination and a complete generation of unpleasure, involving a complete expenditure of defence, may be described as 'psychical primary processes'. On the other hand, these processes which are only made possible by a good cathexis of the ego and which represent a moderation of the primary processes may be described as 'psychical secondary processes'. It will be seen that the *sine qua non* of the latter is a correct exploitation of the indications of reality and that this is only possible when there is inhibition on the part of the ego. (Freud 1954: 388-389)

In other words, it is the effect of the ego which inhibits regression in the system. The binding effect of 'attention' takes the form of 'secondary modifications' of the mnemic images.[15] In the 'Project', bringing the *Ucs.* under the influence of the *Pcs.* is equivalent to a *semiotic* modification of mnemic-images. The binding of energy produces a change in *signification*.

Energy is *transferred* from the complex to the thinking process itself. In other words, memories and thinking become conscious through 'transference' to speech-signs. Consciousness, Cs., in this schema is represented as: 'a *part* of the psychical processes in the neuronal system—namely, of the *perceptual* processes (ω-processes)' (Freud 1954: 427). In Freud's neuronal theory this is represented by an attachment or linking between cathected neurones, involving a transference of a quantity of energy, Q. Transference is—then—a transitive relation between the *signs*: mnemic-images, presentations and speech-signs. Cognition—the act of judgement seeking identity between perceptions, memory-traces, and images—becomes conscious through transference to word presentations and motor-speech-signs ('*Sprachbewegungszeichen*') in the silent act of inner speech. These are then signs of 'thought reality' not of the external world.[16]

The translation of things into words

A letter from Freud to Fliess, dated 6th December 1896, centres upon a diagrammatic representation of the psychic structure as systems of signs—'perception', 'signs of perception', 'unconscious', 'preconscious' and 'consciousness'. Although the graphics follow the convention of western writing—from left to right—the cluster of crosses suggests a *network* structure rather than the serial linearity of the 'telescope' (Freud 1954: 173-181).

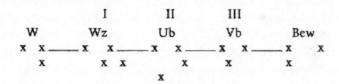

Diagram 3. (Freud 1954: 174)

Freud describes to Fliess what is essentially new about his theory:

> As you know, I am working on the assumption that our psychical mechanism has come about by a process of stratification: the material present in the shape of memory-traces is from time to time subjected to a rearrangement in accordance with fresh circumstances—is, as it were, transcribed.[17] Thus what is essentially new in my theory is the thesis that memory is present not once

but several times over, that it is registered in various species of 'signs'. (Freud 1954: 173)

The first stage of this schema (Diagram 3) shows that the neuronal structure, 'W', gives rise (*'entstehen'*) to perceptions which are not retained. Signs of perception are recorded as the first system—System 'I'—according to relations of simultaneity. This differentiation of perception and signs-of-perception already explains a distinction which is elided in the 'telescope'. System 'II' is the second registration, or transcription according to other relations—including causality. Here the terminology of 'sign' changes to *Ucs. traces.* This transcription contains the earliest infantile memories and constitutes the system *Ucs.* System 'III' represents a reordering of the signs through their attachment to word-presentations (*'Wortvorstellungen'*) (Freud 1950b: 186). Since this transcription may gain consciousness, 'III' represents the 'preconscious', corresponding to the official ego. In this schema, speech-signs and word-presentations—as opposed to the other sign-systems of memory and perception—are clearly shown as belonging to a subsequent epoch of development. But, unlike the analogy of the 'telescope', in which Freud describes the Ψ systems as lenses through which light is refracted, in this semiotic appraisal the governing analogy is of signs 'written' and 'rewritten', as 'transcriptions' ordered according to semiotic laws, a semiotics which includes the syntax of the *Pcs.*

The 1896 schema (Diagram 3) is precisely at odds with the 'telescope' model (Diagrams 1 & 2). In the latter, Freud warns explicitly against the notion that the *Ucs., Pcs., Cs.* represent 'successive transcriptions'. In the context of the 'telescope', 'successive transcriptions' suggests *repetition* of signs in different spatial localities. However, in the diagram from 1896, Freud needs to show that these transcriptions are indeed distinct from each other, but because they correspond to successive *epochs* of life. In this semiotic theory the boundaries between systems I, II, and III arise not from separate psychical localities, but from the re-organisation of signs through 'translation':

> At the frontier between any two such epochs a translation of the psychical material must take place. I explain the peculiarities of the psychoneuroses by supposing that the translation of some material has not occurred—which involves certain consequences... If the later transcription is lacking, the excitation will be disposed of according to the psychological laws governing

the earlier epochs and along paths which were then accessible. Thus an anachronism remains: in a particular province *fueros* are still in force. (Freud 1954: 175)

The adage that there is *no time in the unconscious,* need not deny the significance of this chronology, but only that the passing of time alone does not *change* the memories of experience themselves. Unlike the 1900 'telescope' model of bound energy and secondary modifications of mnemic-images, the 1896 schema sticks to semiotics and tries to account for trauma—and repression—in terms of the translation of signs.

A failure of translation is what we know clinically as 'repression'. The motive for it is always a release of unpleasure which would result from a translation; it is as though the unpleasure provokes a disturbance of thought which forbids the process of translation. (Freud 1954: 175)

Repression—in this model—is the failure to reorder the sign systems from one epoch to another. This process of 'translation' between transcriptions also provides a means of explaining trauma. In trauma, the memory signs have no adequate translation; the traumatic event—as it happened—becomes severed from the affects associated with it. Freud notes: 'We invariably find that a memory is repressed which has only become a trauma *after the event*' (Freud 1954: 413).[18] Learning and understanding is the production of a 'new translation' of the traumatic event, which then leads to the repetition of early memories as if they were occurring for the first time—this is the phenomenon of 'deferred action' (or *'Nachträglichkeit'*).

These ideas of transference and translation have an interesting connection to the philosophy of language proposed by J.S. Mill, whose work Freud translated into German as a student. Mill's descriptive theory of naming bears a close relation to Freud's idea that a perceptual complex is analysed according to the division of subject and predicate (Freud 1954: 390).

In Mill's theory of naming, names are divided according to whether they indicate a singularity or generality, and (further) according to whether they are abstract or concrete. The class of names most relevant to Freud's theory is defined by Mill as the class of 'concrete general names':

The word *man*, for example, denotes Peter, Jane, John, and an indefinite number of other individuals, of whom, taken as a class, it is the name. But it is applied to them, because they possess, and to signify that they possess, certain attributes. These seem to be, coporeity, animal life, rationality, and a certain external form, which for distinction we call the human. Every existing thing, which possessed all these attributes, would be called a man; and anything which possessed none of them, or only one, or two, or even three of them without the fourth, would not be so called. (Mill 1970: 19)

Mill quotes the philosopher Dugald Stewart, in order to explain how names change their extension, a linguistic process which Stewart calls 'transference':

...the letters A, B, C, D, E, denote a series of objects; that A possesses some one quality in common with B; B a quality in common with C; C a quality in common with D; D a quality in common with E; while at the same time no quality can be found which belongs in common to any three objects in the series. Is it not conceivable that the affinity between A and B may produce a transference of the name of the first to the second; and that, in consequence of the other affinities which connect the remaining objects together, the same name may pass in succession from B to C, from C to D, and from D to E? In this manner a common appellation will arise between A and E. (Mill 1970: 442)

Mill also points out that names which are vague in their connotations are especially prone to change their extension through generalisation:

[N]ames creep on from subject to subject, until all traces of a common meaning sometimes disappear and the word comes to denote a number of things not only independently of any common attribute, but which actually have no attribute in common. (Mill 1970: 442)

This concept is close to Freud's use of 'transference' and of 'translation' in the 1896 graphic schema (Diagram 3). Indeed, although Freud's 'translation' appears to have a direction—in that earlier records of signs are translated into the systems of later epochs—this does not exclude the possibility that the translation might be 'undone'. Mill's 'creeping of names' offers a semiotic parallel to the backward movement through the 1900 'telescope' model. Successive transcriptions should be conceived—therefore—as 'overlapping', like a palimpsest, as in Freud's 'A Note Upon the "Mystic Writing Pad"' (1925). Or perhaps we should conceive the same signs as having multiple signification, without being repeated. Applying this idea to the 'telescope' model, the primary processes of condensation, displacement and figuration are signs capable of acting as the tropes of language—metonymy and synecdoche, metaphor and catachresis, homonym and eye rhyme, and so on. Similarly, the account in the 'Project' of the subject-predicate division of perceptual complexes can be understood as a description of signs which can also signify within the syntax of communicative speech.

On the apparent inexhaustibility of signs in dreams, Freud wrote:

The dream-thoughts to which we are led by interpretation cannot, from the nature of things, have any definite endings; they are bound to branch out in every direction into the intricate network of our world of thought. (Freud 1900: 525)

There is at least one spot in every dream at which it is unplumbable—a navel, as it were, that is its point of contact with the unknown. (Freud 1900: 111)

Dream interpretation can become lost in an infinite expanse of associations. But are these associations simply a consequence of the complexity and history of our experience, or is the 'navel' of dream actually a product of the possibilities of language itself? The answer to this question lies—perhaps—not in the telescope model, nor in the schema of the 'Project', but in an even earlier semiotic theory of how language relates to the world. This is the 'molecular' representation of the psyche which is included in Freud's *On Aphasia* (1891). An extract from this work is appended to the Standard Edition version of 'The Unconscious' (Freud 1915: 209-216), in order to illustrate Freud's understanding of the relation between language and perceptions.

In attempting to explain how brain lesions affect speech, Freud formulates three types of aphasia. Speech confusion he attributes to *word aphasia*, disturbances in object recognition he calls *agnostic aphasia*, and loss of intelligibility and meaning he terms *asymbolic aphasia*. Again, it is J.S. Mill's descriptive theory of language which directly informs Freud's thinking on how words refer to the world.[19] In Mill's theory names are *connotative*, meaning that they signify through all their associated predicates or qualities, as opposed to only a small class of 'essential' qualities (Mill 1970: 19-20).

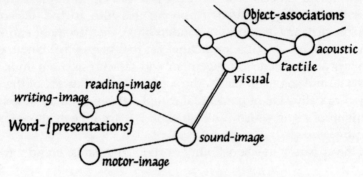

PSYCHOLOGICAL DIAGRAM OF A WORD-PRESENTATION

Diagram 4. (Freud 1915: 214)

In Diagram 4, Freud uses a graphic notation which resembles a diagram of molecular valencies. The basic distinction he draws is between 'object-associations' and 'word-presentations' which, the diagram suggests, form two separate complexes of signs. Word-presentations, in turn, are broken down into pictures of qualities related to sensory perception: sound is represented in the 'sound-image' ('*Klangsbild*'), movement of the vocal apparatus is represented in the 'motor-image' ('*Bewegungsbild*'), and the written and printed words—respectively—in the 'writing-image' ('*Schriftsbild*') and the 'reading-image' ('*Lesebild*'). The most important link, represented by a double bond, lies between the 'sound-image' and 'the visual'. Object associations are similarly represented as a complex association of sensations, but in this case the chain of attributes is conceived as *open-ended*, in contrast to the closed chain of the word (Freud 1993a: 122).

At the heart of this schema is Freud's theory of how speech is expressed or recorded within the psychic structure. Speech is registered as motor-speech innervations (Freud 1915: 210). Learning to speak involves imitating someone, through comparing the heard 'speech-image' with the one we ourselves generate. The key idea here—which reappears later in the 'Project'—is that the infant repeats what is heard until there is an 'identity' of the speech-innervations associated with mnemic acoustic image and the new acoustic image.

These kinds of associations, however, are insufficient to generate *meaning*. The meaning of language, and our understanding of it, depend on the link between words and objects:

> A word, however, acquires its *meaning* by being linked to an 'object-presentation', at all events if we restrict ourselves to a consideration of substantives. The object-presentation itself is once again a complex of associations made up of the greatest variety of visual, acoustic, tactile, kinaesthetic and other presentations. Philosophy tells us that an object-presentation consists in nothing more than this—that the appearance of there being a 'thing' [*das Ding*] to whose various 'attributes' these sense-impressions bear witness is merely due to the fact that in enumerating the sense-impressions which we have received from an object, we also assume the possibility of there being a large number of further impressions in the same chain of associations... The object-presentation is thus seen to be one which is not closed and almost one which cannot be closed, while the word-presentation is seen to be something closed, even though capable of extension. (Freud 1915: 214-215)

Freud thus brings together two systems of representation: the visual, acoustic, and tactile 'presentations' of the object, and the pictures of reading, writing, and so on of the word-presentation. A hierarchy of signs is also suggested by this schema, due to the way Freud privileges the connection between the *visual* signs of the object, and the *sound-image* associated with the word. This idea contains the potential for a semiotic theory of how perceptual signs can become parts of spoken language.

In this 'molecular' representation the 'thing' is epistemological—that is, the 'thing' represents that which is not yet known about the object; it is all the other associations that we have yet to discover. However, as Freud points out, the word-presentation is also capable of extension, through the acquisition of language itself.

To return to *The Interpretation of Dreams*, then, the unplumbable 'navel' of the dream is surely the umbilical (the double-line in Diagram

148   Freud's Interpretation of the Structure of the Psyche

4) which connects sense-impressions and verbal language in the semiotics of the psyche. This is the means by which verbal language is born from semiotic turbulence. It is the very open-endedness of the object-associations, and the equivocation of signs, representation, and language which creates the possibility of meaning from nothingness.

Notes

1 Strachey also translates *'Zeichen'* as 'indicator'.

2 There are several unanswered questions here. First of all, if the need arises in the body, is this *experienced* as a memory 'trace' or 'mnemic-image'? How does the infant distinguish between re-energised perceptual memories and *new* perceptions? How exactly is 'perceptual identity' achieved between an 'image' and a 'trace'? As we will see, these questions were originally addressed in the schema of the 'Project' (1895), which provides further speculations on semiotic relations.

3 In these quotations, the sense of attention is limited to our everyday notion of 'concentration', an effort of will-power. In the 1895 'Project', 'attention' is a primary psychical function fundamentally involved in the formation of the ego as bound energy.

4 *'Sprachzeichen'*, 'speech-signs'. See Freud 1993b: 563.

5 *'Gleichnisse'* is more accurately translated as 'simile'. Freud is careful in his references to linguistic tropes.

6 'Innervation' is another term which appeared earlier in the 'Project'.

7 Here, again, the 1895 'Project' illuminates an area which is hazy in the 'telescope' model. However, the schema in the 1896 letter to Fliess (see below) has the disadvantage of 'successive transcriptions' recorded at different epochs of development.

8 This is Freud's first use of the term 'transference'. Although it appears in a purely technical sense in this instance, the same basic concept underpins his later psychoanalytic understanding of 'transference'.

9 'Cognising' in the German text is *'erkennen'* which brings the meaning closer to 'knowing' than to 'cognition'. See Freud 1950b: 415.

10 The ego and wishing are, therefore, teleological necessities only to the extent that the repetition of 'satisfaction' which they enable fulfils the necessities of life. Viewed as a purely semiotic process, on the other hand, 'attention' is—in fact—a form of negation.

11 *'Man kann davon ausgehen, dass das Zusammenfallen beider besetzungen zum biologischen Signal wird, den Denkakt zu beended und Abfuhr eintreten zu lassen'* (Freud 1950b: 413).

12 The German reveals that this description takes place at the level of the neuronal structure in terms of its state of energy and, furthermore, that the 'signal' is distinct from the 'sign'.

13 *'Am Nebenmenschen lernt darum der mensch erkennen'* (Freud 1950b: 415).

14 As we shall examine, the theory of the acquisition of speech, which underpins the importance Freud attached to the speech-sign, is a hangover from his earlier work on aphasia.

15 'Secondary modification' of highly intense mnemic-images is one of the aims of psychotherapy, as quoted above, p.129, according to the 'telescope' model.

16 *'Die Sprachabfuhrzeichen sind in gewissem Sinne auch Realitätszeichen Zeichen der Denkrealität, aber nicht der externen'* (Freud 1950b: 452).

17 *'Material von Erinnerungsspuren eine Umordnung nach neuen Beziehungen, eine Umschrift erfährt'* (Freud 1950b: 185).

¹⁸ *'Überall findet sich sich, dass eine Erinnerung verdrägt wird, die nur nachträglich um Trauma geworden ist'* (Freud 1950b: 435).
¹⁹ Freud makes an explicit reference to J.S. Mill in Freud 1915: 214.

FREUD'S INFERNAL TRINITY: ON THE VICISSITUDES OF THE 'TRIPARTITE MODEL'

Dany Nobus

Obscurity Triumphant

Freud's distinction between the ego, the id and the superego is probably one of his best known and most widespread accomplishments. This popularisation of what is commonly called the 'tripartite model' or the 'second topography' is mainly due to the development and diffusion of ego psychology in the United States after Word War II. During the 1940s and 1950s American-born analysts such as David Rapaport, and European immigrants such as Heinz Hartmann, tried to establish psychoanalysis as a genuine science of the mind. The second topography was deemed very appropriate for this purpose, because it comprised all the aspects of psychic functioning, from the darkest regions of the drives, to the conscious world of perception, to the moral standards of conscience. Through ego psychology, the id, ego and superego also found a niche within the psychodynamic region of general psychology, which contributed to their dissemination as basic concepts of psychoanalytic theory.[1]

However, when Sigmund Freud introduced, described, and graphically represented the three entities in his 1923 essay *The Ego and the Id*, he felt far less enthusiastic about his achievement than his followers. Some months prior to its publication Freud divulged to Sándor Ferenczi that he was deeply dissatisfied with the whole enterprise:

> Now I am in the well-known depression after correcting the proofs, and I am swearing to myself never again to let myself get on to such slippery ice. It seems to me that since the *Jenseits* [the 1920 essay *Beyond the Pleasure Principle*] the curve has descended steeply. That was still rich in ideas and well written, the *Group Psychology* [the 1921 study entitled *Group Psychology and the Analysis of the Ego*] is close to banality, and the present book is decidedly obscure, composed in an artificial fashion and badly written... Except for the basic idea of the 'Id' and the *aperçu* about the origin of morality I am displeased with really everything in the book. (Cited in Jones 1957: 99)

Of course, Freud could not have known what a marvellous future was in store for his obscure speculations, and his own dissatisfaction with the lion's share of the work did not prevent him from further elaborating his ideas on the subject. Indeed, some ten years after *The Ego and the Id*, Freud summarised the most salient points of his original essay in Lecture 31 of his *New Introductory Lectures on Psychoanalysis*, and proposed a modified graphical representation of the relations between the three entities (Freud 1933: 57-80). In 1938, one year before his death, he dealt with the nature and function of the tripartite model again, in the posthumously published *An Outline of Psychoanalysis* (Freud 1940). In this essay he attempted to explain the model's relation to the theory of the drives and the formations of the unconscious, as well as its concrete value for the practice of psychoanalysis.

Many historians of psychoanalysis have explained Freud's initial discontent with *The Ego and the Id* as just another example of the disparaging, self-belittling attitude with which he usually approached the products of his mind. For example, Peter Gay wrote in his widely acclaimed biography of Freud:

> As so often he [Freud] misjudged his own work; *The Ego and the Id* is among Freud's most indispensable texts. In the corpus of his writings, *The Interpretation of Dreams* and the *Three Essays on the Theory of Sexuality* must always hold pride of place, but whatever names Freud might call it, *The Ego and the Id* is a triumph of lucid mental energy... If *The Ego and the Id* seems at all obscure, that is due to the extreme compression of his postwar work. (Gay 1988: 411)[2]

The question is whether this historical account of the unmistakable merits of Freud's essay and its innovative conception of the mind is not derived more from the cardinal importance placed upon it by ego psychology, than from a detailed textual reading of the Freudian corpus itself. Given the overall presence of the model in the mainstream psychoanalytic literature of the second half of the Twentieth Century, Freud could indeed be taken to task for misjudging his own work. But are we allowed to employ this ubiquity of the model as a valid criterion for judging Freud's judgement? For ego psychologists *The Ego and the Id* is undeniably an indispensable text, and for them the tripartite model of the mind holds pride of place as a basic conceptual requisite.

However, does this imply that 'no one would be able to think of the mind's structure' differently anymore, as Ronald Clark has suggested? (Clark 1980: 437).

Against the ego psychological tide, some psychoanalysts have also criticised the tripartite model for its departure from clinical reality and for its theoretical obscurity, thereby endorsing Freud's own opinion of his work.[3] Furthermore, as far as the reliability of his own opinions is concerned, Freud could at times be extraordinarily and needlessly sceptical about the significance of his writings, but on occasion he could also express a certain satisfaction with what he had produced.[4] In the light of this, would it not be more appropriate to analyse his judgements from the perspective of his own life history or in relation to his own psychoanalytic developments, than to reinterpret them according to what became of the concepts on which they were passed?

My main objective in this essay is to investigate the reasons Freud harboured for introducing the 1923 model, and for proceeding with its refinement. This also entails an evaluation of the conceptual framework of Freud's later clinical works because—in contrast to what James Strachey claimed in his editor's introduction to *The Ego and the Id*—there is at least one later essay by Freud which does not 'bear the unmistakable imprint of its effects' (Strachey 1961: 4). The essay in question is 'Constructions in Analysis'. Besides the fact that it is one of the last technical works Freud produced, it is written in pre-1923 terminology, which is most apparent where the goals of psychoanalytic treatment are discussed (Freud 1937b). Why this sudden shift? Was it perhaps because Freud had finally realised that his judgement of *The Ego and the Id* had—after all—been alarmingly correct, despite the enthusiasm of his followers?

Models and their vicissitudes — take one

In his preface to *The Ego and the Id*, Freud indicated that his new work was a continuation of ideas that he had presented three years earlier in *Beyond the Pleasure Principle*. Contrary to the biological arguments around which the latter had revolved, Freud underscored that he was now going to adduce 'the facts of analytic observation' in what was meant to be a 'synthesis' rather than a 'speculation' (Freud 1923: 12). The point from *Beyond the Pleasure Principle* that Freud was most keen to reconsider in 1923 concerned the equation of the ego with consciousness, which had been challenged by the occurrence of unconscious resistances in the patient during psychoanalytic treatment. In 1920 Freud had written:

> The unconscious—that is to say, the 'repressed'—offers no resistance whatever to the efforts of the treatment. Indeed, it itself has no other endeavour than to break through the pressure weighing down on it and force its way either to consciousness or to a discharge through some real action. Resistance during treatment arises from the same higher strata and systems of the mind which originally carried out repression. But the fact that, as we know from experience, the motives of the resistances, and indeed the resistances themselves, are unconscious at first during the treatment, is a hint to us that we should correct a shortcoming in our terminology. We shall avoid a lack of clarity if we make our contrast not between the conscious and the unconscious but between the coherent ego and the repressed. It is certain that much of the ego is itself unconscious, and notably what we may describe as its nucleus; only a small part of it is covered by the term 'preconscious'. (Freud 1920a: 19)

If resistance, defined as everything that opposes itself to the advancement of the analytic treatment, had to be ascribed to the agency responsible for repression—that is, to the ego—and resistance remained largely unconscious, then the ego must indeed have an unconscious part. This was Freud's conclusion in 1920, so despite his claim that the distinction between conscious and unconscious proved inadequate, it was actually the opposition between ego and unconscious that required revision. In the opposition of ego and unconscious, there appeared to be a confusion of different categories of analysis.

From this perspective, Freud's initial project in *The Ego and the Id* was quite simple. His primary aim was to clarify the status of the ego and to investigate how it relates to the previously made distinctions between unconscious, conscious, and preconscious. Contrary to what he had suggested in *Beyond the Pleasure Principle*, Freud now argued that the nucleus of the ego corresponds with Perception-Consciousness (Pcpt.-Cs.), which is spatially or topographically the first component reached if one approaches the mental apparatus from the outside world.[5] Since the manifestations of resistance in the patient were also occurring on an unconscious level, Freud was forced to conclude that the ego extends into the unconscious, thereby embracing the whole of the preconscious.[6] In order to designate that part of the unconscious which does not comprise the ego, but coincides with the repressed, he borrowed a term from the German physician Georg Groddeck and introduced the id (*'das Es'*).[7] This distinction between the ego and the id formed the basis of a new model of the mind, in which the former systems of the unconscious, preconscious and consciousness were transformed into *functions* of the new structures—the ego and the id. Indeed, whereas the ego had previously been defined as the 'dominant mass of ideas' (*'Vorstellungsmasse'*) in the conscious part of the psychic apparatus, it now lost its quality as a specific function of consciousness, and became a relatively autonomous organisation, of which the former system Pcpt.-Cs. is one of the key functions.[8] With the id and the ego as actors, Freud drew a dualistic picture of the mind, emphasising the dynamic relationship between the psychic agencies. This can be inferred from the first graphical representation of the new structural theory, as it appeared in *The Ego and the Id*.[9]

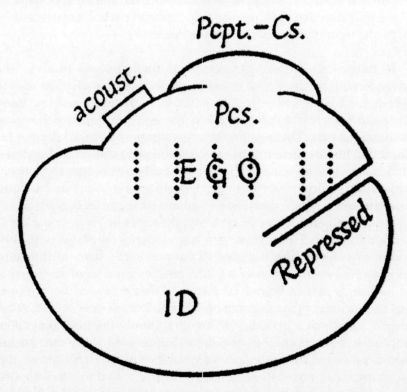

Fig 1: The first graphical representation of the structural theory

Most strikingly, Freud reserved the largest part of this diagram for the id, which was at the same time the least differentiated section. The ego was located in the higher and smaller lobes of the sphere, and seemed to have myriad functions. Whereas the id was spatially dominant, the ego predominated functionally.[10]

However, the apparent straightforwardness of these topographical distinctions was challenged when Freud was called upon to explain how the ego and the id became structurally differentiated from one another. For Freud, a human being was not born with a relatively well-established ego, but rather with a large reservoir of libido or psychic energy that is flowing freely between a wide array of objects. This is in conformity with the mechanism of the pleasure principle, whose aim is the production of lust by means of a process of discharge.[11] The primal state in the ontogenesis of the mind could thus be characterised as a chaotic and unrestrained motion of energy with the aim of pleasure. In that case, what can be held responsible for the modification of this original situation? Freud proposed no less than *three* hypotheses, which were simultaneously explanations of the development of the ego.

The first hypothesis was that the primal state is modified under the influence of stimuli from the outside world. Freud had already formulated this idea in *Beyond the Pleasure Principle*, in which he had argued that the surface of an undifferentiated vesicle is altered both as a protection against the destructive power of external stimuli, and as a means to receive and process external and internal stimuli.[12] In *The Ego and the Id*, he considered the ego as an extension of this surface-differentiation, coinciding with the system Pcpt.-Cs.[13] Because Pcpt.-Cs. is derived from external stimuli, he could also state that the ego-extension is responsible for confronting the pleasure principle with the reality principle, which restrains the unlimited discharge of energy.

Although Freud's second hypothesis on the development of the ego conveys the impression of being simply an enlargement of the first, it actually opened completely new perspectives, which are quite remarkable in the light of his earlier formulations on the ego and topography. Freud wrote that the 'ego is first and foremost a bodily ego', 'not merely a surface entity, but... the projection of a surface. If we wish to find an anatomical analogy for it we can best identify it with the "cortical homunculus" of the anatomists' (Freud 1923: 26).[14] This hypothesis is—in a sense—the corollary of the previous one, because it is a simple matter to situate Pcpt.-Cs., at least in part, on the level of the senses, the organs of which are located on the surface of the body, and thus to contend that the nucleus of the ego is the body, or that the ego is primarily a body-ego. However, in relating the ego to the body Freud connected a psychic region to an anatomical structure, which is radically different from what he had aspired to with his model of the psyche in the final chapter of *The Interpretation of Dreams*. There he had pointed out that he had no intention whatsoever to relate the psychic localities (*'psychische Lokalitäten'*) of the systems—the unconscious (Ucs.), the preconscious (Pcs.) and perception (Pcpt.)—to anatomical parts of the brain (Freud 1900: 536). In *The Ego and the* Id the gap between topography and anatomy became far more narrow, not only because Freud attributed the development of the ego to body-stimuli, but also because he recognised the ego as the 'homunculus'—that is, the little brainperson inside human beings.[15]

Freud emphasised, however, that the ego is not itself a surface, but the *projection* of a surface. Insofar as the body is a surface, the ego equals and supersedes the body. This is because it is a *representation* of the original form, in which the proportions are not necessarily preserved. The ego could be compared with images of the world in an atlas: they present a proportional picture of places and borders, but they are nevertheless deceitful because they derive from a specific projection of the globe on a two-dimensional slate. Freud did not elaborate upon this point in *The Ego and the Id*, nor in any other text, but in some interpretations of his work—notably, in the writings of Lacan—this has been regarded as an important idea for addressing the question of the structure of the ego.[16]

In Freud's third hypothesis, the ego was the result of identifications with objects that had been previously cathected by energy from the id. Freud's account of this process is far more contrived than his linkage of the ego to Pcpt.-Cs. and the body. In several places it is indeed 'decidedly obscure'. A possible explanation for this is that Freud was no longer able to seek solace in biological data, an abstract metapsychological interpretation of 'the facts of analytic observation' (Freud 1923: 12) being the only option.[17] Freud's core idea was that specific object-cathexes stemming from the activity of the pleasure principle in the id have to be relinquished, which entails the disconnection of the libido from the object, the relocation of the libido within an ego-system, and the introjection or identification by the ego-system with the object. Freud also mentioned that not all of the id's object-cathexes had to be abandoned; when the ego starts to recognise them as such it can either fend them off or tolerate them. Yet how can the ego first be 'aware' of object-cathexes, and then be 'formed' through the process of their abandonment? In explaining the mechanism of the development of the ego, Freud *presupposed* what he was trying to account for. The difficulty could be tackled if the 'first ego' (the one that is aware of the object-cathexes) is identified with Pcpt.-Cs., and the 'second ego' (the one that results from abandoned object-cathexes) with the extension of Pcpt.-Cs.. Of course, in this case there are two different egos, and the first ego implies a return to the original problem of Freud's essay, namely the relation between ego and consciousness. Moreover, it must also be explained how Pcpt.-Cs. can distinguish between tolerable and intolerable object-cathexes, considering the fact that it is the ego proper which installs the reality principle. This conceptual difficulty reappeared where Freud considered the object-cathexes as proceeding from the id, since the notion of the id *already* implies the presence of an ego. In other words, the original object-cathexes cannot be related to the id sending out libido if there is no ego-structure as yet. And, if the ego develops through the identification with abandoned objects, then which agency is responsible for putting these identifications into motion?[18]

Freud eventually postulated a *primary identification* 'which takes place earlier than any object-cathexis' (Freud 1923: 31) and which is at the same time the origin of the ego ideal.[19] This brought him to a further differentiation within the original topographical model of ego and id, because the ego ideal—which Freud identified with the superego—was regarded as a third separate structure in the mind. Primary identification had already been touched upon in the 1921 study *Group Psychology and the Analysis of the Ego*, in which Freud had claimed that there are at least three types of identification. Of these, identification with the father, which is more like an incorporation, is chronologically the first (Freud 1921: 105-110). As such, this proposition of a primal identification with the father followed from his mythological explanation of the constitution of social organisation in *Totem and Taboo*. There he had speculated that a fundamental breach had occurred in the history of humankind when members of the primal horde assassinated the mighty and monstrous primal father ruling over them, erecting a totem to commemorate him and eating his flesh during the totem-meal. Before the murder and the incorporation of the father's body, there had been no social organisation whatever, but merely subjection to power. After the murderous act, prohibitions and commands, norms and values came into operation, and a socio-cultural environment had been established (Freud 1912-13: 142-143). In *The Ego and the Id* Freud transferred this phylogenetic myth to the ontological process, adopting the Haeckelian stance that ontogenesis is a repetition of phylogenesis by indicating that primal identification takes place during 'personal prehistory' (Freud 1923: 31).[20] Around this incorporation of the father, new identifications could be formed, contributing to the development of the ego, but also to the creation of the super-ego.

Freud's enquiry into the distinction between the ego and the id was now transformed into the issue of how to separate dynamically the ego and the super-ego. The difficulties Freud experienced in answering this issue become clear if one compares the several formulae he drew up concerning the relations between these structures. On the one hand, he claimed that the super-ego was a modification of the ego, under the influence of an identification with the mother and the father during the dissolution of the Oedipus complex (Freud 1923: 34). Again, the issue arose as to which mechanism could be held responsible for these identifications. In *The Ego and the Id*, Freud initially argued that the abolition of the id's object-cathexes of the father and the mother, which actually coincides with the dissolution and repression of the Oedipus complex, was the task of the ego-ideal (Freud 1923: 34). Yet here we are confronted with the same paradox as in the case of the constitution of the ego. How can the super-ego be both the instigator and the result of the dissolution process? Shortly after writing *The Ego and the Id*, and probably due to this patent incongruity, Freud attributed this mechanism to the intervention of the ego, acting upon castration anxiety. However, in this way the problem was only partly solved, because now he had to explain the origin of castration anxiety.[21]

On the other hand, Freud also claimed that the super-ego was a delegate of the id:

> Whereas the ego is essentially the representative of the external world, of reality, the super-ego stands in contrast to it as the representative of the internal world, of the id. (Freud 1923: 36)

But how can the super-ego be at once a transformation of the ego and a representative of the id? Even if one considers the ego as the 'agent provocateur' of the super-ego, it is difficult to see how a structure which is dominated by Pcpt.-Cs. and by the reality principle could transform part of itself into a representative of the id and thus become an avatar of its own major opponent. Both modification of the ego and spokesman of the id, the super-ego appeared as a highly ambiguous structure, which could explain Freud's reluctance to localise it in his model of the psychic apparatus. Indeed, he admitted the topographical problem of the super-ego in the clearest of words:

> It would be vain, however, to attempt to localise the ego ideal, even in the sense in which we have localised the ego, or to work it into any of the analogies with the help of which we have tried to picture the relation between the ego and the id. (Freud 1923: 36-37)[22]

Whereas Freud's explanatory power was too weak to justify both the origins and the dynamics of these three structures in the mind, his description of their functions and features was much more perspicacious, especially as far as the ego and the super-ego were concerned. According to Freud, the ego had both strengths and weaknesses. Midway between the id and the external world, the ego was mainly responsible for controlling the unlimited and inconsiderate flow of psychic energy coming from the id. The principal strengths of the ego included: (i) an ability to introduce a temporal order into the mental processes; (ii) a capacity to subject the mind to the reality principle; (iii) efficiency in preventing immediate discharges of energy. However, the ego was under continuous attack from three sources: the external world, the id, and the super-ego. Each of these besieged the ego's headquarters, trying to undermine its sovereignty and to take over psychic control (Freud 1923: 55-56). Hence the ego was not weak in itself, but because it had to cope with a triune, destabilising force, its mastery was relative.

The reason the ego had to fight against the super-ego was the latter's ferocious, ruthless character. In Freud's view, the super-ego manifested itself in the form of prohibitions and commands, the nature of which he compared with Kant's categorical imperative (Freud 1923: 35).[23] Whence this extreme severity? For Freud, it resulted from the (male) child's identification with the father as part of the dissolution of the Oedipus complex and the particular type of identification this involves.[24] As I have already described above, Freud claimed that identifications stem from the elimination of object-cathexes. Within the energy used for these cathexes, he postulated a fusion of Eros and Thanatos (the sexual and the death drive) and speculated that the elimination of object-cathexes is carried out via a de-sexualisation, entailing a defusion of the drives and a reinforcement of Thanatos.[25] In sum, the super-ego is so severe owing to the convergence of the power associated with the father on the one hand, and the invigorated death drive on the other.

Yet from this vantage point, the ego ought to be a severe structure as well, since it also derived from identifications—at least, according to the third hypothesis, mentioned above. Freud noticed this difficulty at the end of *The Ego and the Id*, where he raised the question as to how the ego could keep itself from perishing under the power of the death drive. Again, his answer opened up more questions than it solved. He suggested that the ego also 'becomes the representative of Eros and thenceforward desires to live and to be loved' (Freud 1923: 56). Once again, Freud's explanations failed, but the descriptions remained firmly in place. Whereas the ego was striving to be moral, the super-ego was cruel and pitiless in its ultra-morality. In confrontation with the super-ego, the ego could only experience guilt, which could be conscious as well as unconscious, in accordance with the way in which the ego extends between the unconscious and Pcpt.-Cs.[26]

In the final paragraph of *The Ego and the Id*, Freud also described the most important features of the id, although in a strictly negative way. He stressed that the id was beyond love and hate, and that it had not developed a unified will. From the fact that he had already allocated the introduction of temporality to the ego, and of morality to the super-ego, it followed that the id had no time-structure, and that it was amoral.

Models and their vicissitudes—take two

Some ten years after his initial attempt at constructing an integrated model of the mind, Freud had another try in his *New Introductory Lectures on Psychoanalysis*, in a chapter called 'The Dissection of the Psychical Personality' (Freud 1933: 57-80). On the one hand, this lecture contains a summary and a simplification of the earlier positions but, on the other hand, it displays a number of interesting departures from the 1923 essay.

In summarising his earlier points of view, Freud mainly restricted himself to a description of the three systems in the mind, shifting the explanation of their origin and development into the background.[27]

This resulted in a new graphical representation of the structural theory.

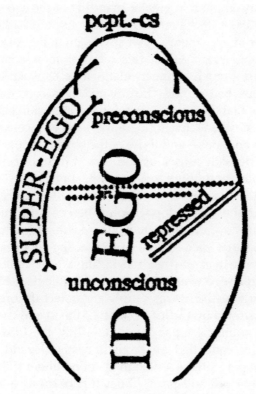

Fig 2: The second graphical representation of the structural theory

A comparison of this model with that from *The Ego and the Id* reveals at least five differences. Certainly, the most significant is that the superego was now graphically represented, as a structure stretching out from the unconscious to Pcpt.-Cs. and covering the ego. Secondly, whereas the first model had an opening on the level of repression, the second model has an opening on the level of the id. Indeed, except for this minor opening on the right-hand side, the 1923 model was closed, whereas the new model shows a major aperture at the bottom. Freud explained this by commenting that the id was 'open at its end to somatic influences' (Freud 1933: 73).[28] Thirdly, the 1923 model had two 'lobes', one pertaining to Pcpt.-Cs. and the other to Pcs. and the ego. The new model contained only the lobe of Pcpt.-Cs. Although this may seem a minor difference at first, it was actually vitally important. Freud observed that his new model was misleading due to this, and required further modification: the 'space occupied by the unconscious id ought to have been incomparably greater than that of the ego or the preconscious' (Freud 1933: 79).[29] Fourthly, the unconscious had not figured in the first model at all, whereas now it was unambiguously situated in the heart of the diagram. Again, this variation may seem only a detail, but it conveyed a much stronger relationship between the id and the unconscious than before. Both the first and the second graphical representation show that there is *no* one-to-one relationship between the elements of the so-called 'first topography'—that is, conscious, preconscious and unconscious—and those of the second topography. The ego did not coincide with consciousness; the id did not correspond with the unconscious; and the super-ego was not simply preconscious. Inasmuch as the systems of the first topography became *functions* of new systems in the second topography, then each function in the second topography covered more than one system. However, it would be wrong to claim that each system in the second topography was also inhabited by more than one function, for this was not true of the id. The ego and the super-ego were both conscious and extended beyond consciousness, whereas the id was simply and solely unconscious. This is amply demonstrated by the localisation of the id and the unconscious in the second graphical representation. Fifthly, the 1933 model of the mind no longer contained an acoustic system. Freud continued to emphasise that perceptions settled in the mind under the form of memory-traces, but he did not specify the nature of these residues.

Besides these five differences, which arise from a close comparison of the two drawings, the 1933 text also contained at least three new perspectives on 'psychic personality'. The first innovation derives from what Freud claimed at the beginning of the lecture, concerning the splitting of the ego:

> The situation in which we find ourselves at the beginning of our enquiry may be expected itself to point the way for us. We wish to make the ego the matter of our enquiry, our very own ego. But is that possible? After all, the ego is in its very essence a subject; how can it be made into an object? Well, there is no doubt that it can be. The ego can take itself as an object, can treat itself like other objects, can observe itself, criticise itself, and do Heaven knows what with itself. In this, one part of the ego is setting itself over against the rest. So the ego can be split; it splits itself during

a number of its functions—temporarily at least. Its parts can come together again afterwards. (Freud 1933: 58)

The concept Freud used to grasp the internal division of the ego is 'splitting' (*Spaltung*)—that is, a fissure or separation through which a unity is divided in two. The concept had already appeared in Freud's study on 'The Neuro-Psychoses of Defence' (Freud 1894), and *Studies on Hysteria* (Breuer & Freud 1895). It had made its entry again in the paper 'Fetishism' (Freud 1927). In the former works, Freud had discussed 'the splitting of consciousness' (*Spaltung des Bewußtseins*) in hysteria (Freud 1894: 46-7; Breuer & Freud 1895: 12), whereas in 1927 he had introduced the notion to account for the coexistence of two contradictory attitudes towards the problem of castration in the mind of the fetishist (Freud 1927: 156). Yet the splitting to which Freud referred in 1933 was something completely different, although this is hardly ever recognised by scholars tracing the meanders of the concept.[30]

In 1933 Freud insisted on the possibility of a splitting between the ego as object and the ego as subject, in which the latter takes the former as an object of study. Of course, one could point out that this 'ego-subject', which Freud called 'the observing agency', is but another name for the super-ego. Yet it is remarkable that Freud drew attention to the *temporary* splitting in the case of ego-object and ego-subject, whilst the superego was meant to be a *permanent* structural splitting *off* of the ego. What Freud described as a splitting of ego-object and ego-subject is more likely to be related to the process of *self-awareness*, and could thus form the basis for the expansion of the second topography as a quadripartite model.

The second innovation of Freud's 1933 model concerns the description of the id. In 1923 Freud had characterised the id in a purely negative way, and this was largely maintained in 1933:

[The id] has no organisation, produces no collective will... The logical laws of thought do not apply in the id... There is nothing in the id that could be compared with negation; and we perceive with surprise an exception to the philosophical theorem that space and time are necessary forms of our mental acts. There is nothing in the id that corresponds to the idea of time; there is no recognition of the passage of time, and—a thing that is most remarkable and awaits consideration in philosophical thought—

> no alteration in its mental processes is produced by the passage of time. (Freud 1933: 73-74)

It is precisely this time-structure of the unconscious which required further exploration:

> Again and again I have had the impression that we have made too little theoretical use of this fact, established beyond any doubt, of the unalterability by time of the repressed. This seems to offer an approach to the most profound discoveries. Nor, unfortunately, have I myself made any progress here. (Freud 1933: 74)

At this point Freud opened a door towards a more positive typification of the id, towards the acknowledgement of a specific order in the chaotic movements of the id's energy, and perhaps towards a time-structure that is different from commonplace chronology.[31]

The third innovation is possibly even more important than the previous two, because it encompasses the whole rationale for the creation of the second topography. In 1933, Freud commenced his presentation of the psychic personality with a discussion of the super-ego, as if remembering that this structure had proved the most problematic in *The Ego and the Id*. Freud now regarded the super-ego as a composite structure containing the ego-ideal, conscience and the function of self-observation. Hence, the super-ego was no longer identified with the ego-ideal, the latter being reduced to one amongst other functions within a larger system. Of crucial importance, however, is that Freud ascribed the mental processes of *resistance* and *repression* to this new version of the tripartite super-ego:

> The resistance can only be a manifestation of the ego, which originally put the repression into force and now wishes to maintain it. That, moreover, is the view we always took. Since we have come to assume a special agency in the ego, the super-ego, which represents demands of a restrictive and rejecting character, we may say that repression is the work of this super-ego and that it is carried out either by itself or by the ego in obedience to its orders. (Freud 1933: 68-69)

The startling consequence of this position is that Freud's main reason for embarking upon *The Ego and the Id*—and introducing the second topography—disappeared. Indeed, the original problem was that the ego could not be opposed to the unconscious since its repressions and resistances frequently remained unconscious themselves. The whole plan of *The Ego and the Id* had proceeded from the problem of the unconscious ego. Now, however, Freud considered the super-ego to be the nucleus of repression and resistances, which challenged the necessity to distinguish between the ego and the id, and opened up new questions about the status of the ego.[32]

Revisionism revisited

At the beginning of the fourth chapter of *The Ego and the Id*, Freud wrote that the distinction between the ego, the id and the super-ego 'ought to enable us to understand more thoroughly the dynamic relations within the mind and to describe them more clearly' (Freud 1923: 40). I have tried to show that Freud's discussion of the dynamics between the three structures leaves several questions unanswered, and that his success is situated more on the level of description than of explanation. If understanding 'the dynamic relations within the mind' is the purpose of the second topography, it occurs to me that we have every reason to think this objective has not been realised. Of course, the original purpose of the second topography was slightly different, and consisted in the clarification of the relation between the ego and the unconscious. Yet in this respect also, the result of the consecutive models is rather meagre, if only because the issue lost its incisiveness once Freud attributed resistance and repression to the super-ego.

Despite these inadequacies, and despite his own repudiation of the 1923 essay, Freud continued to use the structural theory in the 1930s. This can be inferred from 'Analysis Terminable and Interminable', which appeared in June 1937. In this essay, he presented what is probably the most pessimistic view on the clinical value of psychoanalysis ever written. Adversaries of psychoanalysis could skilfully use it to argue that the father of psychoanalysis himself eventually admitted to the worthlessness of his invention. In 'Analysis Terminable and Interminable', Freud testified to the disappearance of all his hopes for an efficient psychoanalytic technique and an adequate psychoanalytic treatment for the neuroses. He asked himself how much change psychoanalysis can produce in the patient, and had to concede that its extent was altogether negligible. Thereupon he proceeded by asking whether the small changes that could be produced were permanent, and again he was forced to answer than this was not the case. The same general pessimism governed the answers Freud gave to questions about the prophylactic action of psychoanalysis and those concerning its power to eliminate external and internal obstacles.

In this pervasive aura of aridity and despondency, Peter Gay has read a sign of the times, both of the apocalyptic political climate in Austria at the end of the 1930s, and of catastrophic events in Freud's personal life (Gay 1988: 614-618). Others, like Isabelle Stengers, have interpreted Freud's pessimism as a confirmation of the impossibility of psychoanalysis, not only as a profession—which Freud himself emphasised—but also as a science (Stengers 1992: 77, 81).[33]

In my opinion, Freud was suffering merely from an effect of the second topography. The master was doomed to acknowledge that the therapeutic power of psychoanalysis was negligible because he had asked himself the question whether psychoanalysis was capable of resolving conflicts between unconscious drives and the structure of the ego. He was obliged to recognise that psychoanalytic practice was weak because he asked himself whether it could reinforce the ego, transform 'permeable repressions' (Freud 1937a: 229) into 'reliable and ego-syntonic forms of mastery' (Freud 1937a: 227) and correct the original process of repression. These questions stemmed from a certain view of the goal of psychoanalysis, which was itself the result of dynamic relationships between the structures of the second topography, theorised in 1923.

In *The Ego and the Id* Freud initially claimed that 'analysis does not set out to make pathological reactions impossible, but to give the patient's ego freedom to decide one way or the other' (Freud 1923: 50 n.1).[34] Later on, he progressively emphasised the psychoanalytic goal of strengthening the ego's control over the id, which resulted in the famous formula of 1933: 'Where id was, there ego shall be' (Freud 1933: 80).[35] Peter Gay has expressed surprise over the fact that Freud seemed to question this goal in 'Analysis Terminable and Interminable', or even abandon it altogether (Gay 1988: 615). But could Freud have done anything else? The tripartite model required the ego to be built out of the same materials as the id, which puts, *a priori*, an embargo on the ego's independence. The second topography leads to a fundamental block if it is applied to the practice of psychoanalysis, and this is what Freud encountered in 'Analysis Terminable and Interminable'.

Therefore, he was justified in confessing to Ferenczi that he was 'displeased with really everything' (Jones 1957: 99) in *The Ego and the Id*, except for the notion of the id and the ideas on the origin of morality. The essay was not only a failure in the light of its own major purposes, but also led to a theory of the mind which reduced the practice of psychoanalysis to ruins.

If Freud's pessimism in 'Analysis Terminable and Interminable' originated in the impossibility of a specific theory of the psychic apparatus, this did not entail the impossibility of the psychoanalytic enterprise. The proof is that Freud continued to work on his invention after the disaster of 'Analysis Terminable and Interminable', as if nothing had happened and as if the second topography had never been developed. In December 1937, Freud's final paper on technique, 'Constructions in Analysis', was published, in which there was not a trace of the ego, the id, or the super-ego (Freud 1937b). Freud returned to the concepts he had used *before* the introduction of the second topography, stating that psychoanalysis aimed at the patient's remembrance of what had been repressed. Hence, Freud's acknowledgement of defeat in 'Analysis Terminable and Interminable' was only partial, because it did not affect the theory that had been developed before 1923. It did affect the second topography, however, because after 'Analysis Terminable and Interminable' Freud did not publish any further theoretical or technical papers in which the dynamics of the ego, the id and the super-ego were refined. One could object to this that there is the posthumously published *An Outline of Psychoanalysis*, of which many sections rely on the structures of the second topography (Freud 1940). To this argument I can simply retort that Freud did not include any important new ideas in this book, and that of course he would present his concept of the second topography in what was meant to be a general survey of psychoanalysis.

With the disintegration of the new model of the mind, 1937 signalled a return to chaos in Freud's theory. Against this background, the drama of ego-psychology becomes all the more conspicuous, because the ego-psychologists have turned into a principle that which gives rise to the impossibility of their own discipline. They have made absolute the 1933 exhortation 'Where id was, there ego shall be', disregarding the implicit message of 1937, which read: 'Where ego was, there id shall be'.

Notes

[1] For a general discussion of the historical circumstances and the specific aims of ego psychology, see Hale 1995: 231-244.

[2] Similar views have been defended by Norman Kiell and Ronald Clark. See Kiell 1988: 485, Clark 1980: 437.

[3] See, for example, Schafer 1976, 1983; Klein 1976. The most violent criticism of Freud's second topography and of ego psychology can be found in the works of Jacques Lacan, who devoted most of his post-1950s contributions to a revival of the 'subject' in psychoanalysis, against the centrality of the ego. See, for example, 'The Function and Field of Speech and Language in Psychoanalysis' (1953), in Lacan 1977: 30-113.

[4] For example, in a letter to Lou Andreas-Salomé, dated 27th July 1916, Freud seemed quite satisfied with *The Psychopathology of Everyday Life*. See Pfeiffer 1972: 51.

[5] It should be noted here that the idea of a topographical representation of the various functions of the mind had already appeared in a letter Freud sent to Wilhelm Fliess on 6 December 1896—a letter also known as 'Letter 52'—and had reappeared in the final chapter of *The Interpretation of Dreams*. In the latter work, Freud had compared the mental apparatus to a microscope or camera, in which each of the stages in the formation of the image corresponds to a certain place (*'Örtlichkeit'*) or region (*'Gegend'*) within the apparatus, albeit without any material, tangible substratum. See Masson 1985: 207-215; Freud 1900: 536.

[6] In 1923 Freud defined the preconscious as the latent unconscious, or as that part of the unconscious that has found a connection with word-presentations (*'Wortvorstellungen'*), which are themselves mnemic traces of mainly acoustic perceptions. For Freud, words entered the mental apparatus through their expression as sounds, which opens an interesting perspective on the relationship between Freud's thought and the ideas of Ferdinand de Saussure, for whom words are basically acoustic images or signifiers. See Saussure 1983.

[7] It is strange that Freud should write in his preface that he did not have to express any acknowledgements for the topics under discussion, yet in the main text Groddeck was explicitly mentioned as the inventor of the id. For a short but instructive biographical statement on Groddeck, see Grotjahn 1995: 308-320. For more detailed studies of Groddeck's life and works, see Grossman & Grossman 1965, Will 1984, Lewinter 1990.

[8] The ego is defined as the 'dominant mass of ideas' in Breuer & Freud 1895: 116.

[9] Freud referred to the 'structural conditions of the mind' (*'Strukturellen Verhältnisse des Seelenlebens'*) in *The Ego and the Id* and to the 'structural relations of the mental personality' (*'die Strukturverhältnisse der Seelischen Persönlichkeit'*) in Lecture 31 of the *New Introductory Lectures on Psychoanalysis*. Expressions such as 'structural theory' and 'structural concepts' have been promoted especially by Heinz Hartmann, Ernst Kris and Rudolf Loewenstein in some very influential papers from the late 1940s. Compare Freud 1923: 17, 1933: 78 and Hartmann, Kris & Loewenstein 1946, 1949.

[10] The dotted lines which cross the ego vertically were not labelled by Freud, but can be regarded as indications of the mnemic traces left by perception, in accordance with the model of the psychic apparatus in the final chapter of *The Interpretation of Dreams*. See Freud 1900: 538-541.

[11] The pleasure principle can be defined as follows. Every living being aims at a maximum of pleasure (*'Lust'*) and a minimum of unpleasure. Unpleasure is everything associated with an increase of tension; pleasure is everything associated with a decrease of tension. Maximum pleasure is a constant level of low tension (or rest). Tension is transformed into rest through the discharge of energy.

[12] See Freud 1920a: 26-29. Freud had explicitly rejected the possibility of a protection against *internal* stimuli, suggesting that the organism could use its protective shield against these stimuli by treating them as external—that is, by *projecting* them onto the outside world.

[13] Hence Freud's doubts as to the nature of the ego's nucleus. In *Beyond the Pleasure Principle* he had regarded it as being unconscious, which makes sense if one considers the material from which the ego is built. In *The Ego and the Id*, however, he identified it with Pcpt.-Cs., which also makes sense, from the perspective of the ego as an extension of the modified surface.

[14] At the very end of the second chapter Freud repeated this phrase, but restricted the bodily aspect of the ego to its conscious part.

[15] This radical change of perspective embraces the entire philosophical debate on the relationship between mind and body, which is currently being revived in the fields of artificial intelligence and the study of consciousness. For an interesting review of recent studies and the plethora of questions involved see Searle 1997 (which includes exchanges with D.C. Dennett and D.J. Chalmers). For a focused discussion of Freud's 'body-ego' see Wollheim 1993: 64-78.

[16] Lacan claimed that the ego is formed through the child's imaginary identification with the (*de facto* inverted) mirror-image of the body, during the so-called 'mirror stage' experience. See 'The Mirror Stage as Formative of the Function of the I as Revealed in Psychoanalytic Experience' (1949), in Lacan 1977: 1-7. For discussions of Lacan's views, see Nobus 1998 and Jalley 1998.

[17] As becomes clear from the clinical examples Freud provided, these 'facts' are taken mainly from the study of melancholia and obsessional neurosis.

[18] In her recent book, *The Psychic Life of Power*, Judith Butler has shown that Freud was not the only thinker to presuppose the 'psychic form' he attempts to explain. Similar problems pervade theoretical accounts of the origin of the subject in the works of Foucault, Althusser and others. For Butler, the solution lies in the subject's 'passionate attachment'—that is, its dependency upon subordination. This solution has been disputed by Slavoj Zizek, who has endeavoured to derive answers from the philosophical writings of Schelling. See Butler 1997, Zizek 1996, Schelling 1997.

[19] A similar conception of a primal condition triggering an actual force had appeared in Freud's metapsychological study 'Repression' (1915), in which he had proposed a primal repression ('*Urverdrängung*') behind the repression proper ('*eigentliche Verdrängung*'). See Freud 1915: 141-158.

[20] For Haeckel's theory see Haeckel 1892, Gould 1977: 76-85.

[21] See Freud 1924: 171-179. Castration anxiety became one of the central points of concern in Freud's essay *Inhibitions, Symptoms and Anxiety* (Freud 1926: 75-175), and again in Lecture 32, 'Anxiety and Instinctual Life' (Freud 1933: 81-111), which immediately followed the retake on *The Ego and the Id* in Lecture 31.

[22] The analogies to which Freud refers emerged throughout the 1923 essay and were continued in Lecture 31 of the *New Introductory Lectures on Psychoanalysis*. For example, in *The Ego and the Id* he compared the ego with a man on horseback, where the ego is the rider and the id is the horse. In the final chapter of this text, he compared the ego alternately to a constitutional monarch, an analyst, a politician, and a unicellular creature. One could also use the 'topographical problem of the super-ego' to explain why Freud left the super-ego out of the title of his essay. However, perhaps it makes sense to say that this could also be due to the initial difficulty of the relation between ego and consciousness, which had prompted Freud to write the essay and introduce the id.

²³ For Kant, the categorical imperative is both *unconditional* (not determined by specific circumstances but only by itself) and *universal* (valid under all circumstances). For an illuminating discussion of Freud's references to Kant, see Assoun 1995: 207-223, 342-348.

²⁴ Since girls were not supposed to identify with their fathers if they wanted to grow up as 'mature women', Freud was forced to conclude that the feminine super-ego is weak, and that its dimensions of conscience, morality and self-criticism are underdeveloped in females. This has provided feminists with more than enough evidence to accuse Freud of misogyny. For Freud's views on female sexual development see Freud 1931: 221-243, Freud 1933: 112-135. The secondary literature dealing with Freud's views on women is too vast to mention. The reader who is simply looking for a thought-provoking exchange of ideas on the female super-ego will most certainly enjoy Millot 1984, and its subsequent discussion.

²⁵ This dualism of the drives was introduced for the first time three years before *The Ego and the Id*, in *Beyond the Pleasure Principle* (Freud 1920a: 52-53). The strength of the drives—like the strength of the ego—is relative, and dependent upon their interrelation. For example, the withdrawal of Eros makes Thanatos stronger, because the force of the latter is no longer challenged.

²⁶ On the topic of guilt, Freud produced a highly provocative and extremely stimulating idea when he pointed out: 'In many criminals, especially youthful ones, it is possible to detect a very powerful sense of guilt which existed before the crime, and is therefore not its result but its motive. It is as if it was a relief to be able to fasten this unconscious sense of guilt on to something real and immediate' (Freud 1923: 52). In the seventh chapter of the 1930 essay, *Civilisation and Its Discontents*, he returned to this point in order to state that guilt—in relation to the super-ego—compels a need for punishment (Freud 1930: 123-133). A magnificent description of this process has been provided by P.D. James in *Innocent Blood*: 'He felt again the sick excitement of the ten-year-old boy standing on the wet sands under Brighton pier with the roar of the sea in his ears, and holding in his small hands the spoils of his latest thefts. Then, as now, he felt no guilt. It was extraordinary that during the years of innocence he had lived under a perpetual burden of guilt; paradoxically, only when he became a thief had that weight lifted. It was the same with Julie's death. He knew that when he drove the knife into Mary Ducton's throat he would drive out guilt from his mind for ever' (James 1989: 210).

²⁷ Concerning the origin of the ego, Freud repeated that it was a part of the id which had been modified under the influence of Pcpt.-Cs, and a precipitate of identifications. The hypothesis of the bodily ego was absent from this account.

²⁸ Elaborating on this point, one might suggest that Freud's decision to leave the model open on the side of the id followed from his thesis that the id is dominated by the drives, which are both physical and psychic. A further interpretation might be that—in the *New Introductory Lectures*—Freud substituted the bodily id for the bodily ego.

²⁹ Through detailed study of Freud's manuscripts, Ilse Grubrich-Simitis has discovered that the drawing published in *New Introductory Lectures* had four predecessors, which proves that Freud had great difficulty in drawing a satisfactory model. However, in none of the preliminary sketches did the id occupy a greater space than the ego, and the super-ego was included in all but one. Freud seemed to have had particular trouble finding an adequate means of situating the ego in his new model. See Grubrich-Simitis 1996.

³⁰ Neither the authoritative compendium by Laplanche and Pontalis, nor the more recent encyclopaedias of psychoanalysis edited by Kaufmann, and by Roudinesco and Plon mention the fragment from *New Introductory Lectures*, in which Freud discusses the splitting of the ego. See Laplanche & Pontalis 1973: 427-429; Kaufmann 1993: 68-69; Roudinesco & Plon 1997: 180-181.

[31] On the basis of Lacan's discussion of this issue in his seminar XI (Lacan 1994: 32) I have elsewhere tried to develop a threefold time-structure of the unconscious (Nobus 1993). For an excellent critical survey of Freud's views on time, see Laget 1995.

[32] Is this the reason why Freud hesitated so much in trying to localise the ego in his new graphical representation?

[33] Stengers' text is a reprint of a paper that was first published under a different title. See Stengers 1989.

[34] This idea corresponded to what he said about the goal of psychoanalysis in his case-study of a homosexual woman. See Freud 1920b: 151.

[35] For a similar view in *The Ego and the Id,* see Freud 1923: 56.

THE SCHEMA L

Darian Leader

In 1954 a series of seminars on the use of mathematics in the social sciences was held at Unesco in Paris, under the auspices of the International Social Science Council. Claude Lévi-Strauss, who organised the meetings, spoke on formalisations of marriage and kinship structures. Among the other speakers, Piaget dealt with the use of group theory in the psychology of thought, and Benveniste addressed current problems in linguistics. Lacan chose the title 'Logical Patterns in the Practice of Psychoanalysis' and although this lecture was never published, the title, together with Lacan's participation in the seminar, gives an idea of the interest he had at that time in formalisation.[1] This interest would bear many fruits in Lacan's work, and it was in the same year that he would introduce to his seminar the logical pattern that he called the Schema L.[2] From its introduction in May 1955 (Lacan 1978: 275-288), where it condensed much of the teaching of that and the previous year, it would undergo metamorphosis, in 1958, into the Schema R of the paper 'On a question preliminary to any possible treatment of psychosis' (Lacan 1977: 179-225) and then continue to serve as a reference point for the schemas in 'Kant with Sade' (Lacan 1963 [1989])] and such later formalisations as the four discourses.

Just as the title of the 1954/5 seminar, 'The Ego in Freud's theory and in the technique of psychoanalysis', juxtaposes a reference to theory with one to technique, Lacan's introduction of the Schema L demonstrates this same preoccupation: formulating the principles of the theory of psychoanalytic treatment, and elaborating their consequences at the level of clinical work. If the Schema L sets out the relations of the imaginary and the symbolic, it was not simply a question, for Lacan, of formalising a theoretical development, but also, in deducing the technical implications of a theory. We can thus ask two questions: firstly, What sort of logical pattern does Schema L map out? And secondly, What does this pattern indicate in terms of clinical practice?

The status of diagrams

Despite the frequency with which diagrams are used in works of exposition and formalisation, it is curious how little is actually said about their status as representations or presentations of structure (cf. Shin 1994a). We are often told what a diagram means, but less often what a diagram is. The most sustained work on the logical function of the diagram was that of C.S. Peirce, a thinker dear to Lacan, and yet even in the supposedly comprehensive histories of logic by Bochenski (1961) and by Kneale and Kneale (1962) there is no discussion whatsoever of his contributions to this question. Although Peirce's work may be seen as the development of a tradition in the history of logic which stretches back to Sylvester and Clifford, who were interested in diagrams to deal with algebraic invariants, his work on logical diagrams remains largely of interest today to the historian rather than the philosopher of logic. As a recent commentator points out, diagrams may be introduced for the purposes of illustrating the categorical syllogism in textbooks of logic, but the kind of graphs that Peirce developed (and that Lacan would later take up), are rarely used or even discussed (cf. Shin 1994b). People tend to prefer algebras here, and we can note that Lacan would also turn to an algebraic treatment of structure only to lose interest relatively swiftly in favour of other modes of formalisation. When the Schema L is first introduced, it is described by Lacan as 'simply a way of fixing our ideas, called for by an infirmity in our discursive faculty' (Lacan 1978: 284). It is not even a model. Later on, as Lacan moved from algebraic ideas to topologies and knot theory, he would come to see the diagram as something closer to the real, not as a representation of a structure but as the structure itself, understood in the sense of a set of relations of invariance. In this sense, he is perhaps close to the Peircian idea of formalisation not as a metaphor or evocative image but as part of the very object of study itself, real in embodying the relations themselves with the inscription of the diagram. It is true that the first introduction of the Schema L makes few of the claims that would later be made on behalf of Lacan's knots, yet the passage to formalisation is none the less continuous. We might thus ask the question of why diagrams should matter to psychoanalysis in the first place.

Although psychoanalysis is a practice based on speaking, it deals with variables which cannot be identified purely and simply with words. It is difficult to find any psychoanalytic thinker who held that what psychoanalysis is concerned with is reducible to language, but rather than constructing a kind of mystique of the non-linguistic, Lacan was interested, on the contrary, in finding ways of tackling this field and in finding ways to express something about its structures. If Lacan is often associated with a kind of linguistic pantheism, it may be observed that the structural linguistics he appeals to invites consideration of that which is not words for the simple reason that if elements in a linguistic system take on their value through their difference from one another, there must be gaps in between elements. What speaking beings do with these gaps is one of the research questions that interested Lacan, particularly crucial given the fact that what speaking beings have to deal with in their lives revolves around encounters with what cannot be apprehended immediately within language. What matters to speaking beings are the moments of encountering something that does not have a preassigned place and that cannot be understood, like the problems of sex, reproduction and death. Infantile theories, as Freud called them, may be put into these gaps, covering them over with a signification, but, and this is the point Lacan would take up, when something cannot be assumed as a meaning it will take on the form of a relation. Logical relations come into play at exactly those points in the subject's life where meaning and understanding break down, and thus at the horizon of such structures will always be a set of impossibilities, impossible in the sense of contradictions and in the sense of impossible to say or make mean. Where words fail something else is appealed to, and in his early work Lacan identifies this with certain privileged images, later on revising this to include the libidinal object in phantasy, object a. Thus, wherever we find the subject of language S, we are likely to find another heterogeneous element, as in the formula for phantasy $ \$ \Diamond A $. And if an element is deemed 'non-linguistic', it will still have a relation to language, for example, as a limit point or an exclusion. In other words, while giving a central place to speech, it is the category of *relation* which now becomes paramount. We find here an elaboration of the idea implicit in much of the structuralism of the late 1940s and early 50s, that what cannot be expressed as a proposition takes on the form of a relation. A contradiction between A and B may thus take on the form of a further contradiction between C and D, the second pairing functioning not as a solution, a meaning given to the first contradiction, but a comparable impossibility. In Freudian terms, these contradictions will involve something unbearable to assume psychically - for example, the contradiction between the idea of mother as object of love and the idea of mother as a sexual being.

Relations this occupy a central place in any formulation of psychoanalysis which acknowledges that suffering makes many things unbearable. Lacan refines these considerations with the idea of a disparity of disparity of levels: the imaginary, the symbolic and the real, the subject, the image and the object. When a point of failure is encountered at one level, an element of another level will be introduced, and thus, although the initial framework will be set out in symbolic terms, the response to it will involve terms which are not strictly speaking symbolic. Lacan's early use of diagrams seems to be a response to the challenge of formalising such changes of level, while at the same time attempting to keep the transmission of psychoanalysis on its toes. Rather than encouraging his students to turn to the textbooks of psychoanalysis for answers, he invites a distancing from the imaginary functions of swift comprehension, and agenda that is maintained through his continual reformulation and changing commentaries on the formalisations he produced. Russell had pointed out that 'symbolism is useful because it makes things difficult', but Lacan tried to explain why exactly this should be the case: symbolism does not just make things difficult, it makes things difficult for imaginary assimilations, which have the function of blocking access to structures. Formalisation, for Lacan, was linked with this 'passage to the real', the letters of his schemas dislodging the place of words and thus, he argued, corresponding to an emptying out of meaning. And if meaning is a function of language, his schemas are the logical development of a theory of psychoanalysis which holds that not everything is reducible to language. If every major theory of psychoanalysis is in agreement that this is the case, it is a question as to why it is only Lacanian psychoanalysis that has elaborated, in serious fashion, a set of diagrams and a logical symbolism.

Since our subject here is Schema L, we can try to situate the context of its introduction in terms of this debate about the role of formalisation. The 1940s had seen the introduction of three basic domains of mathematical thought into what had traditionally been known as the human sciences: topology, structures of order, and algebra. Sharing an ideal with many contemporary mathematicians, thinkers like Lévi-Strauss were interested in formulating invariants, resulting less from the inductive study of objects than from the refining of models, to give access to structures considered as sets of relations between objects. During his stay in New York during the 1940s, Lévi-Strauss was working on the problem of kinship structures and realised that the sort of serious formalisation he needed was to be had from the mathematician. The first one he approached told him that he had no interest in marriage, but the second one, André Weyl, said that although he had no interest in marriage, he was very interested in the relation between marriages: it was this a question, as both Weyl and Lévi-Strauss understood, of sets of relations between elements rather than the priority of the 'element' itself (marriage). Particularly important to this project was the mathematical theory of groups, which allows the expression of invariance across a family of models. Groups are algebraic structures, and Lévi-Strauss attempted to demonstrate that kinship could best be studied within this framework. Marriage and descent are identified with operations that can be combined and inverted, as operations become linked to other operations. In addition to the algebraic current, there was also an interest in structures of order which dealt with choices, hierarchies and classifications, and topology with its concern with neighbourhood, proximity and barrier, notions that could make more precise the algebraic and order considerations. These methods can be traced in the work of Lévi-Strauss, and they would also be central to Lacan's reformulations of analytic theory and practice.

Such formal methods were the main tools emerging in anthropology and the new science of cybernetics, methods designed to treat not quantity but quality, not to measure but to ascertain relations. In their enthusiasm for these mathematical references, as Lévi-Strauss pointed out, what mattered was not just the use of mathematics itself in areas which had always been deemed 'non-mathematical', but rather the use of a new kind of mathematics, not new within mathematics itself, but new in the sense that relations of quality were being separated from those of classical measurement (Lévi-Strauss 1954). Scholars like Lévi-Strauss were interested, for example, in the formal developments of games theory since it seemed that such techniques shared a common problem with the field of linguistics. For example: if linguistics treats of the exchange of messages and if this exchange is homologous with the exchange of goods and services studied in economics, the two fields could admit of the same formal treatment, supplied in this instance by games theory. And similarly, if the state of a speech system is always governed by the immediately preceding states, language could be linked to the theory of servo-systems which constituted the field of study of cybernetics. It was thus a question of a mathematics of discontinuity, of changing states, rather than one of continuity and quantity, which charted, nonetheless, invariance over an apparently diverse range of phenomena.

Lacan would give a lecture at the Société Française de Psychanalyse in June 1955 on psychoanalysis and cybernetics, just a month after his introduction of the Schema L and shortly after his UNESCO intervention on logical patterns. Before examining the logic of the schema, we should note that its form appears close to that of diagrams used by Lévi-Strauss and by the cyberneticians. In 'The Elementary Structures of Kinship', we find the following schema for generalised exchange, which takes up the form of many previous diagrams found in the anthropology of kinship:

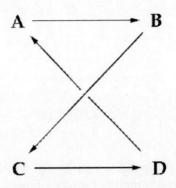

Source: Lévi-Strauss 1969: 178

And in cybernetics texts we find schemas such as the following[3]:

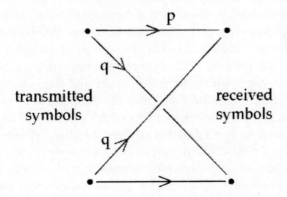

Source: Shannon & Weaver 1949: 76

The first version of Schema L is as follows:

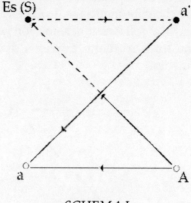

SCHEMA L
Source: Lacan 1978: 284

The Lévi-Strauss schema seems linked with Lacan's only if it is interpreted as a group, a mode of interpretation that Lévi-Strauss himself claims was absent from the use of his diagram, but the cybernetics example seems closer to the kind of question Lacan is dealing with at the time of the introduction of Schema L, as it represents a problem in the theory of discrete channels. On the left-hand side of the schema we have transmitted symbols, and on the right received symbols. The problem under consideration is the formalisation of message and noise, how a message becomes distorted in its transmission. As we will see, Lacan reformulates this in terms of the effect of the ego on the message of the unconscious. The cybernetics references are certainly important in trying to understand the conceptual framework in which Lacan is working, as can be seen from his adaptation of two further terms, the quilting point and the fading of the subject. Fading is a term taken from machine theory that was often used in cybernetics texts, and Lacan's 'point de capiton' seems to be a translation of the cyberneticians 'quilting point'.[4] Given his interest in both structural anthropology and cybernetics, it is curious that in Lacan's first attempts at formalisation we find little reference to the specific areas of mathematics which they privileged. Norbert Wiener's *Cybernetics* (1949) and Lévi-Strauss' *Elementary Structures of Kinship* (1949 [1969]) turn for a large part of their formalisation to algebra, but Lacan seems only to experiment with an explicitly algebraic approach in his seminar on object relations in 1956, several years after his encounter with the texts of cybernetics and the work of Lévi-Strauss, and his interest seems to be short-lived. It would be interesting to investigate the reasons for this. The article on the case of the Rat man, 'The Individual Myth of the Neurotic', does contain an algebraic thread, but it remains implicit, and the formulas which would appear in 1956 are not yet elaborated in this text (École de l'Orientation Lacanienne 1994: 128-48; Leader 1993). What seems to interest him in the early and mid 1950s is less the kind of massive introduction of algebras that we find, for example, in Wiener, than the use of diagrams which these texts made so important. Diagrams which, as we have seen, are concerned with relations between objects, not with objects as such.

The imaginary and symbolic axes

The Schema L is introduced by Lacan in May 1955 as an illustration of 'the problems raised by the ego and the other, language and speech' (Lacan 1978: 285). There are two central axes, a-a^1 of the imaginary relation, and S-A of the symbolic relation. The first line represents a formalisation of Lacan's theory of the ego as it had been developed since the late 1930s.[5] The mirror phase theory had shown how the human infant attains a mastery of its motor functions through capture in an image. An image is assumed which is first of all outside, be it in a mirror itself or in the image of another child. This identification, Lacan argues, will set the framework of the ego, a false identity made up of images which cover over the fragmentation and disunity of the body. a stands for the ego, and a^1 for the image of the other, indicating that the constitution of the ego always takes place in reference to the other, the specular little other whose image the subject has appropriated. The arrow goes from a^1 to a to indicate that the ego is first of all the other, that it is the image of the other that will constitute our own identity. This imaginary matrix will give the measure of the objects within the narcissistic field, and any addressee of the subject's speech will be caught up in this. As Lacan says, 'In so far as the subject brings them into relation with his own image, those with whom he speaks are also those with whom he identifies'.

The second axis of Schema L formalises what lies beyond the imaginary relation, the symbolic vector $\overline{AS}$. Once again the arrow goes from A to S, just as in the axis a-a^1 the arrow had gone from a^1 to a, indicating that what determines the subject comes not from within, but from without. In a sense, one could say that the axis S-A condenses the perspective of the structuralism of the late 1940s and early 1950s, with its notion that the human subject is merely an effect, a product in the dynamic of symbolic forces. The subject S will be strictly determined by the social structure and organisation, for example, of his or her culture. But the Other here refers not only to the set of elements that make up the symbolic world the subject is born into, but also the symbolic place which is present each time that someone speaks. Speaking, Lacan argues, supposes the presence of a place from which one is heard, which, even in the simplest case, may aim at a point beyond the flesh and blood listener.

It is this place which will determine the message of the subject, pinning down its meaning and providing a signification which may be very different from what the speaker 'intended'. Meaning comes from the Other, whether the subject knows it or not, a place which brings him into being and identifies him with certain fundamental significations. In his reading of the Rat Man case, for example, Lacan focuses on the details of the marriage of the patient's parents, demonstrating that the obsessional trance pinpointed by Freud could be interpreted as a reshuffling of these initial elements. All the tomfoolery about paying back the lieutenant and the lady at the post office might invite a host of interpretations in terms of object relations, but it can only be properly situated once it is linked to the family constellation preceding the subject's birth, which concerns an unpaid debt of the father. The linguistic Other made up of all the elements that were there 'before' the subject would thus have determining effects on his existence. Hence Lacan's definition of the Schema L in 1958 as 'signifying that the condition of the subject S (neurosis or psychosis) depends on what is unfolding in the Other A'(Lacan 1966: 549).

This unfolding in the Other, Lacan says:

> ...is articulated like a discourse (the unconscious is the discourse of the Other), whose syntax Freud first sought to define for those fragments that come to us in certain privileged moments, in dreams, in slips of the tongue, in flashes of wit. (Lacan 1966: 549)

These moments show that another discourse is breaking through, undoing the unity and coherence with which we wish to characterise our actions: another discourse which interrupts our intended messages, a discourse which is Other both in the sense that it is strange, that it seems to come from another level of our existence, and also in that it is linked to the discourse of our parents and family members, their desires and demands haunting our speech and structuring our lives even if we are completely unaware of their presence. The Other of the Schema L here is, as Lacan repeatedly points out, an 'absolute Other', beyond imaginary misrecognition, something which we fundamentally do not know, yet which, once its function is revealed, situates the true interlocutors of discourse: for example, the figures from one's childhood to whom one's actions may still be a demonstration.

But why, Lacan asks, should the subject be so interested in this discourse? The answer to this question gives Lacan a definition of the Schema L itself, and indicates the split nature of the speaking subject. He is interested as:

> ...a participator ...stretched out over the four corners of the schema: that is, S, his ineffable and stupid existence, a his objects, a^1 his ego, that is, that which is reflected of his form in his objects, and A, the place from which the question of his existence may be posed for him. (Lacan 1966: 549)

The received notion of the 'patient' or even the 'speaker' thus becomes dissolved: such imaginary ideas cannot be identified strictly with any one point on the schema as their unity is broken down into the four different places or, more precisely, the different sets of relations involved. At the Geneva Congress of the International Psycho-Analytic Association in 1955, Paula Heimann had set as the aim of analytic intervention an answer to the question 'why is the patient now doing what to whom?' (Heimann 1956: 307). Although this is no doubt a worthy agenda, it leaves 'the patient' as the one point in the sentence which lacks a question mark, and the Schema L may be read as an unpacking of this one term which is taken as a given. This might seem to suggest that the schema is simply a way of formalising identifications. The imaginary constitution of the ego is separated from the subject, implying that we need to know from which place a speaker is speaking. Dora's symptoms, for example, might make sense if we realise she is articulating them from the place of Mr K or her father. But the schema in fact concerns much more than the field of imaginary identification. Lacan had been developing for some years the idea that neurosis is equivalent to a question, formulated here in a general sense as 'What am I there?', with the 'there' referring to the discourse into which he is born. This question is the basic problem of his sex and what Lacan calls 'his contingency in being', the fact of whether he should be there or not, whether he was desired or not, wanted or unwanted: in other words, his value for the Other. Thus, beyond the register of identifications there is the question of the sense they might have assumed in a larger structure. If an imaginary element like an image is assumed, it is coming into the place of a gap in a more general framework, be it the place of an absence of meaning or of the point at which the Other fails to recognise the subject. And as this will naturally involve the relation of the subject to the desire of the parents, to his ideals and, in a broader sense, to the Oedipus complex itself, Lacan will expand the Schema L into the Schema R in 1958 (Lacan 1966: 553), and then offer a variant for the clinic of psychosis, the Schema I.

The technical question

The problem which the Schema L articulates is that we are blocked off from any kind of access to the key symbolic elements due to the imaginary axis of the ego. If there is a message to the unconscious linked to our childhood, our complexes and so on, the field of the imaginary acts as a kind of barrier which prevents their emergence. As Lacan says, the schema shows 'the interruption of full speech between the subject and the Other, and its detour by the two egos, a and a^1, and their imaginary relations'(Lacan 1981: 23). This recalls Freud's well known discussion of resistance in the transference. When the chain of free associations stops, Freud had argued, the subject has a particular image in his or her mind, probably linked to the analyst. The development of speech is thus blocked by the emergence of an image, and Freud would insist, in his technique, that this image be verbalised, and thus linked to the dialectic of speech. Lacan's conception of analysis at this stage of his work shows a concern with a similar problem, but it is not only the image of the analyst that is at stake, but rather the series of images which have amalgamated to constitute the ego. Thus in the Dora case, for example, Lacan points to the importance of the image of the brother, a pole of imaginary identification and an image through which she establishes a relation to her own body. As an image, it must be made to emerge in the chain of speech and thus, once spoken, it can enter the dialectic of the speech relation itself (Lacan 1966: 221).

The Schema L thus does more than simply formalise the contemporary theories of the imaginary and the symbolic relations. As its form indicates, what matters are the points of contact and resistance between the two vectors $\overline{a'a}$ and $\overline{AS}$. Lacan, after all, did not simply draw two axes, S-A and a-a¹, but rather a schema of their intersections, intersections which have consequences at the level of clinical practice. At the most immediate level, Lacan's schema is an indicator at the technical level of the handling of transference. The subject speaks of himself, sees himself, in the form of the *a*, the imaginary entity of the ego, and those to whom he speaks will be drawn into the field defined by the narcissistic relation, the analyst included. But rather than attempting to interpret all the references to the person of the analyst in the patient's speech, Lacan's schema supposes an Other, an unknown, absolute interlocutor, beyond the imaginary field. Colette Soler discusses one of Lacan's clinical examples which illustrates this attention to the function of the Other beyond the immediacy of the patient's supposed object relations. A man complains of an inability to use his hand, interpreted by his first analyst as a defence against the wish to masturbate. But, as Colette Soler points out, 'Lacan stresses the fact that, as listeners, we always have to ask ourselves what position the subject occupies with respect to the symbolic order that envelops him' (cf. Soler 1996: 47-55). In this case the man was brought up in the Islamic faith, and his father had once been accused of a crime, the punishment for which would have consisted in the loss of his hand. Thus, between subject and listener, the function of the Other, as symbolic context, is introduced, linked to the Koranic formula 'A thief must have his hand cut off'. The son's relation to the father is situated in this field with symbolic co-ordinates, and it is no doubt in the dynamic between these different elements that the analytic intervention should take place, introducing the symbolic terms beyond the imaginary relations the subject may be constituting. True speech here will constitute the link of subject and Other, working against what Lacan calls the 'wall of language', which moves in the contrary direction, tending towards 'the objectified other', the fact that language 'is there to found us in the Other (as well as) to drastically prevent us from understanding it' (Lacan 1978: 286). We can note that Lacan's work at this point involves something much more subtle than a simple division of the imaginary register of the ego and the register of language. Language is seen here as having a side which supports the objectifications of the ego, while the side which works against them is given a separate term, speech.

The difficulty of registering this latter view, that the opposition of ego and language is not so clear cut, is seen in the muddled questions and comments of the audience at the end of the year's seminar (Lacan 1978, chapters 22 and 24 passim). Just as language has a side which includes us, which makes us think we know what we are saying and that we have a place, there is equally the other side, which makes the terms strange to us, demonstrating, in true speech, that this is indeed an alien inclusion. True speech is thus situated at the juncture of the wall of language that Lacan refers to, in the moments when our mode of inclusion suddenly takes on a very new and altered sense or lack of sense.

Once speech is distinguished from language and the unknown interlocutor situated as its limit, the indications for transference become clear. If the function of the Other is to emerge as 'absolute Other', rather than interpreting the transference classically, it would make more sense to bet on the fact that when the patient's material seems to concern the person of the analyst, there is nevertheless something beyond. This technical implication is both Freudian and a real challenge to the practitioner. When the associations seem to concern the analyst, what could be more tempting than to interpret, especially as the material appears to concern him or herself. But Freud had pointed out in his paper 'The Dynamics of Transference' that the portion of the unconscious material which most satisfies the resistance will be the portion brought forward into the transference. The ideas which become affiliated with the analyst will not be those which exhaust the unconscious complex, but rather those most suited to resistance. Lacan's situating of the A beyond the axis a-a^1 formalises this notion, indicating that it is always necessary to aim at the unknown 'absolute Other' beyond the figures of the subject's ego. What a psychoanalysis should aim at, according to Lacan, is a true speech, a speech which links S to A, and thus undermines the imaginary axis as such: hence Lacan could posit as one of the goals of analysis, be it only a virtual one, the abolition of the ego (Lacan 1978: 287). Later in the seminar, Lacan elaborates this in greater detail, opposing the tendency of transference to operate between a and a^1 with the true axis S-A. The idea of an abolition of the ego is now refined into an idea of 'agreement', not in the sense of an understanding or a pact but rather in that 'it can be treated in the same way' (Lacan 1978: 374). The ego now can become something that it was not, it can 'get to the point where the subject is'.

This conception of analysis supposes the possibility of a real intersubjectivity: if the subject is to find his real interlocutors beyond the field of the ego, the line SA will be constituted, and the fact that there are subjects 'other than us' will be recognised. Lacan calls this his basic assumption, that 'authentically intersubjective relations exist' (Lacan 1978: 285), and in his discussions of this the terms 'true Others' and 'true subjects' are juxtaposed. The Other, at this stage of Lacan's work, is ultimately a subject, or, more precisely, the possibility of a subject, an idea that Lacan will not abandon until after his year long exploration of transference some six years later. From then on, Lacan will elaborate the thesis that at the heart of the Other is not a subject but an object, thus modifying radically the earlier theory that analysis involves as its limit an authentic intersubjective relation: it is now less a question of a link of subject to subject than a link of subject to object $\$ \Diamond A$, that is, the construction of phantasy. Since this object is not a subject, but a dumb condensation of libido, there cannot be an intersubjective relation.

The 1955 thesis of the course of analysis is very different from the ideas of Lacan's contemporaries, and the presentation of the schema in Book Two of the Seminar is clearly designed to serve as a critique and corrective to the principles of analysis elaborated by his contemporaries, particularly Maurice Bouvet (Bouvet 1968: 9-96). When Lacan's work was referred to in the late 1940s and early 1950s in the French language literature, it was generally linked simply to an emphasis on identifications, just as today it is often caricatured in terms of an exclusive concern with language. Reduced to this, it was relatively harmless, and could be cited by thinkers like Bouvet in the course of arguments about the progression of treatment turning around the centrality of the image of the analyst.[6] As the main site of projection, the analyst would play host both to ideals and to internal objects, and the ongoing task for the analyst would be to regulate the 'distance' between himself and the patient, where distance is defined as 'the gap which separates the way in which a subject expresses his instinctual drives from how he would express them if the process of "handling" or "managing" these expressions did not interfere' (1958: 211). Lacan calls this a 'perverted inflection' of analytic technique: the subject is urged to aggregate the fragmented parts of himself, be they pregenital elements, partial drives or the succession of partial objects, into the ego. And if the technical focus is on the imaginary and the pregenital, these parts will be channelled through the intermediary of the image of the analyst. In terms of the Schema L, the key variable is a^1, through which all the messy bits and pieces of the partial drives will be bound together, not A, the symbolic reference beyond the axis a-a^1. What this leads to, Lacan says, is a strange kind of communion, illustrated literally in the image of the phallic host taken from Bouvet.[7] As partial objects are assumed through the image of the analyst, the latter will finally be consumed himself in a eucharistic gesture: the one is swallowed by the other. Later, in the seminar on 'Formations of the Unconscious' (1957-8), Lacan will take up this reference once again, but this time with a focus on the role of the castration complex, as it is ignored in Bouvet's elaborations, and he will reformulate Bouvet's theory of distance in Seminar XI (1963-4) in terms of the distance between I and a. Where Bouvet aims to reduce distance to zero, Lacan argues for precisely the opposite, to maintain distance between I and a, just as in the Schema L it is a question of working against the assimilation of A to a^1.

Transformation

In 1956, Lacan could call Schema L a 'schema of analytic communication' (Lacan 1981: 181). It formalised his work on the relations of the imaginary and the symbolic and provided a kind of compass for plotting the transference. But by early 1958, he is working on redrafting the schema, which will eventually take the form of the Schema R. After its introduction in the Seminar Two, Schema L is used once more in the seminar on the psychoses to illustrate the particular circuit of the speech relation in the celebrated 'Truie' example that Lacan studies in such detail. The S of the schema may be referred to in two ways: by an address to the Other and subsequently receiving one's message in an inverted form, or by allusion. In the 'Truie' example, Lacan argues, there's no Other functioning, which throws the subject back onto the imaginary axis a-a^1: what concerns the S is not received from the Other but is actually said by the little other, the a of the schema. The 'Truie' alludes to what she is as a subject. If the S is 'the thing which has no name'(Lacan 1981: 182) as such, it may be named once the circuit from S to A has been completed; but if in psychosis, this circuit is ruled out to start with, in its place the naming can emerge from the little other which is the subject itself. This use of the Schema L to clarify clinical material is continued in the following year, where Lacan takes object relations as his theme. In his readings of Freud's cases of the female homosexual and of Dora, it functions to map out the different places which are at play in the material, an equilibrium which, in both cases, is disturbed at precise moments. With Dora, we find the following schema:

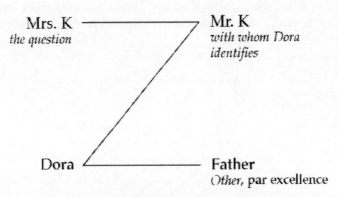

Source: Lacan 1994: 143

Mrs K is in the place of the S, the father in that of the Other, and Dora and Mr K share the imaginary axis a-a^1. We might be surprised to see that it is not Dora herself who is in the place of the S, but this is not to say that she is not concerned: Lacan is showing how the subject is in a sense stretched out over all four corners of the schema, not just in the imaginary axis, but also in between the two crucial symbolic co-ordinates of Mrs K and the father. The schema shows why Mr K's remark that his wife does not count for him had such disastrous effects: Mrs K is loved by Dora's father beyond Dora, just as Dora, or so she thinks, is loved by Mr K beyond Mrs K. When he devalues his wife with the ill-judged remark, she no longer has a place in the circuit and the carefully maintained triangles collapse. If Dora is not loved by Mr K beyond Mrs K, then Dora's own place in the triangle with her father, herself and Mrs K is suddenly put into question.

Lacan's readings of these cases indicates the direction of his interests at this point in the 50s. The Schema L is setting out the dynamics of imaginary and symbolic axes, but the material of the cases is adding something more: basically, the Oedipus complex. It is possible to understand Lacan's development of the Schema now as an attempt to add the Oedipal structure to the imaginary-symbolic dynamic, not in the sense that it was ever properly absent, but rather implicit in the formulation. The original version of the schema contains as one of its poles the Other, but now the question is to formalise those co-ordinates which 'identify the Other in the Oedipus complex' (Lacan 1966: 551).

In other words, to combine the paternal metaphor with the Schema L. If the Other involves the functioning of the father, this has to be added and situated in relation to the other poles of the schema, the mother, the phallus, the ideal and so on. Thus the lower right hand corner of the Schema L - the A - becomes redrafted in the more complex topology of the new schema.

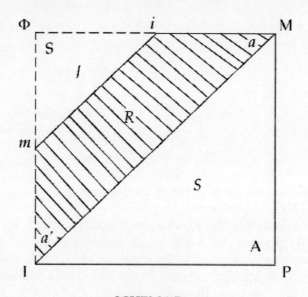

SCHEMA R
Source: Lacan 1966: 553

The original terms S, a, a^1, A are present in the new schema, but they are each capped with a second term: Φ, M, I, P respectively, with Φ as the phallus, M as 'the signifier of the primordial object', and P as 'the position in A of the Name of the Father' (Lacan 1966: 553). The basic structure is thus not abandoned but enriched, to provide a schema for the structuring of the subject's reality. Whereas in the earlier version, it was a question of the imaginary and symbolic, now the real is added and the function of the father in binding the orders together is emphasised. In psychosis, if the Name of the father is foreclosed, this schema will be fundamentally different, and Jacques-Alain Miller has studied the process of transformation which turns the Schema R in to the Schema I, in which the Ideal comes into the place of the missing Name of the Father (Miller 1979).

What Lacan first introduced as a schema of 'analytic communication', elaborated during the period of his interest in cybernetics would thus serve not only to render the theory of the first two seminars more succinct, but also as a kind of instrument to measure the orientations of technique. Even as his ideas would evolve and often differ markedly from earlier formulations, it maintains a robustness in Lacan's work which is testified to by its incorporation into the Schema R and, one might argue, into later formalisations. This is not only an indication of the value of the semantics of the Schema, but also of the power of its structure. Its repeated reformulation in his work shows the commitment to formalisation which is characteristic of Lacan's approach and supports the view he would put forward in 'Kant with Sade' that any formalisation of the structure of the subject must be, given the function of the unconscious, quaternion (Lacan 1966: 774).

Notes

[1] See International Social Science Council Report 1953-59: 30. Claude Lévi-Strauss kindly supplied me with details of these seminars.

[2] It is curious that Lacan chose the term 'pattern' in his title, given its associations not just in psychoanalytic theory but in psychology. Cf. Lacan 1981: 29.

[3] To see how contemporary theories of communication were appropriated by the analytic community in a way very different from that of Lacan, one may consult Rapaport's review of Wiener's *Cybernetics* (Rapaport 1950).

[4] Gerry Sullivan pointed out that the concept 'quilting point' comes from the work of Ashby.

[5] See the special issue of *La Lettre Mensuelle*, No. 50 (École de la Cause Freudienne 1986).

[6] See, for instance, Bouvet 1953.

[7] Lacan's critique of Bouvet must be one of the most sustained polemics in the history of psychoanalysis, stretching from the early 50s to the start of the 60s. The Bouvet case with the reference to the phallic host is 'Incidences thérapeutiques de la prise de conscience de l'envie du pénis dans la névrose obsessionnelle féminine' (Bouvet 1950).

AUTISM AND TOPOLOGY

Bernard Burgoyne

The autistic child struggles to give expression to what other people find simple. The complexities confronting the child facing such difficulties seem miles away from the assumed ease of expression of the others. 'I'—'you': simple. 'You force me to hide my love for you': easy. 'You want me to cut off my love for you, as if it has no right to exist': no problem. A child who struggles with such problems may well be confronting aspects of the human condition that other people prefer to leave unexpressed.

The first formulations given to the structure underlying the suffering of the autistic child were proposed by Kanner in the 1940s[1]: many clinicians still work closely with Kanner's differentiations even today. Kanner organised the structure of the difficulties of the autistic child around a small number of significant symptoms: the autistic child has difficulty in relating to others, and suffers from particular disturbances of speech. Such a child 'hates inconsistency, incompleteness, or ambiguity' and likes things to stay in the same place: people upset this, and so the child usually prefers contact with its objects to involvements with others. Words are tied rigidly to their first context; often there is echolalia (the echoing of the speech of others); there is regularly present a systematic confusion in the use of pronouns—particularly of 'you' and 'I'.

The radically different ways in which the autistic child and the neurotic or normal person experience the structure of their world have struck commentators: 'The child's experience of the world differs radically from ours'.[2] Of course, what is begged here is any cogent notion of 'experience' and 'world', and this refusal to problematise either affects both conceptualisation and diagnosis. The disturbances of speech have a four-to-one sex ratio—more boys than girls. Thus there is here an early indication that there is something in play which has to do with the reality of sexual difference, as it becomes determined by the conflicts of Oedipal loves. There is a passion for sameness: so, already, there is in such a child's life a problem of differentiation—a problem of differentiation in space. Love, space, and speech. In the original psychiatric handling of these problems, no one in the vicinity of an autistic child had any idea how to relate these terms. Some—like

Bettelheim—tried, and their work is what has so far sustained new directions of work in this field.

The autistic child has problems of relating to others; has problems of language; and has problems in the structuring of space, and of time. The challenge presented to the psychiatric world by these children was daunting, but even where it has been perceived, it has not been given an adequate response.[3]

Kanner took some while to develop his ideas, and in turn it took some time for them to have a pervasive effect in the domains of psychiatry and of psychotherapy. It has taken even longer before any serious attempt has been made to address the questions of mathematical structure that underlie the symptoms of this kind of suffering. From the start, Freud's project had related the fields of passion, suffering, and structure, but after this start, the field of 'finding words to say it' had become more and more divorced from an investigation of the way in which human beings are caught up in the effects of structure.

The response in the world of psychoanalysis has—in the Anglo-Saxon world—been given its main outline by a split, a division between two terms. The two terms were known to the Greeks: *pathema* and *mathema*—the latter term defines that which can be structured and transmitted to new generations, while the former term represents the suffering associated with this transmission. The links between the two in English analytical culture have long been lost. Some schools erect an artificial divide between the two, establishing a self-denying ordinance which leaves important tools permanently outside the consulting room: 'ultimately, it is beyond the power of mind to study itself, or to express non-verbal mental experiences in words' (Tustin 1986: 168). One effect of this divorce of structure and feeling is to force on clinical conceptualisation a form of grasping at presumed 'poetical' forms of expression. The following fairly representative example shows some of the limitations of this analytical approach: '"flowing-over-at-oneness" is the process by which the illusion of "primal unity" is maintained' (Maiello 1997: 10).[4]

How can we tell what is going on with these children? Many analysts want to answer this question by remaining within the domain of their 'common sense'. There are indications in Freud that such approaches have limitations[5]—limitations which are so severe that adopting such an approach to this problem forfeits all chance of gaining co-ordinates that do anything other than stay within the surface of the symptoms from which the child suffers.

In his book *The Empty Fortress*, Bettelheim draws an outline of the pain and isolation of the autistic child. He describes, in particular, the world of Laurie, one of the children at his school, who, when she arrived, had not spoken for over four years. Bettelheim and his co-workers eventually brought her to what he calls 'the verge of speech', before she was withdrawn by her parents. Laurie was voicing words, but weakly: she was uttering them so weakly that her therapists were not 'sure she had said them', and her parents, it seems, did not want to risk the experiment of listening to what she was now about to put into words.

Marcia also was mute when she arrived at the school; she learned to speak, but not in any 'organised language'. Her staring into space was interspersed with murmurings: Bettelheim comments on her whispered phrase 'udder/mudder' with its allusion to mother and murder. He links her dawning ability to distinguish separately parts of her body with her becoming able to speak—particularly with her starting to develop the use of pronouns: 'as with all autistic children Marcia's difficulties with pronouns had to do with her struggle to separate herself... from her world' (Bettelheim 1967: 209). Yes, but 'has to do' is very vague, and how it is that children can build a world as they acquire a facility in language? How it is that the outlines of this world are already built for them? How it is that they inherit problems that the adults blithely assume to be soluble, given the resources of discrimination, heedlessness and disregard freely available to the adult? All these questions are left in the air by Bettelheim's formulations. He focuses on language in almost every circumstance: in relation to the body, in relation to the children themselves, in relation to their involvement with others. His belief in 'true speech' being fairly lacking in problems—pretty 'crystal-clear'—leaves him somewhat uneasy in the way that he treats language; but with much detail of this kind in all of his cases he effectively presents the autistic child as having a problem in distinguishing 'normally' separated signifying terms.[6]

Joey was a child who learned a systematic reversal of pronouns: he called himself 'you' and 'the adult' that he was talking to 'I'. Bettelheim is aware that this requires considerable skill—skill that he describes as 'logical'. It is not easy, says Bettelheim, 'to not once make the mistake of using pronouns "correctly"' (Bettelheim 1967: 243). Somehow Bettelheim was aware from the start that these problems of language and logic were connected, and that the question of their relation went beyond the means he was bringing to bear on these issues. He flags these problems in almost every paragraph that he writes, while being unable to formulate or to resolve them. Still, he persevered with the children, and in his determination he sought further than most for some solutions in this domain.

Bettelheim quoted from the French psychoanalyst Edouard Pichon. To be sure, he had not read Pichon directly, but he was astute enough to realise that a passage in the work of Despert drawing on Pichon's work in a commentary on Kanner, has a central importance. The passage is as follows:

> Pichon, in his studies of language development, has pointed out that the first and foremost requirement for language to arise and develop is what he calls 'la fonction appetitive'—the appetition for language... meaning literally 'the direction of desire towards an object or purpose' ...Appetition for language is manifested in infants long before language is constituted and sentence formation in its most rudimentary form appears. In fact, it can be said that it precedes the first phonetic forms and represents the first stage of speech as a means of communication. This appetition for language is conspicuously lacking in the autistic and schizophrenic child, even though coincidentally the child may have acquired an extremely large vocabulary... (Bettelheim 1967: 428)[7]

Bettelheim does not generally consider questions of language in relation to, or in connection with, problems of space. Autistic children, he says, withdraw from the difficulties of relating space and time, so that only problems of space remain[8]: 'this they try to master through sameness or boundary behaviour' (Bettelheim 1967:52). There are two topological properties here: lack of separation, and structuring by boundary or frontier. In Laurie's case, says Bettelheim, her torn strips of paper 'set down boundaries between... her world... and the rest of the world'; she tore a very long strip of paper, and 'used it to connect her buggy to her bed. Next what she had thus linked together became a boundary that separated her very own world from the rest of the room' (Bettelheim 1967: 136-7). The desperate difficulties encountered by the child in constructing a world and, within it, a separate place for its own being repeat case after case. Bettelheim gives astute and lovingly focussed attention to the children in his care. The eyes and ears of this physician are acutely attuned, but they function separately; on the one hand the child has problems about space; on the other hand there is something in its use of language that is not quite right. If he had worked with access not only to the work of Pichon, but also to the later developments of formalisation in the French School—brought into being and then articulated by Lacan—he would have been able to move towards the concept of a space of signifying terms, of phrases equipped with the spatial structure given to them by assignations of meaning, and its shift.[9]

Aware that his scattered responses need some kind of link, Bettelheim attempts to give some connection to the problems of language and of space, towards the end of his book. He recognises that there is some dependency on language and representation in the successes of autistic children in differentiating and adopting such categories as 'above', 'below', 'underneath', and 'to the right'. He falls back on what is effectively a psychological jargon in order to describe this—'they have conquered', he says, 'representational space'.[10] Bettelheim knew that no such notion was well developed in the United States in the 1960s. The situation has not changed even today.[11] He fools himself a little, developing his argument as if, to progress further, these categories need to acquire some substance. 'Perhaps' he says 'the "failure" of development should be fixed at a point of transition between the first creation of a world of inner representation, and the use of those representations as symbolic tools of thought' (Bettelheim 1967: 457). He knows that these terms are only loosely fictive representations of the real world of the child, and that not much can be hoped of them. A real formalisation at this point would be a considerable achievement, but, instead of proceeding in this direction, he concludes: 'the children's use of symbols is weak and spotty. Their inner world of representation is not stable enough'.

The passion of Bettelheim's account of the children he worked with drove him to seek conceptualisations of their distress: his search was wide-ranging and devoted. But conceptual instruments of greater clarity are needed if such subtle and disturbing phenomena are to be caught in a net that will provide an adequate response to the suffering of these children. Freud's early development of the concept of unconscious structure provides such an apparatus.

Freud was impelled to develop the notion of structure in the context of his early work with hypnotic theory and practice. In the early years of the 1880s, he had been particularly impressed by the hypnotic phenomenon of negative hallucination, in which a person can be induced to fail to perceive consciously what on some other level they can actually perceive. Freud rapidly extended this phenomenon from the hypnotic domain to the realities of everyday life, by establishing that the defence of repression produces exactly the same effect. Unconscious knowledge and perception, once created by repression, produce the conditions for a conscious failure to perceive. In this situation, to find the real connection between events in consciousness often demands an access to inaccessible material; this real connection is then unavailable, and the ego confronts a gap in consciousness. Freud claims that the ego seems to be impelled to a compulsive filling-in of such gaps, and that when such real connections are unavailable, the ego fabricates connections—fictive and distortive accounts of the world—simply because it cannot bear to construct an account that bears more closely on the real nature of the world.[12]

Freud found this concept of false connection to be associated with the phenomena of negative hallucination: these in turn held a central place in the ideogenic theories of hypnotism, and Freud gave this functioning of false connection a central place in the conceptual apparatus of psychoanalysis. Repeatedly Freud comes back to these twin phenomena—of negative hallucination and false connection—that had most struck him in his work with Bernheim. It is this concept of hallucination around which he attempts to construct his notion of consciousness.[13] It is also this step—of placing false connection at the heart of the functioning of consciousness—which challenges the classical world-view of psychological science.

Since repression in neurosis and normality is ubiquitous, it seems that there is no escape from the effects of false connection, no domain which is sheltered from its consequences. In everyday life, and in the arts and sciences—everywhere that theory is constructed—fabricated reality takes the place of access to what is real in people's lives. This is an epistemological problem: if one stays in the domain of consciousness, according to Freud, it seems that no co-ordinates exist that would allow one to navigate the world.[14] Freud's formulation, then, is that everyday consciousness fabricates realities which misrepresent the nature of the world: that underneath such errant reality lies the structure of the unconscious.

Two questions arise. Firstly, does this underlying structure give a more reliable orientation to the world? Freud's answer is 'yes'. Secondly, since structure is found also in the world of mathematics, what relations exist between unconscious structure and the structure of mathematics? Freud is strangely silent on this question: other analysts have tried to answer it for him.

This is the central divide which has separated Latin and Anglo-Saxon schools of analysts. The wager taken up by the Anglo-Saxon schools has been that somehow the effects of false connection can be evaded—somewhere, according to this bet, there is a domain of the conscious ego where it is free from unconscious conflict, where it can be trusted. In such a domain, sciences can be built,[15] foundations laid out for common sense. Latin psychoanalysts will have nothing to do with this wager—they leave this field to those whose clinical orientation is consistent with that of ego-psychology, whose work was organised around a flight from the consequences of false connection, both in the clinical and in the conceptual domain.

However, Franco-Hispanic schools have their own wager. It is that the ego, far from escaping from this distortive domain, is characterised by its operations: if any way out of this field is to be found, it will then have to come from what Freud termed the field of structure.

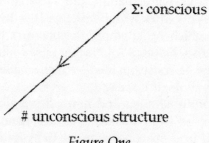

Figure One.

This way of formulating Freud's project sees the direction of analytical work as moving from the shifting field of false connections characteristic of consciousness—a field that includes the level of the symptom and its displacements—to the relatively stable level of unconscious structure that causes the symptom and underlies it. Pathways are opened up from the domain of consciousness to the underlying structure, by the processes that Freud called 'free-association': all these processes have in common the outwitting of the ego, which seeks to block the advance of such pathways by forms of resistance. In so far as they gain access to material otherwise cut off from association, Freud calls these pathways 'logical threads'[16] and, in so doing, he is proposing that there exists a close connection between forms of analytical technique and the functioning of logic. It is this claim that needs some investigation: the logic that Freud is actually appealing to is the classical 'dialectical method'[17] invented by Socrates—but how Freud came to formulate the psychoanalytical situation in these terms is rarely explained.

Freud took up the theory of Socratic dialectic from the translation that he made in 1879 of Mill's lengthy review of the text that his friend Grote[18] had produced on the primary importance of the technique of Socratic dialectic in the development of Greek political theory and in the development of Greek science.[19]

Grote and Mill carefully distinguished the Socratic Plato—the Plato of what they called 'negative dialectics'—from the later Plato of 'dogmatic' ideals. They cherished the former, and had great suspicion of the latter.[20] In his first drafting of his *Autobiography*, Mill wrote: 'I have ever felt myself, beyond any modern that I know of except my father, and perhaps beyond even him, a pupil of Plato, and cast in the mould of his dialectics'. It was this position that Grote was to surpass in the mid 1860s; and Freud in turn was to take up this mantle from Grote before the end of the following decade.

Freud's argument is that 'negative dialectic' operates on pathological defence, producing by its action a field of connections to consciousness that had been cut by the activity of defence. His early theory of defence centres round the structure of neurosis being organised around the functioning of repression. The unconscious is constructed by the ego finding certain representations intolerable,[21] and so relegating them, hiding them away so that they are outside the domain of critical enquiry. However, if the ego can be forced to enter into a connection with this repressed material, then the unconscious will be brought into logical contact with the representations of consciousness, and such logical threads will have re-established the functions of logic in the human soul. The means that Freud introduces in order to achieve this all fall under the category of 'catching the ego unawares'. Such a functioning of surprise is built into the clinical protocol for his method of free association, and the whole gamut of what he will subsequently call 'recommendations for technique'.[22]

In this approach to things, Freud is concerned with two domains, the one—governed by the conscious ego—separated completely from the other. It is this spatial separation of the conscious ego from the repressed material that constitutes the unconscious, which gives Freud his first clearly topological problems. He has a space that is disconnected: his aim is to build pathways between its two parts. What makes up the material of this particular space? *Representations*[23]—not concepts, not images, not ideas, and not feelings. The topological formulation of the problem is that of establishing connectivities between two otherwise disjoint domains of representation—a problem which is the same as that of re-establishing a domain of critical reason where previously the dominant dynamic was that of neurotic flight.

What has all of this to do with the plight of the autistic child? In the case of the adult, Freud is committed to searching for the topological realities that underlie and in fact cause neurotic suffering. In the case of the child, beneath the everyday suffering there is a structure with which the child struggles. There are these indications in Freud that the problem is topological. The topological structure of the child's unconscious is what it inherits from the world of the adults and, in the case of autism, it is this underlying structure that we intend to find.

Theodor Gomperz was the intermediary who introduced Freud to the world of Socratic logic.[24] In his youth, this eminent philosopher suffered from just the kind of inheritance of structure to which children are subject in relation to those that they love. In his relation to Mill, Gomperz had played out, recapitulated, and—in some ways—almost exactly repeated the stage-setting of Mill's childhood loves. John Stuart Mill's father, James Mill, had been born into the family of a blacksmith working on the estate of a Scottish laird. He was seen to show promise, and was taken in by this noble family and educated by them. When they moved to London in 1802 to participate in London politics, he moved with them. He fell in love with their daughter: a quite impossible love at that time for two people coming from such different social backgrounds. Even if she had known of this love and had responded, it would have been impossible. Mill named his son after this impossible love: the Scottish laird was Sir John Stuart, and the son born to James Mill in 1806 was given as his first names the name of this other 'father'. Destiny had already set a direction for John Stuart Mill decades before he was born. The man who was to become England's leading theorist of freedom, the theorist who maintained that established directions of policy are always alterable by discourse, struggled against this framework all his life. In questions of politics he would challenge fixed opinion, in his personal life his nervous breakdowns, and—in particular—his falling in love, recapitulated the phantasies and the dreams of his father.

James Mill chose a wife—Harriet—who was 'thoroughly obedient to her lord' (Bain, cited in Kamm 1977: 11). John Stuart Mill in his turn fell impossibly in love with a married woman—one with the same first name as his mother—a woman who swept him off his feet at the first glance. Harriet Taylor became the pole star around which his love revolved. For seventeen years this love was impossible to realise: only after her husband's death would they marry.

This was the family that Theodor Gomperz visited when he travelled to England to see Mill. He had fallen impossibly in love with Harriet Taylor's daughter, Helen. After the death of Harriet in 1858, her daughter Helen had devoted herself to caring for Mill. In the summer of 1862, as Harriet and Mill returned from a holiday in Greece, they called on Gomperz in Vienna: he was their guide to the city.

Gomperz had fallen in love with Helen in this summer of 1862. He followed the couple to London later that winter, nurturing the aim of gaining her hand. Throughout the winter months he lived with the torture of this impossible love. Finally, in mid-April, he proposed to Mill that he visit them in Avignon, in the hope that his approaches would be well received. (Mineka & Lindley 1972: 854) Mill's response to his letter was brusque: 'come... if you like'.

The rebuttal to his hopes became clearer as the summer approached. By May or June Gomperz was the victim of delusions of persecution. At first Mill was surprised, but by the end of July was actively trying to persuade Gomperz to face the reality of his situation, whilst offering him some consolations. 'I do not think you have any chance'; 'You are not 'maligned'; 'What makes this delusion so painful to us is the measure it gives us of what you are suffering from other causes' (Mill to Gomperz June 16th & July 29th, 1863 in Mineka & Lindley).

By September, Mill was continuing to urge clarity, while increasing the range of real contact that he could offer to his colleague. 'The only way to clear up misunderstandings is to speak plainly about them'— this while offering to Gomperz the German language publication rights to *Utilitarianism*.[25]

This was the man then who was later to offer Freud the chance of translating the material of the final volume of his German edition of Mill's *Works*. One of the four essays in this volume was Mill's commentary on Grote's account of dialectic. Freud was later to have Gomperz's wife as an analysand, and to try to adduce his son Heinrich to become a philosopher of the analytical movement. This great series

200 *Autism and Topology*

of events—this history of love—contained one key event: Freud's translation of Mill's extensive commentaries on Socratic dialectic. By means of these links, the method of deductive logic was put into a central place in the protocol that Freud devised for the analytical relation.

The detail of such a method is not readily available to a child. These histories of Mill and Gomperz show that even the adult—perhaps more than the child—is caught up in the signifying world of others. Like the autistic child, John Stuart Mill and Theodor Gomperz each found themselves in turn caught in a net of signifying terms set up and maintained by a previous generation.[26] Any individual finds that this net builds the world from within which they negotiate—adequately or badly—the problems and the destinies of their loves. In all of these histories, adults and children are caught up in determinations that interrelate history, structure, and love.

In this context of the dependency between structure and love, Lacan introduces two stories about Achilles.[27] The first is a fable, the second a version of the Homeric history of Troy: both stories involve the structure of a space.

In one of the paradoxes of motion devised by the Greeks—as part of what can be seen as the movement towards a science of physics, governed by rules of criticism and consequence—the proposition is that Achilles is racing a tortoise, which has a head start.[28] The problem is to determine the process by which Achilles closes the gap, and then to determine the limit point at which Achilles catches up with the tortoise. As with any analysis, there are many ways to do it: I will stay—as does Lacan—with the paradoxical form given to it by Zeno. Suppose Achilles first halves the distance; he will still have some way to go. After he has halved the remaining distance, there is still some work left for him. In fact, in this account, he has an *infinite* labour before he can be abreast of this other creature. Such infinities are part of everyday life—work or play. The notion put forward by mathematicians in order to analyse them is that of a limit, of a bounding or end point.

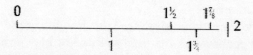

Figure Two. Given any containing region or 'neighbourhood' of 2, all the points after a given point will be caught in it.

Achilles sets himself his end—to achieve his aim he finds that he has first to go through this 'infinity' of steps. Unless something inhibits him, the act will take place, even though it has this infinite series of prerequisites. His action, in other words, is already caught up in the structure of a space.

Lacan's other story is in many ways somewhat similar. This time it concerns the involvement of Achilles with another creature—his girlfriend, Briseis. She has been stolen by his chieftain, Agamemnon. When Achilles returns to camp and discovers the theft, he rushes to confront his warlord, and is about to draw his sword. Now, even in Greek times, this would have been called an imprudent act. A modern commentator might suggest that prudence alone might have determined what came next; but this was not the type of explanation sought for by the Greeks. The goddess Athena swept down from the sky and, grabbing Achilles by the hair, pulled him back. It is difficult to draw a sword when you are being pulled back like that. So here there is a limit, a point that is seemingly impossible to reach: in this case it leads to an action that is not taken.

Freud introduces such themes in his discussion of the sexual drive: the sexual drive, he says, has an end, or aim.[29] A series of points are passed through as preliminaries to achieving this aim: Freud calls these points of *Vorlust*—forepleasure.

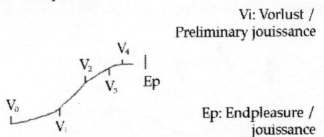

Vi: Vorlust / Preliminary jouissance

Ep: Endpleasure / jouissance

Figure Three. Given any neighbourhood of Ep, all Vn, after a certain n, will be caught in it.

Such points are staging points for lingerings at points preliminary to the limit-point of the sexual aim. One form of sexual perversion described by Freud is defined by such topology—that of a limit point not reached. Other forms of perversion—such as extension of the bodily zone aimed at[30]—have similar topological determinations.

Lacan asks us to consider the infinities of these sequences in the context of the sexual relation between Briseis and Achilles. The two are in bed together. Achilles is making love to her; Lacan asks us to envisage the proceedings. Achilles is approaching a point of orgasm: he cries 'that's it; we've got there'. Is it then over? The woman's response says Lacan, is *'encore'*: 'no, that's not it, *encore'*. Are these then the kinds of limits experienced by a woman? For the woman—says Lacan—there is something in addition to *this* limiting process, something more—*en plus*. She demands the approach to another limit, something not initially envisaged by the man. These spaces of sexual excitation and satisfaction—or dissatisfaction—are embedded in a world of phrases—signifying spaces.[31] Throughout this process, her response is 'more': as it reaches its end, her response is the same. The woman and the man are involved in a dispute—a quarrel about limits.

In any space—not only in signifying spaces—a sequence of points can determine a limit. The spatial structure can be generated by means of these limits: but there exists a range of other operations that can generate the structure of a space. One notion that is able to generate the field of topology is that of an open set[32]: an open set protects its members from intrusion from points of the exterior. Take any collection, or set, of points—where the points can be phrases, they can be points of excitation, they can be re-transcriptions of memory, they can be whatever constitutes the material of the space you wish to investigate in this way. Then an open set is any set such that all sequences of points in the exterior of the set have limit points that fail to penetrate into the set.

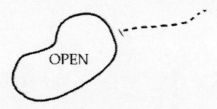

Figure Four.

You can formulate this property in terms of an interdiction: 'S is open' means that the limit of any sequence approaching from the outside of S is forbidden to be in S. S can be a collection of phrases being struggled with by the child: S can be any state or moment of the human soul.

An important notion which stems from that of an open set, is that of a neighbourhood. A neighbourhood of a point has the property that there always exists within it an open set surrounding that point. That is, a neighbourhood of a point always gives the ability to retreat to a collection within it that protects from intrusion from outside.

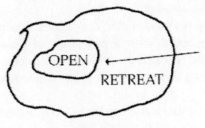

Figure Five.

In a space of phrases, a neighbourhood of a particular phrase would allow a retreat into a collection of phrases within, any point of which is protected from intrusion by sequences of phrases in the exterior. These notions are more than sufficient to formulate the notions grasped at by Bettelheim: 'a world of representations... as symbolic tools of thought' (Bettelheim 1967:457). The phrase that most succinctly describes what Bettelheim was groping for is that of a space of signifiers. Open sets are as able as limit points to determine the properties of the space: if you know the open sets that are available, then you know all the topological properties of the space.

If one needs to retreat, in the above sense, the question that is pertinent, often urgent, is how many open sets are available in a given space. There may be few, or many. The ability to retreat will depend upon whether there are many or few of these open sets, and where they are located: even if there are many around, they may not be all that accessible.

The same collection of phrases can be equipped with different spatial properties. So the class of phrases that a child is using can have different topological properties, and in particular, the child may acquire different discriminatory abilities as the topology that it is provided with undergoes change.

A child is threatened by the words used by the others. It is not that the words in themselves are used as a threat: even the most loving phrases may have consequences that threaten what the child most cherishes. The phrases are the vehicle of negotiation for loves and desires which touch the deepest levels of the child. Already this gives the child an interest in hoping that the phrases are embedded in a topological space adequately equipped with open sets. In such spaces the child can retreat as it tries to face up to the demands addressed to it in the words on the lips of the others. A retreat of this kind has the characteristics of what Freud called defence: it is therefore pertinent to the structure of the unconscious.[33]

The way that a mathematician constructs a path through this problem is as follows. Start with a collection of phrases—the signifying terms that the child is confronting. This set can be furnished with many different topologies dependent on what collection of open sets it has been given.

The strongest spatial structure that can be forced upon any set is one that comes from having all of its subsets open. Alternatively, the opposite way of going about would be to produce the weakest spatial structure: the way to produce this smallest topology is to have no proper subset open at all. The smallest topology is called the indiscrete topology, because there are no neighbourhoods: nothing in such a space protects against intrusion. The richest one is correspondingly called the discrete topology: everything here can be separated from everything else. A child who is trying to separate or distinguish what it previously could not, is, it seems, facing the problem of moving from encountering a small provision of open sets to a region that is much more provident.

In a discrete space, any set is a neighbourhood, and protects: the range of spaces, increasing in separation strength, that moves from the poorest topology towards the richest is called by mathematicians the lattice of topologies. At the lowest end of the lattice of topologies there is the indiscrete space; then all the spaces with only one open set, followed by all the topologies that have at least two. At the other end of the lattice, adjacent to the discrete topology, are all the topologies that are very well furnished with open sets—spaces where there are very few sets which are not open.

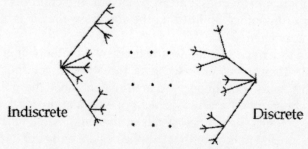

Figure Six. The Lattice of Topologies.

The autistic child is caught in the regions of the spaces that 'adjoin' the location of the indiscrete space. Thus, in a range of topologies or spatial structures, the coarser ones cannot differentiate certain points, whereas richer or finer topologies can distinguish them. The problem of the autistic child then becomes why this range of richer topologies becomes inaccessible,[34] why some children become stuck in the ruts of a signifying space. The lattice of topologies then gives co-ordinates for the transmission of structure in the domain of love. Some pathways through the network of topologies are too hard, and this is the predicament of the autistic child immersed in the spaces of signifying terms.

A person who is struggling to overcome autistic problems of communication is, according to this hypothesis, caught up within the lattice of topologies, and trying to move through it, towards the richer end. In trying to further their progress they may face obstacles, they may even be forced to regress. Even whether such retreats are even possible depends on the place that the child is in on the lattice of topologies. In many predicaments involving discrimination in love, a human being suffers by not being able to move towards this finer end; the autistic child is caught up near the coarser end—its aim is to move towards regions that other people already inhabit. Its progress may be unbearable, and a space without the problems of talking to adults may cause less pain. This problem of progression and regression through the lattice of topologies probably better represents the problems of differential diagnosis than do Abraham's phases or stages—with progression or regression through them—that have led, in the main, to developmentalist interpretations of drive functioning. Topological spaces allow for the structural investigation of the organisation of the drive; at the same time, problems of frustration and privation in relations of love can be formulated using the same apparatus.[35]

In his Seminar at Vincennes in the spring of 1970, Serge Leclaire concluded that the effects of castration are 'impossible' to subject to measurement. His formalisations are very fragmentary: it is doubtful if he had in mind at the time the notion of measure as used in the metric function in a topological space.[36]

Eric Laurent takes these themes much further, in his commentary on the presentation of thirteen cases of autism in children.[37] His account greatly advances the state of theorisation of autism as a clinical structure. Towards the end of his summary, he proposes the following commentary, which he organises around the notion of a phallic function:[38]

But also this symbolic... is equipped with a topology... When the child goes, at the same time, to look at the eye and the window, and they're equivalent for him, we should grasp hold of a space at play which is not constructed with an inside and an outside—limited and bordered by the house—but rather like the torus, where from the point of view of its surface, the internal circle and the external circle are both external. You can look towards the centre: you are always in the process of looking towards infinity. It's this kind of [structural] paradox that leads techniques of empiricist mumbo-jumbo to assert that the autistic child suffers from bad visual perception.[39] When a child is so palpably terrified as he sees an aeroplane passing in the sky, that he acts as if it were next to him, is taken to be an indicator that he has perceived it badly. Then a debate starts: is it really bad visual perception, or is it rather not the child's auditive perception that is going wrong? You can make all the empirical tests in the world: they will all be forced to admit that there is a space at play, which is not metric. What we are involved with are subjects who move around in spaces where the neighbourhood and the infinite can be equivalent. The hole that yawns open next to them is equally open to infinity. Metric spaces only come much later, after the arrival of the metric-standard,[40] that is, the phallus. In so far as phallic signification is not there, there is no measuring of the world. Truffaut has put it very well: I have to say I haven't seen any better way of putting what is at play in the construction of a metric space. Such a space isn't constructed, as Piaget would have it, by the integration of cognitive rules. Truffaut puts it thus: 'the legs of women are the compass which allows us to measure the world'. (Laurent 1992: 143)

Laurent is claiming that there is a topological difference between the spatial structure in which points can separated by means of their distance from each other, and those spaces in which such forms of measure are just not possible. Some spaces are far too subtle to be able to bear such a structure. Take two signifying terms, Sa and Sb: if they exist in a metric or distance space, then it makes sense to talk of the distance between them d(Sa, Sb).[41] Laurent asserts that this makes no sense within the spaces that the autistic child is inhabiting. This is an interesting claim. Whether it makes sense to say that non-autistic people can discriminate spatial distance because this is equivalent to having achieved a phallic function of separation is quite another matter.

This idea of a metric space is a very strong spatiality. There are very many spaces which allow some degree of separation of their points, but by means that are necessarily much weaker than the (attempted) imposition of a distance measure. Such spatial realities allow a series of claims to be made about the autistic child. It is very likely that the autistic child is having difficulties with this kind of separation; so let us look a little at how separations that are weaker than distance functions relate to this more general level of metric-standard, and to each other.

Take two phrases Sa and Sb set in a signifying space: if every open set in the space that contains one of these phrases also contains the other, then the two phrases are absolutely indistinguishable in terms of their spatial properties. For any distinguishability to emerge which can start to separate these phrases, then some open sets must include one of these points, and fail to include the other. It is this struggling for a distinguishability to emerge, against the background of the ever-available option of choosing not to distinguish, that characterises the terrified anxieties of the autistic child.

Let us look at this question a little more closely. In autism, a child is seeking to distinguish two phrases, but failing. In a metric or distance space, such distinguishing can always be achieved: the phrases can be separated by means of circles whose radius is smaller than half the distance between the two phrases. If the linguistic world of the child were like this, separation would be, as it were, very easy.

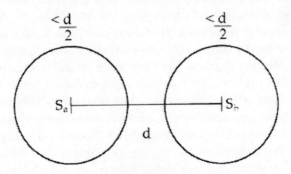

Figure Seven.

Most children, many adults, and certainly all autistic children find themselves confronting much greater difficulties than this. The autistic child must, then, be living in a space which is weaker than a distance space: let us see what kinds of these spaces there are.

Topologists distinguish at least four levels of separation in order to make some structural sense of these problems. They are usually called T-n levels, after the German word *Trennung*, separation. I will use the usual labels, and call the four types of space I want to look at T0, T1, T2, and M spaces. T0 has some separation properties, but they are very weak; T1 has somewhat stronger separation properties; T2 has built into its structure considerably stronger separations; and M is just a name for the familiar metric spaces we have already looked at—separation properties in M are very strong indeed. I will draw these things in a table: what I am claiming is that the autistic child is attempting to make its way down this table, but cannot, because of the pain of what that would mean. (See Figure Eight.)

In a T0 space, given any two phrases Sa and Sb, then *either* there will be an open set that contains Sa and not Sb, *or* there will be one that contains Sb and not Sa: nothing in the structure of the space guarantees which of these will take place, but what it means for a space to have this strength is precisely that one or the other of these forms of separation is available. In a T1 space there will always exist an open set surrounding Sa that excludes Sb, *and* also there will exist an open set around Sb that excludes Sa.[42] Any T1 space is in this sense stronger than a T0 space, and the child needing to adopt these separation properties in confronting its anxieties can have greater confidence if its history has allowed it to gain access to such spaces.

A T2 space has a stronger property: that given any two phrases Sa and Sb, there is an open set surrounding Sa and excluding Sb, and also another open set surrounding Sb and excluding Sa, such that these two open sets are totally separated from each other—they have no point in common.[43] All metric spaces have this T2 or Hausdorff property—simply take balls—around any two points, as in Figure Seven—that have radius one third of the distance between the points. This will separate the points in the Hausdorff sense: in other words, any metric space has this Hausdorff separation property. So, of these kinds of space, in the order that I have given them, any one is stronger than each of its predecessors. Neurotic and normal children are able to accede to the Hausdorff strength of space, and beyond. So the problem of autism lies in the body of this table of forms of strength of separation, at levels lower than the separation strength of a T2 space.

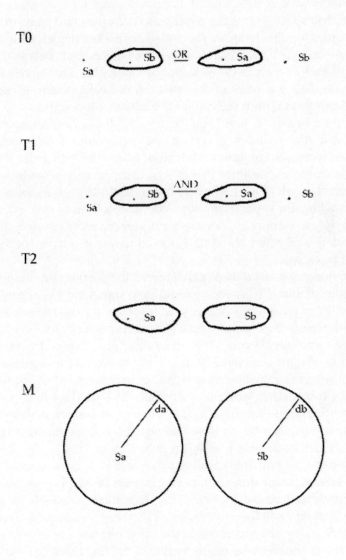

Figure Eight.

A simple way of understanding this latest separation property is to remember that in Hausdorff spaces, any two points can be 'housed off'. This housing off is what the autistic child fails to do: so it is at a level of separation weaker than that of T2 spaces—and much weaker than that of metric spaces—that the psychosis holds the child in its grip. It now becomes feasible to locate the autistic child's struggles with more precision—not just 'near' the indiscrete space, but between the Hausdorff and T0 regions of the lattice of topologies. This table—in its drawing on the arras-work of the lattice in its background—gives the child a destiny set within the web of the lattice of topologies.

Take the phrases 'I' and 'you'; if the child can find an open set around 'you' that excludes 'I', and an open set around 'I' that excludes 'you', then it can start to differentiate itself from others. In order for the spatial structure to guarantee that this can take place, it must have the separation strength of a T1 space. If the child finds itself in a space of signifiers where the separation properties have a weaker strength than this, then he or she may be lost in a world where relations with others are excluded, and where the child is forced to live in a world of aloneness that is 'extreme'.

The children who find themselves forced to take their orientation to others from within a T0 space can find guarantees only of separating either the 'I' from the 'you', or the 'you' from the 'I'—but in such a way that they have no choice as to which of these is possible. In this kind of space, the 'you' may become the orientating pole, where the retreats the child needs are available. That is, its own retreats to regions that pacify its anxieties may be possible, but only in terms of the pronoun 'you'. I say this space is 'extreme'—a phrase often used for the isolation of autistic children—because if the separation property were any weaker than this, then the child would be totally adrift, unable to have any faith in distinguishing himself from any other.

The separation principles at play in T0 and T1 spaces seem to provide the terrain where differentiations between schizophrenia, autism, and paranoia can be established. The separations available in a T0 space are precarious[44]; those found in a T1 space give a structure where 'you' and 'I' cannot be separated in the same phrase.

Something different becomes available to the child once it has claimed possession of spaces with separation properties that are stronger than any made available by T1 and T0 structures. The Hausdorff (T2) level of separation between signifiers is richer than that existing in either of these more feebly separated spaces. In such a space a child can at the same time establish differentiations—that have zones of retreat—between any two phrases in its world of meanings.

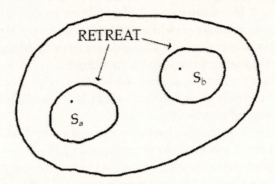

Figure Nine.

All metric spaces are Hausdorff, as we saw earlier. So a question arises: in this progression of spaces T0-T1-T2-M, where is the 'phallic' level described by Laurent? The phallic register is there when an equivalent exists of the famous *Fort-Da* game—the game described by Freud as he observed the play of one of the children of his daughter Sophie. These two signifiers *Fort* ('Gone') and *Da* ('Returned') are brought into play with a bright alacrity by this little boy Ernst. They are not distinguished by Ernst only while each alone is present—they are brought *together* in his binary play. He goes beyond the holophrase of 'Here(ness)' or that of 'Gone(ness). He brings them together as he presents them to the attention of the adults: 'Here—Gone'. The two signifiers brought together—yet separated—in this phrase represent the phallic principle, and the order of separation that they embody is T2.[45]

The phallic measure then sought by Laurent is to be found on the T2 level in the child's world. The phallic level of separation is richer than that available to the autistic child: the problems of autism are encountered at lower levels of separation than T2. In this context, Laurent is right to claim that where there is no phallic structure there is no metric measure; however there can be a phallus—a phallic 'compass'—without a metric, within the confines of a T2 space. It is this class of spaces, rather than metric spaces, which sets a limit to what the autistic child can bear.[46] The T1 spaces that the autistic child inhabits cannot be strengthened without his or her experiencing unbearable pain.

Freud's theory of defence can now be tested, in terms of the differentiations of structure that it proposes, by means of structures of separation in topological space.[47] The structure of the lattice of topologies also plays a role in producing spatial co-ordinates that allow the navigation of territory where previously analysts were 'all at sea'.[48] A pair of compasses was needed: but also some further instruments, capable of some discriminations unavailable to compass and rule.

The world of autism has at work within it principles of considerable power. The suffering of the autistic child is so striking because this world is its setting, and its fate.

I have proposed structural solutions in this paper that draw on discussions and results in the field of language. I have not considered the question of relations between biology and language, but clearly, this is a necessary next step.[49] The solutions proposed here need also to be subjected to an apparatus of test. It ought not to escape the wit of the adult world to put together proposals of this kind. There are enough references to phallic structure in the psychoanalytic literature, there are enough children still struggling with these difficulties, and there are enough adults suffering these limitations, to make this movement towards test an imperative. As with Kant's imperative—or that of the Delphic oracle—the emergence of structure out of the pain of the soul indicates a point where the scientific structure of space takes on a bearing which is ethical.

Notes

[1] See in particular Kanner 1943, 1946, 1951 and 1973. These themes are recapitulated and augmented in Bettelheim 1967 and Trevarthen et al. 1998.

[2] Bettelheim 1967: 4. Such a formulation is effectively found in most commentaries. See for instance, Frances Tustin: 'Let us now... [have] a deeper look into the world in which such children live' (1986: chapter 10).

[3] Ignorance conveyed with authority is the style of typical forms of psychiatric response. In DSM III-R for instance—and this example could be multiplied a hundredfold—you find the term 'reciprocal social interaction' at the head of the 'abnormalities' found in 'autistic disorder'. The theorists producing these textbooks have no clear idea of what they mean by 'social interaction' let alone its subclass 'reciprocal social interaction': however this does not stop them from refusing to investigate this complex term, while continuing to persuade the whole world that they understand it perfectly.

[4] Maiello is describing the way in which a term used by Imre Hermann—who embedded his own work in an investigation of the relation of clinical and mathematical structure—was taken up by Frances Tustin in the development of her conceptualisation of autism.

[5] Effectively, the functioning of what Freud calls 'false connection' vitiates any attempt to proceed in such a direction: some of the consequences of Freud putting this term at the centre of his work will be taken up later in this text.

6 Of course, he does not use the phrase 'signifying term': what he does is time and again come back to problems that have each of two components—that of language, and that of space.

7 Despert's commentary was a response to Kanner's article on the structure of language disturbance in the autistic child. Edouard Pichon was one of the founders of the French Psycho-Analytic Society: he was one of the first of the French psychoanalysts to extend psychoanalytical problems into the domain of linguistics. With his uncle, Jacques Damourette, he constructed a philological grammar of the French language (published, in seven volumes, between 1911 and 1940), and, between 1925 and 1938, he published a series of articles on the relation of grammar to the unconscious, on the functioning and structure of negation, and on the analysis of the personality in terms of the functioning of pronouns. A good description of this is in Roudinesco 1982: 297-320; further references to Pichon's relation to Lacan are to be found in Roudinesco 1986.

8 'Time' he says 'is the destroyer of sameness. If sameness is preserved, then time must stop in its tracks. Therefore the autistic child's world consists only of space' (Bettelheim 1967: 84).

9 In what follows, whenever I the use the term 'phrase' I shall use it in this sense, equating it with Lacan's term 'signifier'; I shall not go into the question of whether this is a happy or an unhappy choice of terminology—I shall simply go ahead and use it.

10 The notion of representation (*Vorstellung*) that Freud found in Herbart's work of the early 1800s is far from the sense that Bettelheim intends to give to the term. Herbart's work later led Riemann to develop a generalised theory of space—this being the first step of a series of mathematical developments unknown to Bettelheim that form a preliminary to the analysis of psychic space. For more details of this in relation to Freud, see Burgoyne & Leader 2000.

11 The work of Colwyn Trevarthen is beginning to change this state of affairs. For a study of the problems of interaction with the language of others that gives them a priority within the context of the physiological building of the brain, see Trevarthen et al. 1998.

12 See Breuer & Freud 1895, particularly the case of Emmy von N. For the pre-history of this problem see Freud 1888 and Freud 1889.

13 See Freud 1917.

14 This philosophical problem is a central question in the philosophy of science. A tradition that stems from the pre-Socratics to Karl Popper therefore forms a backcloth—despite the 'conscious' reservations of Popper—to the work of Freud and Lacan.

15 This was certainly the aim of Hartmann's construction of ego-psychology; the English style of formulating these questions relies more on an assumption of the rationality of common sense.

16 See Freud's concluding theoretical chapter to *Studies on Hysteria* (Freud & Breuer 1895).

17 The aim of the Socratic dialectic is to introduce a procedure by which someone can be led to loosen their attachment to certain of their opinions. Socrates claimed to have discovered a process—other than the imposition of someone else's values or opinions—which achieved this. In so far as the analyst is trying to loosen the attachment of the analysand to certain sexual opinions or fantasies, he is, at least in the initial part of the analytical work, in the position of working with Socratic dialectic.

18 Grote was a leading member of the group of 'Philosophical Radicals' representing the Benthamite position in politics in Westminster from the 1820s until 1841. Grote, together with James Mill, John Stuart Mill, and David Ricardo, developed a politics centred round the critical alteration of political opinion and established institutions. Of these activists, Grote in particular was the one who produced the detail of the 'Socratic' theory of change brought about in theories subjected to criticism of their consequences. The focus of the group was on social, political and economic institutions, as well as on scientific and popular culture. Grote first

met James Mill in David Ricardo's house in 1819; his friendship with John Stuart Mill started in the next few years. In 1822 Grote was 28, Mill a precocious 16, and of the two elder statesmen—each some twenty-odd years older than Grote—Ricardo was nearing the end of his life, but not of his influence. See Grote 1846-56 for the construction of his account of the motive force behind the advance of Greek civilisation, and Grote 1865 for his account of the detail and the effects of the process of Socratic cross-examination. It is this latter text that Mill reviewed in April 1866, and that Freud translated at Gomperz's request in 1879.

[19] See Mill 1866 and 1880.

[20] Of course, the division itself is contestable, and has been contested. Irrespective of any question of the 'true' Plato, the influence on Freud of the Socratic theory of dialectic is all that concerns us here. Many traces of this influence can be found in Freud's early writings on technique, up to the time of the First World War. In psychoanalysis as in mathematics, the operation of the dialectic reveals the underlying structure: I do not wish here to go into the question of whether some aspects of this structure are themselves fairly fixed, that is, relatively immune to criticism.

[21] Freud—almost as if by a slip—equates two terms that link logic with psychic pain: *Unerträglich* ('unbearable') and *Unverträglich* ('incompatible'). His early theory of the ego assumes that the ego takes out of logical connection what it finds unbearable.

[22] From this perspective, Freud's commentaries on technique are aimed at producing the circumstances from within which the analysand can be led to recognise the absurdity of the consequences of their fantasies. The logic introduced in this way operates through allusion and wit, and with what Freud calls 'working through'.

[23] In choosing this term—*Vorstellung*: representation—Freud is drawing on the much earlier groundwork introduced by Herbart. Bettelheim would have needed this background in order to make sense of the child's struggles with problems of symbolisation and representation.

[24] Accounts of Gomperz, and his relation to Mill, are to be found in Weinberg 1963.

[25] A focusing on the content of words had been a constant of Mill's replies, even where this was likely to confront Gomperz with hard conflicts: 'You say that I have two different languages to you' (Mill to Gomperz, July 29th in Mineka and Lindley). Gomperz had earlier talked of being 'maligned'.

[26] For details of central conflicts in Mill's life see Levi 1949 and Hayek 1951.

[27] See Lacan 1975, particularly chapter one.

28 It is not a new formulation of the classical roots of modern science to perceive them as lying in the (proto-Socratic) forms of searching for consequences, and in the mathematical notions that emerge as solutions to the contradictions and paradoxes of this method of cross-examination. At the origins of classical science, and the subsequent redevelopment of science during the Renaissance, there is to be found a dual process: a founding method of question and answer, and a later introduction of (mathematical) structure. The mathematisation of the physical world was well under way by the time of Galileo; in relation to the more hidden world of the soul, psychoanalysis can be seen as following the same trajectory. There is a wide literature on these problems of the history of science: for a formulation of some of the extensive range of themes involved see Vlastos 1975.

[29] It also has an object, a pressure, and a source; of these he says that the object is the least central to its structure. The Greeks, he says, had a clearer notion of the drive. They did not idealise the object to the extent that is done in the modern world. This fourfold division is already a structuring of the apparatus of the drive; it is not the only structure the drive is equipped with. There are, in addition, partial drives, which can be united by becoming subjected to what Freud calls 'forms of organisation'. These forms are vastly neglected in Anglo-Saxon work—at worst they are taken as biologically determined stages of development.

Their structure in Freud is much more complex than this, involving many of the above considerations of boundary and limit. What Freud calls the components of the drive structure are made up of the fourfold sub-structure of the (partial) drive, the variety of partial drives, as well as the forms of organisation to which they are subject. Strachey's translation of Freud's *Partialtrieb* ('partial drive') as 'component instinct' makes a mockery of this terminology, and has led to long-standing confusions about Freud's drive theory in the Anglo-Saxon world.

30 See Freud 1905, particularly Section I (2).

31 Lacan's Seminar XX (Lacan 1975) is devoted to establishing the nature of a space of *jouissance* of satisfaction of the excitation of the sexual drive. In this paper I will restrict my attention to the kind of space that Lacan was committed to investigating a quarter of a century earlier—to what can be called the space of the signifier. Of course, there exist relations—important relations—between the space of the signifier and the space of *jouissance*: the aim of the drive after all needs a representation to give it form. None of these relations will be addressed in this paper.

32 Equally topological structure can be obtained by considerations of boundary or frontier. There exists a range of topological notions, all of which can be demonstrated to be equivalent in having this power to generate the structure of a space: where there are limitations on this equivalence they raise questions about the foundations of topology and the foundations of mathematics. The equivalent notions include the concepts of neighbourhood, interior, closure, closed set, net, limit, filter, and ideal.

33 Needless to say, what is just on the lips turns out to be not something that is actually said.

34 The introduction in this paper of the notion of 'space of signifiers' attempts to respond to the questions raised in Kanner's clinical work with the construction of a mathematical structure that can grasp its problems.

35 Lacan—in his Seminar IV: *La Relation d'Objet* (Lacan 1994)—uses these concepts of privation, frustration and castration as instruments for building an account of object relations which returns to the corresponding theory established by Freud. Freud's object relations theory is not straightforward or easy to reconstruct: it effectively revolves around the concept of *Versagung*, a term traditionally—and inadequately—translated into English as 'frustration'. Lacan's starting point is, as usual, a critical evaluation of the advances brought about by Anglo-Saxon analysts—in this case, of the work of Winnicott and Jones.

36 See Leclaire 1971, particularly Part II, Section 6; for the detail of metric structure see below, and in particular, footnote 41.

37 See Laurent 1992, in which there are also extensive commentaries on the general nature of theories of autism developed within the IPA, and in turn their comparison with Lacan's account of autistic structure. (See Section II. 2, particularly 'Le Savoir sur l'Autisme dans l'IPA', by Dominique Miller, and 'Les Références de J. Lacan à l'Autisme', by Marc Strauss.) The final section of the book contains valuable commentary on the question of differential diagnosis in childhood psychosis (Laurent 1992: 267-295).

38 The term 'phallic function' could do with some explanation. From early in his work Freud had become aware that the term 'phallic' was used in classical and antique mythology to designate the function of loss and subsequently restored possession. This principle of loss and restitution is the core of the idea of the phallic function. In the *Minutes of the Vienna Psychoanalytical Society*, particularly the session of March 29, 1911, the anthropologist David Oppenheim described the nature of phallic Gods and Demons (see the Minutes of the Vienna Psychoanalytical Society Vol. III). The Sun, the Moon, rising and setting stars, all bird Gods, all Deities that disappear before being restored, are phallic Gods—as are Christ and Osiris. The only organ in the human body that visibly and palpably possesses this function of loss followed by restitution is the penis—not however the erect penis, but the penis in a state of detumescence. It is this loss built into the functioning of the penis that gives it its phallic allure. A woman's body also contains organs that suffer this phallic loss and resurrection, but

they are more hidden. As Freud progressively disabused himself of his confusions between phallus and penis, he was able to formulate the phallic function as the principle at play in the loss of the primary love attachment to the mother—that is, in the field of (Oedipal) anxieties of loss of love, and the pathways that go beyond such loss into the field of sexual identity.

39 Laurent is not only discarding the typically Anglo-Saxon (indeed particularly British) notions that spatial problems which concern the child can be formulated in terms of 'inner and outer worlds', but also indicating that much child psychology makes assumptions about the nature of physical and psychic space that lead to desperately erroneous diagnostic decisions being brought bear on the child.

40 *Metric-Standard: Mètre-étalon'*: there are a few jokes involved in this phrase. In the French, metre (*Mètre*) is homophonous with master (*Maître*), referring to the mastering which introduces itself into the soul of the child as he takes into himself the structure of Ideals. This field of Oedipal conflict and its refusal is also invoked by the fact that *étalon* is French for stallion. Finally there is a more oblique reference to what French schools of psychoanalysis see as the tendency of some of their British counterparts to want to reduce psychoanalytic reality to standardised versions of theory and technique.

41 For those who are mathematically inclined, the usual rules followed by this 'distance function' are:
1. $d(x, y) = 0$ always when $x = y$, and never otherwise;
2. $d(x, y) = d(y, x)$ always; and
3. $d(x, y) + d(y, z) \geq d(x, z)$ always.

This last rule simply says that the sum of two sides of a triangle is greater than the third. Any function whatsoever that obeys these rules is a 'distance' function; it follows that some such distance functions will be familiar, and that some will be very unusual.

42 The greater provision of open sets that allows for such increasing ability to separate or distinguish in T1 spaces also, of course, allows the child greater freedom to retreat—to retreat from the overwhelming anxieties that it at times experiences as unbearable.

43 This T2 kind is often called a 'Hausdorff space'. Felix Hausdorff was—together with Maurice Fréchet—one of a small number of brilliant developers of the topological theory of space in the years before the First World War. He wrote philosophical commentaries and poetry under the pen-name of Paul Mongré, combining his work in this field with his publications in mathematics until 1910. He and his wife killed themselves in 1942 in order to escape deportation to a Nazi death camp. In the Mathematics Institute of the University of Bonn there is the following commemorative plaque: *The mathematician Felix Hausdorff 8.XI.1868—26.I.1942 worked in this University from 1921 to 1935. The Nazis drove him to death because he was a Jew. Let all victims of tyranny, force, and war be honoured with him. Never more war and the reign of force.*

44 In such a space the differentiation of the 'I' cannot be established. There are topological structures that are even weaker than T0 spaces. A topological space which is not T0 may allow for T0 separation—or even stronger separations—of some of its points. But there will be—critical—points where the separation fails.

45 There are five divisions here: not T0/T0/T1/T2/M; they represent a field of division between the neuroses and the psychoses, and a principle for differentiating one psychosis from another. As I have said before, it is this kind of division that Abraham was struggling towards in his 'developmental account' of the forms of organisation of the libido—towards a spatial structuring, rather than a biological principle.

46 Laurent's hypothesis—that this limit is set by the class of metric spaces—seems to be one level of separation too high. It is this work of Laurent's, which follows on from the proposals in Lacan's Seminar on Identification (Lacan 1961-2), that has set the conditions for further formalisation and advances in this field.

47 It may be that spaces even weaker than topological structures are needed in order to fully take account of the choices facing the autistic child; such spaces would become topological in the presence of particular further relations.

48 'Adrift'; 'at sea': these terms are repeatedly used by psychoanalytic commentators on autism, from Bettelheim to Tustin (used sometimes of the child's experience, sometimes of their own).

49 This topic is broached in Colwyn Trevarthen's work (Trevarthen 1998).

A CALCULUS OF CONVERGENCE[1]

Nathalie Charraud

This session from the treatment of a young woman allows a clear distinction to be made between the main points which preceded the statement proffered by the analyst, and the effects of the interpretation.

Rejection

The analysand starts the session by telling me that she can't continue coming, because it's her friend who pays for the sessions. She doesn't want this situation to carry on any more—she has to get rid of this bloke. The bloke in question is living with another woman, and she has a position of 'mistress'.

At a second point in the session she tells me a dream she had the previous night—it is as follows: *She is going down a corridor which is straight, and has a high ceiling. This corridor gives out onto a desert. It's dreadfully hot, she's stifling.* She wakes up, very much wanting to vomit. This leads her to the washbasin where, however, she will not vomit. But she is surprised by this nightmare, because never before has one of her dreams given rise to such a violent physical reaction.

The third point in the session concerns her delicate situation with regard to her 'papers'. With a foreign passport, she needs a work permit in order to be able to stay in France. She's not short of job-offers, having gained the necessary qualifications for her work, but she can't bear the idea of going to the Prefecture to make this request for a permit, and has asked a lawyer to do it in her place. The lawyer is taking plenty of money from her, but with no result. What she wouldn't be able to bear—but what she feels will happen—is that if she goes to the Prefecture herself she will be confronted with a refusal. This state of affairs has already arisen on a number of occasions, at the times of her previous visits to Paris. Each time she had left, because she was setting about the task of putting her papers in order badly.

It's at this moment that I intervene, saying: 'there's rejection'.[2]

This term 'rejection' came to me through what I knew of the patient's life. Originating from a family which was very orthodox in its beliefs, she was destined—as were the other daughters—to marry someone from her own faith. While waiting for this to happen, she was supposed to devote herself to reading the Bible. She was forbidden to continue her studies, and to sit for the *baccalauréat*. Wanting—in spite of everything—to continue with her studies, she had endured some extremely violent conflicts with her parents. She left them at the age of eighteen to set herself up, finally, in the United States. She sees herself as the black sheep of the family, excluded from the circle of her own people.

However, after the session was over, I perceived that this signifier 'rejection' carries a particular weight,[3] from the fact that it was placed at the centre of the knot made up from the three preceding phrases. For her it was a matter of leaving both her boyfriend and me; secondly, in her dream, of vomiting something up; and thirdly, of encountering a refusal from someone at the Prefecture. She leaves, she is excluded, she vomits. These significations turn about a central signification, which one might describe as a point of convergence of the terms that have followed one another: that of rejection. This point of convergence has two aspects: a signifying aspect, which can be pinpointed by the term rejection, and a real aspect, that of the oral object which was looming up in the nightmare, and which she fled by means of waking up and wanting to vomit.

If I had interpreted with something more precise on the level of meaning—'you fear a rejection', or 'you're producing a rejection', or even 'there's a rejection'—I think that the real dimension of the object would have been much more obscured. 'There's rejection' kept open all the ambiguities, whilst not brushing aside the object of rejection. In particular, my statement played on the equivocation introduced by the terms which arranged themselves around this signifying term. Consequently, after a silence, she starts with a question: 'Rejection? On whose part?' I reply to her with a 'Yes?' of encouragement, and in the remainder of the session what one can take to be the effects of the interpretation unfold.

The first is an effect of remembering. Important material is brought into the session about the way in which she left at the time of the rejection of her family. It is not important to go into this here. A second effect, which was a consequence of this remembering, is a reactualisation by means of affect. This second part of the session was, in fact, centred around a kind of actualisation or staging, around the themes of her nightmare and of recurrent elements in her life. Very agitated by this evocation of the rejection of her father—labelled as 'definitive'—she sat up on the couch, explaining that she was suffocating (as in her dream) and that she wanted to leave. She said that she no longer knew what to hang on to but, noticing a print on the wall of my consulting room, that she caught onto it, and that this allowed her to lie down again. She had chosen her studies in the same way, she continued. Some posters had appealed to her, and this had led her towards her profession. So we have here, successively, a 'bringing into the present' of the unbearableness of the real aroused by the dream (feeling ill); the imaginary solution—recurrent in her life—of leaving; and the catching hold of a symbolic element—a poster—of which the content is relatively unimportant, but which allows her to return to the signifying chain.

The question arises of whether to explain—as I have done here—the signifying term which seems to produce a point of convergence, and of whether or not to offer this to the analysand. Consider, for instance, the case in which a signifier is clearly set out, and around which the analysand attentively develops her associations. In such a case it's not worth adding any more; it's more a question of cutting, of lightening the discourse... In other cases, the central signifier is in the position of $S(\cancel{A})$, which designates the lack in the Other, and which wants at the same time to fill it in. To bring this to the attention of the analysand risks encouraging the suturing tendency. The same holds for the phallic signification which underlies every discourse. A joke or play on words here limits the interpretation to this phallic signification and leads, it seems to me, towards a complicity in the analytical relation. The signifier 'rejection', in the case of my analysand, is clearly a master signifier, which represents her in the vicinity of a certain number of other signifiers, S_2 (her family, the Prefecture, various consulates and embassies). But it isn't reducible to this function. It also designates the gap between S_1 and S_2, because it's attached to the oral drive, and sticks itself against the place of the object. This double function of the signifier 'rejection' will come into play in what I want to put forward now—that this intervention possesses the central characteristics of an interpretation.

Meeting with the desire of the analyst

In his abstract of his *Ethics* Seminar, Lacan provides us with some sound benchmarks regarding what he calls 'reasoned interpretation', as opposed to 'wild interpretation', or the 'spontaneous interpretation' made by the dream in the dream-work.[4] (Lacan 1984). His commentary was produced in relation to dreaming, but it seems to me equally true applied to interpretation in general. 'Reasoned interpretation can do no better than to have appear the weakness that the phrase denotes'. Deciphering 'shows a defect of signification, and it's in no other way that it achieves the connotation of a desire'. 'Anxiety breaks up sleep when the dream is about to lead onto the real of what is desired.' (This is particularly verified in the dream of my patient.)

In thinking, after the event, about this interpretation, it seemed to me to indicate something of the 'real object of the desired' of this analysand. This object demonstrates its oral component in the dream reported here, an aspect which had already appeared in the preceding sessions. The 'stifling' (when confronted with the scorching desert) is translated—by the intermediary of the anxiety—into 'wanting to vomit', which shows that this desert emptiness (which is encountered once again in 'I don't know what to catch on to') designates equally well the proximity of the oral object that is to be rejected, to be vomited out. Lacking the signifier—too full of the object. It's another nourishment to which she aspires, and this is just as recurrent in her discourse. The 'lack of air' is correlative to a disgust at 'too much'. (She repeatedly says that she has made too many efforts in her life. She commented a while before that she has the impression she's 'swelling up'.)

The 'defect of signification' is found in the equivocation, the logical functioning, around the fact of knowing who rejects whom, or what.

The 'weakness' of the discourse is approached through the term 'rejection', and the effects of the statement 'there's rejection' seem to me explicable as effects of displacement—but not of metonymic displacements. A sliding is operative in the very weakness of the discourse, as it becomes caught up—a little further on—in the spiral of meaning which itself turns about a hole occupied by the object. That is to say, a new clasping, a new loop, can be noticed in the appearance of the material which is accompanied by affect in the actual session.

It follows from the hypothesis of the phantasy as an axiom for meaning that these spirals all roll parallel to the same initial circle, and that they are all consequences which follow from the statement of the phrase of the phantasy. An Antigone of modern times, with her will to educate herself against her father's diktat, having recourse to a law other than that of the father—a law more in keeping with our times; but actually, it's Iphigenia with whom she compares herself, even from the moment of the preliminary interviews. Her ideal image is certainly that of the emancipated woman, yet her place in the phantasy is that of the sacrificed daughter. Another young woman that she knew was in the same situation, and had obtained, by judicial means, and after a judgement had been given in her favour, the right to sit for her *baccalauréat*, against the wishes of her parents. My analysand told me that she hadn't wanted to follow this pathway, that she hadn't wanted to drag her father through the law courts. Something about the desire of the father had had to be protected. She won't oppose another law to that of her father, but will make herself into a deadbeat, the object of rejection.

Proof already existed that—on the father's part—he was ready to crush all the gifts and inclinations of his children, in order for everything to remain the same, and to follow tradition, in conformity with the sacred texts. The dimension of eternity—in which the paternal phantasy is situated, and to which the daughter responds with the phantasy of being the victim of a sacrifice—was evident. But in this beginning of the treatment, it wasn't practicable to make the phantasy more precise.

To sum up, I can say that I am putting forward this intervention—after the event—as possessing the status of an interpretation, by virtue of the fact that the point of convergence designated in it was not something purely on the level of semblance, on the level of the symbolic. The term indicated at the same time this terrain of the object, a 'weakness in the phrase', and was able to generate, as a result, something in the nature of a 'going beyond'—at any rate, a suspension of meaning. It's this suspension which can be seen in the first reaction of the analysand which is, textually, a double question: 'Rejection? On whose part?' These interrogations cut through the assertive style, which was more usually hers.

There was this going beyond: being at an end-point, and herself being stuck in this story of the Prefecture, my intervention had led her, through her recall of paternal rejection, to the memory of the fortuitous meetings (of images, as with the print in my consulting room) which had determined her choice of profession. Her profession had allowed her to obtain job contracts relatively easily, and in the intervals between contracts she played with her position of being 'deadbeat', 'left over' material. This remembering, which had marked the taking up again of the signifying chain, had not been brought about by the intermediary of a signifying association, but by encountering a detail in the consulting room of the analyst, a detail in the form of the print, which stuck out like a sore thumb within the suspension of meaning.

The effects of interpretation are incalculable, Lacan said, because they concern *jouissance*. And, in fact, it was unforeseeable that it should have been by means of the print, of the look, that the patient would recapture the signifying chain. As an interpretation, my intervention was shown to revolve around the scorched earth, the desert of *jouissance*. But that was not immediately clear to me at the time. Rather, I was only vaguely reckoning on the possibility that she would start speaking again—in relation to rejection—about her father, as indeed she did. But the effect went well beyond this 'expectation' because, from the father's rejection, she passed, she traversed, an empty zone, where only the presence of the analyst—operating as a semblance of the object *a*—could support her.[5] A 'nothing' on the side of the analyst, a print, had been enough for this revival, a relaunching, but not in just any old way, since what was involved designated a crucial moment in her history: the choice of her line of work.

The matheme which guided me in these developments, and which inspired the expression 'convergence' in the title of this paper, is the schema of the flattening out of the Borromean knot, as Lacan presented it at the time of his growing interest in knots.[6] During this period Lacan utilised the Borromean knot as a means of representing something of which it is difficult to conceive: convergence—in the topological sense of this term—defined by means of the notion of a filter.[7] What is a filter? You can represent it as a family of sets, such that successive intersections within the family give something smaller and smaller, something more and more precise. To say that the filter is convergent is equivalent to saying that the limit of this process generates a point. It is in this way that the Borromean knot represents the intersection of at least three rings, which illustrate the convergence towards the point *a*. The three rings are rings of meaning, says Lacan, but— more precisely—they are the meanings of the real, of the imaginary, and of the symbolic, knotted together by the presence of the object *a*. This point is called a 'pinning point', if you regard it as a knot; it's a point of convergence, if you regard it as a topology of signifiers. I'd like to emphasise that, before knots, Lacan had already introduced the notion of convergence, which has the advantage of being situated in the field of the topology of signifiers, and is therefore more accessible with respect to problems of clinical practice.

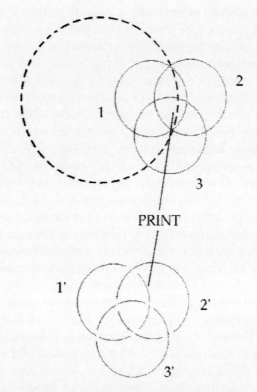

We can return to the development of this session in terms of such a schema. The three 'rings of meaning', the three topological neighbourhoods which are in play at the start of the session, are:

1. To go, to leave, etc. (*partir, quitter*...)
2. To vomit, disgust, etc. (*vomir, dégoût*...)
3. Prefecture, papers, passport, etc. (*préfecture, papiers, passeport*)

My intervention produced a drawing tighter of this convergence, by indicating its limit signifier: 'rejection'. This piece of information could have produced no effect, but the patient integrates it into a fourth ring, that of:

4. Paternal rejection (*rejet paternel*).

The effect which we have located is the suspension of meaning, and the catching hold again of the signifying chain by means of the print.

After that, a new chain unwinds, again determined through three neighbourhoods:

1. To go, to leave my consulting room (*partir, sortit de mon bureau*);
2. To be stifled (*elle étouffe*);
3. How she chose her profession (*comment elle a choisi sa profession*).

What is interesting is the difference between the initial situation and that at the end. The initial structure displays a convergence towards one signifier, that is, a signifying stasis—or, again, a symptom, in the sense of a condensation—where the signifier 'rejection' finds itself stuck to the object. It seems that the effect of the interpretation would have been, on one hand, the unsticking of the signifier in relation to the object—which can be seen in the fact that her problems with her papers will sort themselves out, and that she will not obey her compulsions to leave. On the other hand, there's an effect of subjectivity in so far as she remembers something primordial in her existence—the choice of her profession: primordial in the sense that she had left everything behind, and crossed the ocean in order to bring it into being. A short time after this session, she found herself in the position of being able to pay for her sessions herself.

Notes

[1] This article was first published as Charraud 1987, in the special issue of *Ornicar?* devoted to interpretation. It, and some two dozen other articles, appeared together under the general title: *A Calculus of Interpretation*. The present text is a translation by Bernard Burgoyne. All footnotes to this text are those of the translator.

[2] In the original: '*il y a du rejet*'.

[3] The term *rejeter*, in French, has an extensive field of associations. It means to throw up, to spew out, to cast out, to expel, to discharge, to push back, to repel, to reject, to turn down, to dismiss. It can also have a somewhat different meaning—to sprout new shoots, put out new growth. *Rejet* can, therefore, signify 'rejection', or 'a reject', as well as acting as a vehicle for the other threads of association listed above.

[4] One of the functions of the dream is that of 'interpreting' the dream-thoughts, thereby directing them *away* from the dream wish, whereas the analyst's interpretation attempts to open up a path *towards* the dream wish.

[5] Lacan's formalisation of the object which operates as the cause of desire is this little algebraic letter a. It is located on the edges, at the boundary of the networks woven by the signifying chain.

[6] The matheme is the field of the mathematical relations that exist between formalisations of aspects of human activity and passion. Mathemes allow the analyst a mode of intervention

and interpretation, which is supplementary to the classical Freudian mode of interpretation within the context of a family romance. Differing styles of clinical practice exist within the field of psychoanalysis. In particular, some Lacanian psychoanalysts make extensive use of the structure of mathemes, some less so. Some focus more upon algebraic forms of matheme, some more upon topological forms. The Lacan Seminar to which Nathalie Charraud refers in the text is his Seminar XXI—in particular, the session of 15th January, 1974.

[7] Topology is the modern theory of space, of the most general spaces that are conceivable. So spatial relations between excitations, or between phrases, or between moments in the experience of a human soul, are all conceivable in this mathematical field, and therefore in the topological constructions of mathemes. In this field, frontiers or edges can be used to determine all the topological properties that are in play. Alternatively, there are many other notions that can be used to generate the structure of the space: Nathalie Charraud chooses here the notion of a filter, a notion that Lacan has analogised to that of a love philtre. For a development of a topology utilising another notion—that of 'neighbourhood'—see Charraud 1997, originally published as Charraud 1986.

BIBLIOGRAPHY

Abraham, K. (1948) 'A Short Study of the Development of the Libido', in *Selected Papers on Psychoanalysis*, London: Hogarth Press.
Allers, R. (1944) 'Microscosmus: from Anaximandros to Paracelsus', *Traditio* 2: 319-407.
Assoun, P.-L. (1995) *Freud, la philosophie et les philosophes*, Paris: Presses Universitaires de France.
Bain, A. (1882) *James Mill: A Biography*, London: Longmans, Green, Reader and Dyer.
Benvenuto, B. (1989) 'Once upon a time—the infant in the Lacanian theory', *The British Journal of Psychotherapy* 5, 3: 409-422.
Bernfeld, S. (1985) 'The facts of observation in psychoanalysis', *The International Review of Psycho-Analysis* 12: 341-351.
Bettelheim B. (1967) *The Empty Fortress: Infantile Autism and the Birth of the Self*, New York: The Free Press.
Biblioteca Philosophica Hermetica (n.d.) *The Silent Language: The Symbols of Hermetic Philosophy*, exhibition, Amsterdam.
Bion, W.R. (1954) 'Notes on the Theory of Schizophrenia', in Bion 1967.
Bion, W.R. (1957a) 'Differentiation of the Psychotic from the Non-Psychotic Personalities', in Bion 1967.
Bion, W.R. (1957b) 'On Arrogance'. in Bion 1967.
Bion, W.R. (1958) 'On Hallucination', in Bion 1967.
Bion, W.R. (1959) 'Attacks on Linking', in Bion 1967.
Bion, W.R. (1962a) 'A Theory of Thinking', in Bion 1967.
Bion, W.R. (1962b) *Learning from Experience*, London: William Heinemann.
Bion, W.R. (1963) *Elements of Psycho-Analysis*, New York: Basic Books.
Bion, W.R. (1965) *Transformations: Changing from Learning to Growth*, London: William Heinemann.
Bion, W.R. (1967) *Second Thoughts: Selected Papers on Psycho-Analysis*, New York: Jason Aronson.
Bion, W.R. (1970) *Attention and Interpretation*, London: Karnac.
Bion, W.R. (1977) 'Learning from Experience', in *Seven Servants*, New York: Jason Aronson.
Bion, W.R. (1994) *Cogitations*, new extended edition, London: Karnac.
Bion, W.R., & Rickman, J. (1961) 'Intra-Group Tensions in Therapy', in *Experiences in Groups*, London: Tavistock Publications.
Bochenski, I. M. (1961) *A History of Formal Logic*, Indiana: Notre Dame.

Bouvet, M. (1950) 'Incidences thérapeutiques de la prise de conscience de l'envie du pénis dans la névrose obsessionnelle féminine', *Revue Française de Psychanalyse* 14: 215-243.

Bouvet, M. (1953) 'Le moi dans la névrose obsessionnelle', *Revue Française de Psychanalyse* 17: 111-196.

Bouvet, M. (1954[1968]) 'La Cure Typée', in *Résistances, Transfert*, Paris: Payot.

Bouvet, M. (1958) 'Technical variation and the concept of distance', *International Journal of Psycho-Analysis* 39: 211-221.

Bowie, A. (1993) *Schelling and Modern Philosophy: An Introduction*, London: Routledge.

Breuer, J., & Freud, S. (1895) *Studies on Hysteria*, SE II.

Brierley, M. (1951) *Trends in Psycho-Analysis*, London: Hogarth Press & the Institute of Psycho-Analysis.

Brown, L. (1987) 'Borderline Personality Organization and the Transition to the Depressive Position', in *The Borderline Patient: Emerging Concepts in Diagnosis, Psychodynamics, and Treatment,* vol. 1, (eds.) J. Grotstein, M. Solomon, and J. Lang, New York: Analytic Press.

Brown, L. (n. d.) 'The transitional position', unpublished MS.

Burgoyne, B. (1990) 'Clinical commentary', *The British Journal of Psychotherapy* 6, 4: 480-482.

Burgoyne, B. (1996) 'Lacanian Psychoanalysis', in *In Search of a Therapist - Jitendra: Lost Connections*, ed. E.M. Jacobs, Milton Keynes: Open University Press.

Burgoyne, B., & Leader, D. (2000) 'Freud's Scientific Background', in Leader, D., *Freud's Footnotes*, London: Faber.

Burgoyne, B., & Sullivan, M., eds. (1997) *The Klein-Lacan Dialogues*, London: Rebus Press.

Butler, J. (1997) *The Psychic Life of Power: Theories in Subjection*, Stanford CA: Stanford University Press.

Charraud, N. (1986) 'La topologie freudienne', *Ornicar?* 36: 21-41,

Charraud, N. (1987) 'Un "calcul" de convergence', *Ornicar?* 40: 136-142.

Charraud, N. (1997) *Lacan et les mathematiques*, Paris: Anthropos.

Clark, R. (1980) *Freud: The Man and the Cause*, New York NY: Random House.

Damourette, J., & Pichon, E. (1911-40) *Des Mots à la Pensée*, Paris: D'Artrey.

Despert, J.L. (1946) 'Discussion of L. Kanner, Irrelevant and Metaphorical Language in Early Infantile Autism', *American Journal of Psychiatry* 103.

Dor, J. (1997) *The Clinical Lacan*, New Jersey & London: Aronson.

École de l'Orientation Lacanienne (1994) 'La resolution curative dans le cas du Petit Hans', in *La Conclusion de la Cure*, Paris: Eolia/Seuil.

École de la Cause Freudienne (1986) *La Lettre Mensuelle*, no. 50.

Eissler, K. (1958) 'Remarks on some variations in psychoanalytical technique', *The International Journal of Psycho-Analysis* 39: 222-229.

Emerson, R. (1995) 'Circles', in *The Vision of Emerson*, ed. R. Geldard, Shaftsbury: Element Books.

Fairbairn, W. (1944) 'Endopsychic Structure Considered in Terms of Object Relationships', in Fairbairn 1952.

Fairbairn, W.R.D. (1941) 'A Revised Psychopathology of the Psychoses and Psychoneuroses' in Fairbairn 1952.

Fairbairn, W.R.D. (1943) 'The Repression and the Return of Bad Objects, with Special Reference to the "War Neuroses"', in Fairbairn 1952.

Fairbairn, W.R.D. (1951) 'A Synopsis of the Development of the Author's View Regarding the Structure of the Personality', in Fairbairn 1952.

Fairbairn, W.R.D. (1952) *Psychoanalytic Studies of the Personality*, London: Tavistock.

Fairbairn, W.R.D. (1952) *Psychoanalytic Studies of the Personality*, London: Tavistock. (Published in U.S. as: (1954) *An Object Relations Theory of the Personality*, New York: Basic Books.)

Fairbairn, W.R.D. (1952a) 'Endopsychic Structure Considered in Terms of Object-Relationships', in Fairbairn 1952a.

Fairbairn, W.R.D. (1954) 'Observations on the nature of hysterical states', *British Journal of Medical Psychology* 27: 37-54.

Fairbairn, W.R.D. (1958) 'On the nature and aims of psychoanalytic treatment', *International Journal of Psycho-Analysis* 39: 374-385.

Fairbairn, W.R.D. (1994) 'An Object Relations Theory of the Personality', in D. Scharff & E. Fairbairn Birtles (eds.) *From Instinct to Self*, vol. 2, New Jersey: Jason Aronson.

Ferenczi, S. (1949) 'Confusion of Tongues Between Adults and the Child', in Ferenczi 1955.

Ferenczi, S. (1955) *Final Contribution to the Problems and Methods of Psycho-Analysis*, London: Karnac.

Fink, B. (1997) *A Clinical Introduction to Lacanian Psychoanalysis: Theory and Technique*, Cambridge MA: Harvard University Press.

Fink, B., Feldstein, R., & Jaanus, M., eds. (1996) *Reading Seminars I & II: Lacan's Return to Freud*, Albany: State University of New York Press.

Fordham, M. (1985) *Explorations into the Self*, London: Academic Press.

Fraiberg, S. (1969) 'Libidinal object constancy and mental representation', *Psychoanalytic Study of the Child* 24: 9-47.

Freud, A. (1998) 'Problems of Technique in Adult Analysis', in *Selected Writings by Anna Freud*, ed. R. Ekins & R. Freeman, London: Penguin.

Freud, S. (1888) 'Preface to the Translation of Bernheim's *Suggestion* ', SE I: 73-87.

Freud, S. (1889) 'Review of August Forel's *Hypnotism* ', SE I: 89-101.

Freud, S. (1894) 'The Neuro-Psychoses of Defence', SE III: 41-61.

Freud, S. (1900) *The Interpretation of Dreams*, SE IV & V: 1-627.

Freud, S. (1905) *Three Essays on the Theory of Sexuality*, SE VII: 123-245.

Freud, S. (1912) 'The Dynamics of the Transference', SE XII: 97-108.

Freud, S. (1912-13) *Totem and Taboo*, SE XIII: 1-162.

Freud, S. (1914) 'On Narcissism: An Introduction' SE XIV: 67-102.

Freud, S. (1915) 'Repression', SE XIV: 141-158.

Freud, S. (1915), 'The Unconscious', SE XIV: 159-215.

Freud, S. (1917) 'A Metapsychological Supplement to the Theory of Dreams', SE XIV: 217-235.

Freud, S. (1917) 'Mourning and Melancholia', SE XIV: 237-258.

Freud, S. (1920a) *Beyond the Pleasure Principle*, SE XVIII: 1-64.

Freud, S. (1920b) 'The Psychogenesis of a Case of Homosexuality in a Woman', SE XVIII: 145-172.

Freud, S. (1921) *Group Psychology and the Analysis of the Ego*, SE XVIII: 65-143.

Freud, S. (1923) *The Ego and the Id*, SE XIX: 1-66.

Freud, S. (1924) 'The Dissolution of the Oedipus Complex', SE XIX: 171-179.

Freud, S. (1925) 'A Note Upon the "Mystic Writing Pad"', SE XIX: 225-232.

Freud, S. (1926) *Inhibitions, Symptoms and Anxiety*, SE XX: 75-175.

Freud, S. (1927) 'Fetishism', SE XXI: 147-157.

Freud, S. (1930) *Civilisation and Its Discontents*, SE XXI: 57-145.

Freud, S. (1931) 'Female Sexuality', SE XXI: 221-243.

Freud, S. (1933) *New Introductory Lectures on Psycho-Analysis*, SE XXII: 1-182.

Freud, S. (1937a) 'Analysis Terminable and Interminable', SE XXIII: 209-253.
Freud, S. (1937b) 'Constructions in Analysis', SE XXIII: 255-269.
Freud, S. (1940) *An Outline of Psychoanalysis*, SE XXIII: 139-207.
Freud, S. (1950a) 'A Project for a Scientific Psychology', SE I: 281-397.
Freud, S. (1950b) 'Entwurf einer Psychologie', in *Aus den Anfängen der Psychoanalyse*, London: Imago.
Freud, S. (1954) 'Project for a Scientific Psychology', in *The Origins of Psycho-Analysis, Letters to Wilhelm Fliess, Drafts and Notes: 1887-1902*, tr. E. Mosbacher and J. Strachey, ed. M. Bonaparte, A. Freud, and E. Kris, London: Imago.
Freud, S. (1993a) *Zur Aufussung der Aphasien*, Frankfurt: Fischer Verlag.
Freud, S. (1993b) *Die Traumdeutung*, Frankfurt: Fischer Verlag.
Gay, P. (1988) *Freud: A Life for Our Time*, New York & London: W.W. Norton.
Giegerich, W. (1987) 'The rescue of the world: Jung, Hegel, and the subjective universe', *Spring* 107-114.
Goethe, J.W. (1959) *Faust*, Part Two, tr. F. Wayne, Harmondsworth: Penguin Books.
Goldberg, A. (1983) 'Self Psychology and Alternative Perspectives on Internalisation', in J. Lichtenberg & S. Kaplan (eds.) *Reflections on Self Psychology*, Hillsdale NJ: Analytic Press.
Gould, S. J. (1977) *Ontogeny and Phylogeny*, Cambridge MA & London: The Belknap Press of Harvard University.
Gréco, P., Grize, J.B., Papert, S., & Piaget, J., eds. (1960) *Problèmes de la Construction du Nombre*, Paris: Presses Universitaires de France.
Green, A. (1997) *On Private Madness*, London: Rebus Press.
Grossman, C., & Grossman, S. (1965) *The Wild Analyst: The Life and Work of Georg Groddeck*, New York NY: George Braziller.
Grote, G. (1846-56) *History of Greece*, 12 vols., London: John Murray.
Grote, G. (1865) *Plato and the Other Companions of Socrates (Vols. I-III)*, London: John Murray.
Grotjahn, M. (1995) 'Georg Groddeck (1866-1934): The Untamed Analyst', in F. Alexander, S. Eisenstein, and M. Grotjahn (eds.) *Psychoanalytic Pioneers*, new edition, New Brunswick NJ: Transaction.
Grotstein, J. (1981) *Splitting and Projective Identification*, New York: Jason Aronson.

Grotstein, J. (1984) 'An Odyssey into the Deep and Formless Infinite: The work of Wilfred Bion', in *Beyond Freud: A Study of Modern Psychoanalytic Theorists*, ed. J. Reppen, Hillsdale, NJ: Analytic Press.

Grotstein, J. (1993) 'Towards the concept of the transcendent position: reflections on some of "the unborns" in Bion's "Cogitations"', *Journal of Melanie Klein and Object Relations* 11, 2: 55-73.

Grotstein, J. (1997) 'Bion, the pariah of "O"', *British Journal of Psychotherapy* 14: 77-90.

Grotstein, J. (forthcoming a) 'Bion's "O", Kant's "thing-in-itself", and Lacan's "real": toward the concept of the transcendent position', *Journal of Melanie Klein and Object Relations*.

Grotstein, J. (forthcoming b) 'A clinical and theoretical reassessment of Klein's positions'.

Grubrich-Simitis, I. (1996) *Back to Freud's Texts: Making Silent Documents Speak*, trans. P. Slotkin, New Haven CT & London: Yale University Press.

Haeckel, E. (1892) *The History of Creation*, 2 vols., tr. E. Lankester, London: Kegan Paul, Trench, Trubner & Co.

Hale, N. (1995) *The Rise and Crisis of Psychoanalysis in the United States: Freud and the Americans 1917-1985*, New York NY: Oxford University Press.

Hartmann, H. (1958) *Ego Psychology and the Problem of Adaptation*, New York: International Universities Press.

Hartmann, H., Kris, E., & Loewenstein, R. (1946) 'Comments on the formation of psychic structure', *The Psychoanalytic Study of the Child* 2: 11-38.

Hartmann, H., Kris, E., & Loewenstein, R. (1949) 'Notes on the theory of aggression', *The Psychoanalytic Study of the Child* 3/4: 9-36.

Hayek, F.A. (1951) *John Stuart Mill and Harriet Taylor: Their Correspondence and Subsequent Marriage*, London: Routledge & Kegan Paul.

Heidegger, M. (1992) *Parmenides*, tr. A. Schuwer & R. Rojcewicz, Bloomington: Indiana University Press.

Heimann, P. (1956) 'Dynamics of Transference Interpretations, *International Journal of Psycho-Analysis* XXXVII 156:303-310.

Hermann, I. (1978) *Psychanalyse et Logique*, Paris: Denoël.

Hermann, I. (1979) *La Psychanalyse comme Méthode*, Paris: Denoël.

Hermann, I. (1980) *Parallelismes*, Paris: Denoël.

Hillman, J. (1980) *Egalitarian Typologies versus the Perception of the Unique*, Dallas: Spring Publications.

Hillman, J., et al. (1980) 'Dionysus in Jung's Writings', in *Facing the Gods*, Dallas: Spring Publications.

Holt, D. (1992) 'Reminding, Letting Be, Showdoing: The Organisation of Psychotherapy', in *The Psychology of Carl Jung: Essays in Application and Deconstruction*, Lewiston: Edward Nellen Press.

Hood, J. (1996)

International Social Science Council (1953-59), 'The First Six Years, 1953-1959', Paris.

Jacobs, M. (1995) *D.W. Winnicott: Key Figures in Counselling and Psychotherapy*, London: Sage.

Jaffe, A. (1979) *C.G. Jung: Word and Image*, Princeton: Princeton University Press.

Jalley, É. (1998) *Freud, Wallon, Lacan. L'enfant au miroir*, Paris: EPEL.

James, P.D. (1989) *Innocent Blood*, Harmondsworth, Middlesex: Penguin.

Jones, E. (1957) *The Life and Work of Sigmund Freud. Vol. III: The Last Phase (1919-1939)*, New York NY: Basic Books.

Jung, C.G. (1902) 'On the Psychology and Pathology of So-Called Occult Phenomena', CW 1: 1-150.

Jung, C.G. (1918) 'The Role of the Unconscious', CW 10: 1-48.

Jung, C.G. (1920) 'Editorial Note', CW 6: v-vi.

Jung, C.G. (1921) *Psychological Types*, CW 6.

Jung, C.G. (1929) 'Commentary on "The Secret of the Golden Flower"', CW 13: 1-84.

Jung, C.G. (1932) 'The Hypothesis of the Collective Unconscious', CW 18: 1223-1225.

Jung, C.G. (1935) 'The Tavistock Lectures: On the Theory and Practice of Analytical Psychology', CW 18: 1-415.

Jung, C.G. (1936a) 'Individual Dream Symbolism in Relation to Alchemy', CW 12: 44-331.

Jung, C.G. (1936b) 'Psychological Typology', CW 6: 960-987.

Jung, C.G. (1939) 'Conscious, Unconscious and Individuation', CW 9i: 489-524.

Jung, C.G. (1946) 'Analytical Psychology and Education: Three Lectures', CW 17: 127-229.

Jung, C.G. (1948) 'The Spirit Mercurius', CW 13: 239-303.

Jung, C.G. (1950a) 'A Study in the Process of Individuation', CW 9i: 525-626.

Jung, C.G. (1950b) 'Concerning Rebirth', CW 9i: 199-258.

Jung, C.G. (1954) 'On the Psychology of the Trickster-Figure', CW 9i: 456-488.
Jung, C.G. (1955) 'Appendix: Mandalas', CW 9i: 713-718.
Jung, C.G. (1955-56) *Mysterium Coniunctionis*, CW 14.
Jung, C.G. (1957) 'Prefatory note to 'The Transcendent Function', CW 8.
Jung, C.G. (1963) *Memories, Dreams, Reflections*, ed. A. Jaffe, tr. R. Winston & C. Winston, New York: Random House.
Jung, C.G. (1966) 'The Structure of the Unconscious', CW 7: 437-507.
Jung, C.G. (1973) *Mandala Symbolism*, tr. R.F.C. Hull, Princeton: Princeton University Press.
Kamm, J. (1977) *John Stuart Mill in Love*, London: Gordon & Cremonesi.
Kanner, L. (1943) 'Autistic disturbances of affective contacts', *The Nervous Child* 2: 217-250.
Kanner, L. (1946) 'Irrelevant and metaphorical language in early infantile autism', *American Journal of Psychiatry* 103: 242-246.
Kanner, L. (1951) 'The conception of wholes and parts in early infantile autism', *American Journal of Psychiatry* 108: 23-26.
Kant, I. (1965) *Critique of Pure Reason*, second edition, tr. N. Kemp Smith, New York: St. Martin's Press.
Kaufmann, P., ed. (1993) *L'apport freudien. Eléments pour une encyclopédie de la psychanalyse*, Paris: Bordas.
Kernberg, O. (1974) 'Further contributions to the treatment of narcissistic personalities', *International Journal of Psycho-Analysis* 55: 215-240.
Khan, M. (1954) in Winnicott, (1987) *Through Paediatrics to Psychoanalysis*, London: Karnac.
Kiell, N. (1988) *Freud Without Hindsight: Reviews of his Work, 1893-1939*, Madison CT: International Universities Press.
King, P., & Steiner, R., eds. (1991) *The Freud-Klein Controversies 1941-1945*, London: Tavistock.
Klein, G. (1976) *Psychoanalytic Theory: An Exploration of the Essentials*, Madison CT: International Universities Press.
Klein, M. (1927) 'Symposium on Child Analysis', in Klein 1975a.
Klein, M. (1928) 'Early Stages of the Oedipus Conflict', in Klein 1975a.
Klein, M. (1929a) 'Infantile Anxiety-Situations Reflected in a Work of Art and in the Creative Impulse', in Klein 1975a.
Klein, M. (1929b) 'Personification in the Play of Children', in Klein 1975a.

Klein, M. (1930) 'The Importance of Symbol Formation in the Development of the Ego', *International Journal of Psycho-Analysis* 11: 24-39, and in Klein 1975a.

Klein, M. (1933) 'The Early Development of Conscience in the Child', in Klein 1975a.

Klein, M. (1935) 'A Contribution to the Psychogenesis of Manic-Depressive States', in Klein 1975a.

Klein, M. (1940) 'Mourning and its Relation to Manic-Depressive States', in Klein 1975a.

Klein, M. (1946) 'Notes on Some Schizoid Mechanisms', in Klein 1975b.

Klein, M. (1952) 'Some Theoretical Conclusions Regarding the Emotional Life of the Infant', in Klein 1975b.

Klein, M. (1975a) *Love, Guilt and Reparation and Other Works 1921-1945*, London: Hogarth Press and the Institute of Psychoanalysis.

Klein, M. (1975b) *Envy and Gratitude and Other Works 1946-1963*, London: Hogarth Press and the Institute of Psychoanalysis.

Klossowski de Rola, S. (1988) *The Golden Game: Alchemical Engravings of the Seventeenth Century*, London: Thames and Hudson.

Kneale, W. & Kneale, M. (1962) *The Development of Logic*, Oxford: Oxford University Press.

Kohut, H. (1959) 'Introspection, empathy and psychoanalysis: an examination of the relationship between modes of observation and theory', *Journal of the American Psychoanalytic Association* 7: 459-483.

Kohut, H. (1966) 'Forms and Transformations of Narcissism', in P. Ornstein (ed.) *The Search for the Self: Selected Writings of Heinz Kohut*, vol. 1, New York: International Universities Press.

Kohut, H. (1971) *The Analysis of the Self*, New York: International Universities Press.

Kohut, H. (1977) *The Restoration of the Self*, New York: International Universities Press.

Kohut, H. (1979) 'The two analyses of Mr. Z', *International Journal of Psycho-Analysis* 60, 3: 3-27.

Kohut, H. (1984) *How Does Analysis Cure?*, Chicago: University of Chicago Press.

Lacan, J. (1963-4 [1973]) *Le Séminaire Livre XI: Les Quatre Concepts Fondamentaux de la Psychanalyse*, ed. J.-A. Miller, Paris: Seuil.

Lacan, J. (1947) 'La psychiatrie anglaise et la guerre', *L'Evolution Psychiatrique* 1: 293 - 312.

Lacan, J. (1952[1966]) 'Intervention sur le Transfert', *Revue Française de la Psychanalyse*, XVI, No. 1-2:154-163 (and in Lacan 1966).

Lacan, J. (1953) 'The Individual Myth of the Neurotic', *Psychoanalytic Quarterly*, 48, 1979: 405-25.

Lacan, J. (1954-55 [1978]) *Le Seminaire Livre II: Le Moi dans la theorie de Freud et dans la technique de la psychanalyse*, ed. J.-A. Miller, Paris: Seuil.

Lacan, J. (1955-56 [1981]) *Le Seminaire Livre III: Les Psychoses*, ed. J.-A. Miller, Paris: Seuil.

Lacan, J. (1956-57 [1994]) *Le Seminaire Livre IV: La relation d'objet*, ed. J.-A. Miller, Paris: Seuil.

Lacan, J. (1957-58 [1998]) *Le Séminaire Livre V: Les Formations de l'Inconscient*, ed. J.-A. Miller, Paris: Seuil.

Lacan, J. (1959a [1966]) 'D'une Question Préliminaire à tout traitement possible de la psychose' in *La Psychanalyse*, 4: 1-50 (and in Lacan 1966).

Lacan, J. (1959b [1966]) 'Kant avec Sade' in *Critique* No. 191 (and also in Lacan 1966).

Lacan, J. (1961-2) *Le Séminaire, Livre IX: L'Identification*, unpublished.

Lacan, J. (1963) 'Kant with Sade', *October* No. 51, 1989: 55-75.

Lacan, J. (1966) *Écrits*, Paris: Seuil.

Lacan, J. (1973-74) *Seminar XXI: Les noms-dupes errent*, unpublished.

Lacan, J. (1975) *Le Séminaire, Livre XX: Encore (1972-1973), Paris, 1975*; translated as *The Seminar of Jacques Lacan, Book XX, On Feminine Sexuality, the Limits of Love and Knowledge, Encore 1972-1973*, New York, 1998.

Lacan, J. (1977) *Écrits: A Selection*, trans. A. Sheridan, London: Tavistock.

Lacan, J. (1984) 'Compte rendu avec interpolations du Séminaire de l'Ethique', *Ornicar?* 28: 7-18.

Lacan, J. (1988) *The Seminar of Jacques Lacan - Book I: Freud's Papers on Technique*, ed. J.-A. Miller, trans. J. Forrester, Cambridge: Cambridge University Press.

Lacan, J. (1994) *Le Séminaire, Livre IV: La Relation d'Objet*, Paris: Seuil.

Lacan, J. (1994) *The Four Fundamental Concepts of Psychoanalysis*, tr. A. Sheridan, ed. J.-A. Miller, Harmondsworth, Middlesex: Penguin.

Laget, A. (1995) *Freud et le temps*, Lyon: Presses Universitaires de Lyon.

Laplanche, J., and Pontalis, J.-B. (1973) *The Language of Psycho-Analysis*, tr. D. Nicholson-Smith, London: Hogarth Press & the Institute of Psycho-Analysis.

Laurent, E. (1992) 'Lecture Critique II', in *L'Autisme et la Psychanalyse*, Toulouse: Découverte Freudienne.

Leader, D. (1993) 'Some notes on obsessional neurosis', *Journal of the Centre for Freudian Analysis and Research* 2: 34-43.
Leader, D. (1997) 'Clinical commentary', *The British Journal of Psychotherapy* 13, 3: 405-407.
Leclaire, S. (1971) *Démasquer le Réel*, Paris: Seuil.
Levi, A.W. (1945) 'The "mental crisis" of John Stuart Mill', *Psychoanalytic Review* 32.
Lévi-Strauss, C. (1954) 'The mathematics of man', *International Social Science Bulletin* 4: 581-590.
Lévi-Strauss, C. (1969) *Elementary Structures of Kinship*, ed. R. Needham, London: Tavistock.
Lewin, K. (1936) *Principles of Topological Psychology*, New York: McGraw-Hill.
Lewinter, R. (1990) *Georg Groddeck: Studien zu Leben und Werk*, Frankfurt am Main: Fischer Taschenbuch Verlag.
Likierman, M. (1995) 'Loss of the object: tragic motifs in Melanie Klein's concept of the depressive position', *British Journal of Psychotherapy* 12: 147-159.
Loewenstein, R. (1958a) 'Remarks on some variations in psychoanalytic technique', *The International Journal of Psycho-Analysis* 39: 202-210.
Loewenstein, R. (1958b) 'Variations in classical technique: concluding remarks', *The International Journal of Psycho-Analysis* 39: 240-242.
Maclean, A. (1989) *The Alchemical Mandala: A Survey of the Mandala in Western Esoteric Tradition*, Grand Rapids: Phanes Press.
Maiello, S. (1997) 'Going Beyond: Notes on the Beginning of Object Relations in the Light of "The Perpetuation of an Error"', in Mitrani & Mitrani 1997.
Maizels, N. (1996) 'Working through, or beyond the depressive position: achievements and defenses of the spiritual position, and the heart's content', unpublished MS.
Masson, J., ed. (1985) *The Complete Letters of Sigmund Freud to Wilhelm Fliess (1887-1904)*, Cambridge MA & London: Belknap Press of Harvard University.
Matte-Blanco, I. (1975) *The Unconscious as Infinite Sets*, London: Duckworth Press.
Matte-Blanco, I. (1988) *Thinking, Feeling, and Being: Clinical Reflections on the Fundamental Antinomy of Human Beings*, London/New York: Tavistock and Routledge.
Meltzer, D.W. (1978) *The Kleinian Development. Part III: The Clinical Significance of the Work of Bion*, Perthshire, Scotland: Clunie Press.

Mill, J. S. (1866) 'Grote's Plato' in *Edinburgh Review*, CXXIII, April 1866: 297-364.

Mill, J.S. (1873) *Autobiography*, London: Longmans, Green, Reader and Dyer.

Mill, J.S. (1880) *Gesammelte Werke*, vol. 12, ed. T. Gomperz, Leipzig.

Mill, J.S. (1970) *A System of Logic*, London: Longmans.

Miller, J.-A. (1979) 'Supplement topologique à la question préliminaire', *Lettre de l'École Freudienne de Paris* 27.

Millot, C. (1984) 'The Feminine Superego', tr. B. Brewster, in P. Adams & E. Cowie (eds.), *The Woman in Question*, London: Verso.

Milner, M. (1978) obituary.

Mineka, F., & Lindley, D., (eds.) (1972) 'The Later Letters of John Stuart Mill', in *The Collected Works of John Stuart Mill*, vol. 15, London : Routledge & Kegan Paul.

Mitrani, T., & Mitrani, J., (eds.) (1997) *Encounters with Autistic States: A Memorial Tribute to Francis Tustin*, New Jersey & London: Aronson.

Mollon, P. (1986a) 'An appraisal of Kohut's contribution to an understanding of narcissism', *British Journal of Psychotherapy* 3, 2: 151-161.

Mollon, P. (1986b) 'A note on Kohut and Klein. Idealisation, splitting and projective identification', *British Journal of Psychotherapy* 3, 2: 162-164.

Mollon, P. (1993) *The Fragile Self: The Structure of Narcissistic Disturbance*, London: Whurr.

Mollon, P. (1996) *Multiple Selves, Multiple Voices. Working with Trauma, Violation and Dissociation*, Chichester: Wiley.

Moran, F. (1993) *Subject and Agency in Psychoanalysis: Which Is To Be Master?* New York and London: New York University Press.

Nacht, S. (1958) 'Variations in technique', *The International Journal of Psycho-Analysis* 39: 235-237.

Nobus, D. (1993) 'La struttura temporale dell'inconscio', *La Psicoanalisi. Rivista italiana della Scuola Europea di Psicoanalisi* 14: 27-34.

Nobus, D. (1998) 'Life and Death in the Glass: A New Look at Lacan's Mirror Stage', in *Key Concepts of Lacanian Psychoanalysis*, ed. D. Nobus, London: Rebus Press.

Noel, D. (1995) 'Jung's Anti-Modern Art of the Mandala', in W. Doty (ed.) *Picturing Cultural Values in Postmodern America*, Tuscaloosa: University of Alabama Press.

Nunberg, H. and Federn, E. (eds.) (1962-75) Minutes of the Vienna Psychoanalytic Society, Vols. I-IV, New York: IUP.

Ogden, T. (1988) 'On the dialectical structure of experience', *Contemporary Psychoanalysis* 23, 4: 17-45.

Ogden, T. (1989) 'On the concept of an autistic-contiguous position', *International Journal of Psycho-Analysis* 70, 1: 127-140.

Ornstein, P. (1978) 'The Evolution of Heinz Kohut's Psychoanalytic Psychology of the Self', in P. Ornstein (ed.) *The Search for the Self: Selected Writings of Heinz Kohut*, vol. 1, New York: International Universities Press.

Pfeiffer, E., ed. (1972) *Sigmund Freud and Lou Andreas-Salomé: Letters*, tr. W. & E. Robson-Scott, London: Hogarth Press & the Institute of Psycho-Analysis.

Plotinus (1981) *The Enneads*, ed. J. Dillon, tr. S. MacKenna, London: Penguin Books.

Pontalis, J.-B. (1981) *Frontiers in Psychoanalysis: Between the Dream and Psychic Pain*, tr. C. Cullen and P. Cullen, London: Hogarth.

Rapaport, D. (1950) 'Review of *Cybernetics*, by Norbert Wiener', *Psychoanalytic Quarterly* 19: 598-603.

Rayner, E. (1990) *The Independent Mind in British Psychoanalysis*, London: Free Association Books.

Redfern, J. (1985) *My Self, My Many Selves*, London: Academic Press.

Rickman, J. (1957) *Selected Contributions to Psychoanalysis*, London: Hogarth Press & the Institute of Psycho-Analysis.

Ricoeur, P. (1965) *Freud and Philosophy*, New Haven: Yale University Press.

Roudinesco, E. (1982) *La Bataille de Cents Ans: Histoire de la Psychanalyse en France*, vol. 1, Paris: Ramsay.

Roudinesco, E. (1986) *La Bataille de Cents Ans: Histoire de la Psychanalyse en France*, vol. 2, Paris: Seuil.

Roudinesco, E., and Plon, M. (1997) *Dictionnaire de la psychanalyse*, Paris: Fayard.

Saussure, F. de (1983) *Course in General Linguistics (1906-1911)*, tr. R. Harris, ed. C. Bally, A. Séchehaye and A. Riedlinger, London: Duckworth.

Schafer, R. (1976) *A New Language for Psychoanalysis*, New Haven CT & London: Yale University Press.

Schafer, R. (1983) *The Analytic Attitude*, New York NY: Basic Books.

Schelling, F.W.J. von (1997) *The Abyss of Freedom/Ages of the World*, ed. S. Zizek, Ann Arbor MI: The University of Michigan Press.

Schofer, E. (1972) 'Heidegger's Language: Metalogical Forms of Thought and Grammatical Specialities', in J. Knockelmans (ed.) *On Heidegger and Language*, Evanston: Northwestern University Press.

Searle, J. (1997) *The Mystery of Consciousness*, New York NY: New York Review of Books.

Shannon, C., & Weaver, W. (1949) *The Mathematical Theory of Communication*, Urbana: University of Illinois Press.

Shin, S.-J. (1994a) *The Logical Status of Diagrams*, Cambridge: Cambridge University Press.

Shin, S.-J. (1994b) 'Peirce and the logical status of diagrams', *History and Philosophy of Logic* 15: 45-68.

Soler, C. (1996) 'The Symbolic Order (II)', in Fink, Feldstein & Jaanus 1996.

Steiner, J. (1979) 'The border between the paranoid-schizoid and the depressive positions in the borderline patient', *British Journal of Medical Psychology* 52: 385-391.

Steiner, J. (1987). The interplay between pathological organisations and the paranoid-schizoid and depressive positions', *International Journal of Psycho-Analysis* 68: 69-80.

Steiner, J. (1990) 'The Defensive Function of Pathological Organisations', in *Master Clinicians: On Treating the Regressed Patient*, eds. L.B. Boyer and P. Giovacchini, Northvale NJ and London: Jason Aronson.

Steiner, J. (1993) *Psychic Retreats*, London and New York: Routledge.

Stengers, I. (1989) 'Boîtes noires scientifiques, boîtes noires professionnelles', in C. Le Guen, O. Flournoy, I. Stengers, & J. Guillaumin (eds.) *La psychanalyse, une science?*, Paris: Les Belles Lettres.

Stengers, I. (1992) *La volonté de faire science. A propos de la psychanalyse*, Le Plessis-Robinson: Laboratoires Delagrange/Synthélabo.

Stern, D. (1985) *The Interpersonal World of the Infant: A View from Psychoanalysis and Developmental Psychology*, London: Karnac.

Stern, D. (1993) 'Acting versus Remembering in Transference Love and Infantile Love', in E. Person, A. Hagden & P. Fonagy (eds.) *On Freud's Observations on Transference Love*, Yale: Yale University Press.

Stolorow, R., Atwood, G., & Brandchaft, B. (eds.) *The Intersubjective Perspective*, Northvale NJ: Aronson.

Stolorow, R.D. (1994), *Intersubjective Perspectives*, New York: Aronson.

Strachey, J. (1961) 'Editor's Introduction', SE XIX: 1-4.

Strambaugh, J. (1992) *The Finitude of Being*, Albany: State University of New York Press.

Sutherland, J. (1994) 'Fairbairn's Achievement', in J. Grotstein & D. Rinsley (eds.) *Fairbairn and the Origins of Object Relations*, New York: The Guilford Press.
Trevarthen, C., Aitken, K., Papoudi, D., & Robarts, J. (1998) *Children with Autism*, second enlarged edition, London & Philadelphia: Jessica Kingsley.
Tustin, F. (1986) *Autistic Barriers in Neurotic Patients*, London: Karnac.
Vlastos, G. (1975) *Plato's Universe*, Oxford: Oxford University Press.
Von Franz, M.-L. (1974) *Number and Time*, Evanston: Northwestern University Press.
Von Franz, M.-L. (1992) 'The Idea of the Micro- and Macrocosmos in the Light of Jungian Psychology', in *Psyche and Matter*, Boston: Shambala.
Weinberg, A. (1963) *Theodor Gomperz and John Stuart Mill: Travaux de droit, d'économie, de sociologie et de sciences politiques*, No. 16, Geneva: Ambilly-Annemasse.
Weiner, N. (1949) *Cybernetics: or Control and Communications in the Animal and the Machine*, New York: Technology Press.
Wilhelm, R., & Jung, C.G. (1965) *The Secret of the Golden Flower*, London: Routledge and Kegan Paul.
Will, H. (1984) *Die Geburt der Psychosomatik*, München: Matthes & Seitz.
Winnicott, D.W. (1951) 'Transitional Objects and Transitional Phenomena' in Winnicott, 1987.
Winnicott, D.W. (1952) 'Psychoses and Child Care', in Winnicott, 1987
Winnicott, D.W. (1960) 'Ego Distortion in Terms of True and False Self', in Winnicott, 1990.
Winnicott, D.W. (1971a) *Playing and Reality*, London: Routledge.
Winnicott, D.W. (1971b) *Therapeutic Consultations in Child Psychiatry*, London: Hogarth.
Winnicott, D.W. (1987) *Through Paediatrics to Psychoanalysis*, London: Karnac.
Winnicott, D.W. (1988) *Human Nature*, London: Free Association Books.
Winnicott, D.W. (1990) *The Maturational Processes and the Facilitating Environment*, London: Karnac.
Wollheim, R. (1993) 'The Bodily Ego', in *The Mind and Its Depths*, Cambridge MA & London: Harvard University Press.
Zizek, S. (1996) *The Indivisible Remainder: An Essay on Schelling and Related Matters*, London: Verso.

Index

Abraham, K. 34, 56, 204, 214
acceptance 18,29, 32, 42, 54, 57-8, 60, 69-71, 86-8
adaptation 25-6, 29, 31, 58, 178
affect 10-12, 64, 103, 110, 128, 143, 216, 218
agency 20, 37, 76, 96, 121, 131, 153, 157, 163-4
aggression 58, 65, 75, 79
alchemy 93, 103-4, 114-5
Allers, R. 115
ambivalence 69, 73
analyst 9-11, 16, 18, 47, 75-6, 78-80
analytic communication 186, 189
anxiety 13, 38-9, 42, 60, 75, 84, 90, 218; castration 158, 169; depressive 35; persecutory 34-5
Assoun, P.-L. 170
attachment 20, 64, 67, 130, 141-2, 169, 211, 213
autism 198, 205, 207-8, 210-2, 215, 217
autoerotism 78, 80

baby 11, 23, 30, 90, 125, 127
Bain, A. 199
Benvenuto, B. 21
Bernfeld, S. 15-6, 19
Bettelheim, B. 191-4, 203, 212-4, 217
biology 210
Bion, W.R. 7, 10, 12-4, 16-21, 34, 40, 14, 45-56, 90
birth 28, 37, 57, 103, 180
black hole 53, 63, 69
Bochenski, J. M. 173
bodily ego/body ego 150, 156, 165, 169-70
body 39, 59-60, 69, 80, 83-4, 88, 112, 133, 137, 139, 148, 156-7, 169, 179, 182, 192, 213
body relations 17
body-image 78, 138
body-self 80, 87-8, 90
body-stimuli 156
boundaries 14, 95, 142, 193
Bouvet, M. 11, 185-6, 189
Bowie, A. 113
brain 118-9, 132, 156, 211
brain lesion 145
break in the session 15, 20
breakdown of repression 68, 70, 73-4
breast 23, 29, 59-60, 72, 84, 125
Breuer, J. 163, 168, 211
Brierley, M. 16-21
Brown, L. 54
Burgoyne, B. 21, 213
Butler, J. 169

castration 163, 204, 213; anxiety 158, 169; complex 188
cathexis 125, 131, 134-6, 140
child 23-25, 29, 31-3, 35, 38, 41, 58, 61-2, 64-5, 68, 72, 76, 79-82, 86, 88-90, 122-3, 159, 169, 179, 190-4, 198-200, 203-12, 214
civilisation 18, 212
Clark, R. 152, 168
conflict 12-3, 15, 35, 75, 89, 94, 166, 212, 216; internal 57; intrapsychic 82; unconscious 166, 196
communication 90, 189, 193, 204
consciousness/conscious 20, 69-71, 75, 85-9, 93-5, 97, 108, 110-3, 121, 124, 128-31, 133-4, 139-42, 150, 152-4, 157, 160, 162-3, 169, 194-7, 211
consultation 31-2
Controversial Discussions 10
core 88, 110, 112
couch 219
counter-transference 9
creativity 79, 89

Damourette, J. 213
day-dream 20
death 100, 103, 115, 123, 151, 170, 174, 199, 216
death drive 159-60;
death instinct 37, 43, 50, 53
deconstruction 50
defence 13, 19, 31, 36-9, 41, 43-4, 57, 62, 65, 73-5, 86-7, 140, 183, 195, 197, 204, 212
denial 37, 46
dependence 59, 68, 71, 78
depression 12-3, 42, 45, 85-7, 150
depressive illness 36-7, 39-40, 42-3, 45, 47, 54
depressive position 32, 34-48, 53-6
desire 13, 21, 48, 54, 61, 63, 82, 97, 160, 181-2, 193, 203, 220-2, 225
Despert, J. 193, 213
determinism 37, 40, 53, 55
discourse 16, 111, 180-2, 198, 220-1; alchemical 104; (see also four discourses)
disintegration 68, 69, 167
Dor, J. 21
dream 41, 49, 52-3, 84, 93, 95-7, 99-101, 110, 117-27, 131, 145, 151, 156, 168, 180, 198, 218-21, 225
dream-interpretation 117
drive 37, 50, 53, 55, 57, 82, 150-1, 159-60, 166, 170, 185, 201, 205, 214-5, 220

Index   243

dualism of the drives 170
dyad 69, 75

ego 21, 26, 36, 38-42, 53, 62-5, 67, 70-5, 78, 84, 90, 114, 118, 129, 134-6, 140, 142, 148, 150, 152-71, 178-9, 181-5, 195-7, 214; anti-libidinal 64, 73-4, 76; central 64-71, 74-5; complex 93; control 12; ideal 36, 78-9, 89, 157-9, 164; libidinal 64, 67, 70, 73, 76; nuclei 30; psychologists 82, 90; ego psychology 78, 150-2, 167-8, 196, 213; structure 73
ego-centricity 93
ego-consciousness 103, 110
ego-defence 103
ego-object 163
ego-subject 163
ego-syntonic 166
Eissler, K. 21
Emerson, R.W. 97-8
empathy 11, 31, 79-82, 90
empiricism 18, 95
environment 20, 24-7, 31-2, 71-2, 79, 84, 89, 110, 138
environmental deficit 57
environmental factors 58
environmental stimuli 75
environmental responses 75, 90
envy 83
epistemology 49-50, 55, 106
Eros 57, 159-160, 170
external world, 18, 60, 71, 89, 120, 134, 141, 158-9 (see also real world)

Fairbairn, W.R.D. (Ronald) 10, 36, 43, 50, 57-76, 82
false connection 195-6, 212
false identity 179
false self 27, 90
fantasy 90, 96, 102-3, 110-2, 122-3 (see also phantasy)
father 39, 79, 123, 157-160, 165, 170, 180-1, 183, 187-8, 197-8, 219, 221-3
Father, Name of the 188
feeding 29, 115
Ferenczi, S. 50, 71, 150, 167
Fink, B. 21
Fleiss, W. 118, 132, 141, 148, 168
forepleasure 201
Foucault, M. 169
Foulkes, S.H.
four discourses172 (see also discourse)
four humours 112
Fordham, M. 115

fragmentation 80, 90, 102, 179
Fraiberg, S. 56
Freud, A. 9-10, 15, 21
Freud, S. 9-10, 12, 14-5, 20, 34-7, 42-3, 53, 56, 58-9, 63-5, 74, 78, 82, 90, 99, 102, 111, 117-49, 150-72, 174, 180, 182, 186, 191, 194-201, 204, 211-6, 226

Gay, P. 151, 166
genital level 38
gesture 80, 86
Giegerich 115
groups 12-4, 20, 85, 172, 176, 178, 213
Goethe, J. W. 115
Goldberg, A. 82
Gréco, P. 20
Green, A. 11-12, 20, 24, 29-30, 32
Grize, J. 20
Groddeck, G. 154, 168
Grossman, C. 168
Grossman, S. 168
Grote 197, 199, 213-4
Grotjahn, M. 168
Grotstein, J. 54-6
Grubrich-Simitis, I. 170
Guilbaud 20
guilt 37, 39, 69, 75, 83, 128, 160, 170

Haeckel, E. 169
Hale, N. 168
Hartmann, H. 15, 90, 150, 168, 213
hate 49, 52, 57, 70, 74, 81, 160, 190
Hayek, F. 214
Heidegger, M. 109, 115
Heimann, P. 181
Hermann, I. 9. 19-20, 212
Hillman, J. 101, 112, 115-6
holding 31
Holt, J. 115
homosexual, female 186
homosexuality 171
humour 79, 89
hunger 90, 125
hysteria 117, 163

id 38, 47, 52, 75, 150-71
idealisation 37, 43, 79-80, 179
identification 37, 39-40, 156-9
identity 59, 68, 71, 92, 113, 125, 129, 135-8, 141, 147-8, 179, 216
imaginary, the 172, 175, 179, 181-8, 220, 223
imaginary identification 169, 181-2
impingement 25

independence 166
individuation 57, 93, 99, 103, 114-5
infant 11, 22-3, 25, 27, 29-35, 37-43, 46-7, 49, 51-2, 54-5, 57, 59-64, 67-8, 72, 75, 78, 90, 125, 137, 147-9
integration 30-1, 85, 89, 115, 206
internal body-images 138
internal circle 206
internal saboteur 73
internal stimuli 155, 169
internal systems 121
internal world 158
interdependence 44, 139
interpretation 19, 21, 72, 84, 94, 97, 206, 115, 117, 119, 123, 126, 131, 145, 156, 170, 178, 218-23, 225-6
intersubjectivity 12, 46, 50, 89, 184
introjective identification 41, 43
introjection 39, 42-3, 62, 114, 156
investment 86

Jacobs, M. 23, 33
Jaffe 108
Jalley, 169
James, P.D. 170
Jones, E. 10, 150, 167, 215
jouissance 215, 223
Jung, C.G. 10, 92-116

Kamm 199
Kanner 190-1, 193, 212-3, 215
Kant, I. 50, 52, 95, 98, 113, 159, 170, 212
Kauffmann de Rola, S. 115
Kernberg, O. 89
King, P. 20
Klein, M. 11, 34-44, 47, 49-50, 53-6, 90, 168
Kleinians 46, 50
Kneale W. & M. 173
knowledge 20, 23, 41, 44, 49-50, 52, 92, 97, 119, 131, 138, 195
Kohut, H. 10, 50, 77-91
Kris, E. 168

Lacan, J. 9-10, 13-5, 19-21, 51, 53, 156, 168-9, 171-2, 190, 194, 200-2, 213-6, 220-1, 223, 225-6
lack 9, 31, 142, 221; of differentiation 59; of separation 193; in the other 220
language 9, 91-2, 95, 105, 109, 117-9, 136-9, 145-8, 173-6, 179, 183-5, 191-5, 212-4; of love 59; limits to 12; philosophy of 143; structure of 12; symbolic 106
Laget, A. 171

Laplanche, J. 170
Laurent, E. 205-6, 211, 215-6
learning 38, 138, 143, 146
Leader, D. 21. 179, 213
Leclaire, S. 205, 215
Levi, A. 214
Lévi-Strauss, C. 172, 175-9, 189
Lewin, K. 14, 19
Lewinter, R. 168
libido 65, 78, 80-2, 84, 87, 155-7, 185, 216
Likierman, M. 37, 41, 55-6
Lindley, D. 199, 214
Loewenstein, R. 21, 168
love 49, 52, 57, 59-61, 63-4, 81, 90, 160, 174, 190, 198-200, 202-3, 205, 216, 226; attachment 216; relations 20
Lust 168

Maclean, A.115
Maiello, S. 191, 212
Maizels, N. 41, 54-5
mandala 92-116
manic defence 37
Masson, J. 168
Matte-Blanco, I. 20, 50, 56
mechanism 46, 51, 64, 95; of defence 19, 75; of paranoid-schizoid position 36, 51; schizoid 37
Meister Eckhart 52
Meltzer, D. 37-8, 54, 56
memory 23, 48-9, 53-4, 61, 83, 112, 119, 121, 123, 125, 128, 133-7, 140-3, 202, 222
memory-image 123
memory-trace 124-5, 129, 131, 141, 148, 162
memory-picture 135
merger 84
microcosm 91
Mill, James 198-9, 213-4
Mill, J.S. 143-6, 149, 197-200, 213-4
Miller, J.-A. 188
Millot, C. 170
Mineka, F. 199, 214
mirror 92, 106, 120, 179
mirroring 64, 78, 103
mirror phase 179
mirror stage 169
mnemic image 124-31, 133, 135, 138, 140, 148
mnemic trace 127, 129, 141, 143, 168
Mollon, P. 78, 86, 90-1
Moran, P. 37
mother 11, 29, 31, 37, 39, 41, 43, 46-7, 49, 51, 55, 58-63, 72, 76-77, 83 86-8, 90, 125, 127, 137, 158, 174, 188, 192, 199, 216

mourning 35-6, 40-4, 46-7, 54, 68
multiple personality disorder 86

Nacht, S. 21
Nachträglichkeit 143, 149
narcissism 35-7, 77-80, 82, 84, 86, 88-90
narcissism, primary 37, 42
narcissism, secondary 37, 42
narcissism, pathological 37
neuronal network 118, 133-4
neuronal structure 118, 133-4, 138, 142, 148
neurones 118, 133-4, 136, 139-41, 169, 216
neurosis 13-4, 19, 122-3, 165, 180-1, 195, 197
neurosis, obsessional 169
Nobus, D. 169, 171
Noel, D. 102-3, 115

object 22, 26-7, 30, 34-9, 41, 43-5, 47, 51-2, 55-7, 63, 66-7, 69-70, 72-3, 75, 78, 81, 90, 110, 113, 137, 144, 146-7, 153, 156-7, 162, 174-5, 179, 181, 185, 190, 193, 214, 219-22, 225; *a* 174, 223; cathexis 156-60; choice 35-6; relations 57, 71, 179-80, 183, 186, 215; bad 31, 65, 67, 69, 72, 75, exciting 64, 68, 70, 73 external 40, 67, 69, 72-3; good 38, 40-1, 43-4, 63-4, 67-8, 70, 72-3; ideal 64, 67-8, 70; internal 21, 40, 61-5, 67, 69-73, 75, 82, 185; libidinal 174; part 39, 70; partial 185; primordial 187; rejecting 73; rejective 63-4, 68, 73; transitional 29-30, 33; whole 35-6 39-40, 42, 44, 62-3
object-associations 146-8
object-love 38, 78-9
object-presentation 147
obsessional neurosis 169
Oedipal loves 20, 189
Oedipal phase 75
Oedipal structure 187
Oedipus Complex 13, 17, 39, 65, 158-9, 181, 187
Oedipus complex, negative
Oedipus conflict 38-9, 190, 216
Ogden, T. 47, 54
omnipotence 43
oral drive 220
Ornstein, P. 78

Padel, J. 76
Papert, S. 20
paradox 30, 33, 39, 108, 113, 122, 158, 200, 206, 214
paranoid-schizoid position 32-3, 36, 39, 41-8, 51, 56

passive/aggressive 41
patient 31, 34, 38, 42, 45-7, 51, 54, 61, 69, 76, 78-9, 81-9, 101-2, 111, 122-3, 153, 165-7, 180-1, 183-5, 218, 221, 223-4
penis 215-6
perception 51, 58, 113, 119, 121, 125-9, 133-43, 147, 150, 153, 156, 162, 168, 195, 206
personality 30, 45, 75, 78, 82, 86-8, 93, 110-112, 115, 160, 162, 164, 168, 213
Pfeiffer, E. 168
phallic host 186, 189
phallic function 205, 207, 215, 217
phallic signification 208, 220
phallic structure 212
phallus 188, 206, 211, 216
phantasy 10, 37, 53, 90, 125, 174, 185, 198, 221-2 (see also fantasy)
philosopher 13, 17-8, 50, 103-4, 119, 163 173, 199
philosophy 15-7, 97, 100, 103, 143-4, 147, 169, 213, 216
phobia 75
Piaget, J. 20, 173, 206
Pichon, E. 193-4, 213
Plato 52, 102, 197, 214
Plotinus 93-4
pleasure 86, 121, 125, 127-8, 155, 168
pleasure principle 134, 155-6, 168
Poincaré 52
Pontalis, J.-B. 24, 170
Postmodernism 34, 40, 46, 48, 50, 55
preconscious 20, 121, 129-30, 142, 153-4, 156, 162, 168
primal identification 158
primary care-giver 68
Primary Force 98-9
primary identification 59, 65, 157
primary repression 70
primary process 123, 129, 138-40, 145
projection 17, 20, 40, 90, 102, 114, 155-6 185
projective identification 41, 43, 46-7, 51, 90
psyche 30, 35, 57, 62, 74-5, 80, 83-4, 86-7, 89-90, 92
psyche-soma 22
psychoneuroses 142
psychoanalysis 14-6, 18-21, 44, 46, 51, 55, 78, 91, 95-6, 115, 150-1, 160, 165-76, 184, 189, 191, 195, 214, 216, 226
psychosis 49, 99, 181-2, 186, 188, 210, 215-6
psychotherapy 93, 128-9, 148, 191

Rapaport, D. 150
Rayner, E. 10, 20
reality 152, 158, 188, 190, 195, 199, 216
reality principle 155, 157-9
real world 135, 194 (see also external world)
reconstruction 10, 21, 89, 109
Redfern, J. 115
regression 27, 41-2, 47, 49, 79-81, 84, 90, 119, 126, 129-31, 135, 139, 205
re-integration 71
rejection 87, 218-25
repression 20, 57-8, 61, 64-5, 67-70, 73-6, 78, 84-6, 88-9, 96, 127-8, 130, 143, 153-4, 161, 163-7, 169, 195, 197
Rickman, J. 12-20
Ricoeur, P. 115
Roudinesco, E. 170, 213

sadism 36, 38-9, 43
Saussure, F. de 168
Schafer, R. 168
Schelling, F. W. J. 113
schizophrenia 45, 210
Schofer, E. 109
science 13-9, 21, 44, 52, 97, 018-9, 151, 166, 172, 175-6, 195-7, 200, 213-4
Searle, J. 169
secondary process 140
self 23-5, 27, 37, 47, 54, 57-61, 63-4, 68-71, 75, 77-81, 84-6, 88, 94-5, 99-103, 114-5
self-esteem 71, 77, 86-7, 89
self-object 77, 81-2, 84, 89-90
semiotics 107
separateness 57
sexual development 58, 170
sexual difference 190
sexual drive 201
sexual fantasies 80, 84, 213
sexual libido 82
sexual history 123
sexuality 58, 75, 115
shame 77, 83, 85, 87, 128
Shannon, C. 177
Sholern 52
Shin, S.-J. 73
Sigg, H. 100
skin 55
Soler, C. 183
splitting 26-7, 36-7, 43, 61, 63-5, 67, 70-1, 73, 86, 162-3, 170
Steiner, J. 54, 56
Steiner, R. 20
Stengers, I. 166, 171

Stern, D. 37, 59
Stolorow, R. D. 75, 89
Strachey, J. 148, 152, 215
Strambaugh, J. 115
structural theory, the 154, 159, 165, 169
subject 37-9, 48, 52, 57, 60, 62, 91, 107, 113, 137-8, 144, 151, 162-3, 168-9, 174-5 178-89
subjectivity 51, 59, 94, 96, 112, 225
sublimation 36, 59, 82
Sullivan, G. 189
Sullivan, H. 50
superego 36, 38, 46, 71-5, 89, 150, 158-60, 162-5, 167, 169-70
Sutherland, J. 13, 68
symbolic 172, 175, 180, 183, 186, 188, 206, 222-3
symbology 107
symptom 40, 75, 85-6, 117, 181, 190-1, 196, 225

telescope 118-21, 123-7, 129-35, 138-9, 141-5, 148
Thanatos 57, 159-60, 170
thing-in-itself 50
thing-presentation 12
topographical model, the 157
topography 124, 131, 135, 155-6; first 162; second 150, 162, 164-8
transference 15, 20, 32, 75-6, 81, 86-7, 89, 93, 102-3, 118-9, 126-7, 129, 134, 140-1, 143-4, 148, 182-6
transitional phenomena 22, 25, 27-30, 33
translation 118-9, 141-5, 178, 197, 200, 215, 225
trauma 61, 63, 67, 78, 82, 83, 86, 89, 134, 143, 149
Trevarthen, C. 212-3, 217
tripartite model 150-2, 166
true self 26
Tustin, F. 54, 191, 212, 217

unconscious/Ucs. 13, 19-20, 53, 69, 74-5, 83, 85, 94-6, 102-6, 108, 110, 112-4, 116, 118, 120-1, 123-5, 128, 131, 141, 143, 145, 151-6, 160-2, 164-6, 168-71, 178, 180, 182, 184, 189, 194-8, 203, 211
unpleasure 121, 127-8, 134, 136, 140, 143, 168
uroboric 109, 115

Vlastos, G. 214
Von Franz, 100, 104, 115

Weiner, N. 178
Wilhelm, R. 101, 111
Will, H. 168
Winnicott, D.W. 9-11, 20, 22-33, 50, 90, 215
wish 79-80, 84, 88-9, 119, 121, 124-6, 128, 135, 225
wish fulfilment 119, 123-5, 127, 129, 134-5, 138, 140
withdrawal 59, 170
word-presentation 12, 142, 146-7, 168
Wollheim, R. 169

Zizek, S. 169